A
FIERCE
GREEN
FIRE

A
FIERCE
GREEN
FIRE

The American Environmental Movement

PHILIP
SHABECOFF

HILL AND WANG
A division of Farrar, Straus, and Giroux
New York

Copyright © 1993 by Philip Shabecoff
All rights reserved
Published simultaneously in Canada by HarperCollins*CanadaLtd*
Printed in the United States of America
First edition, 1993

LIBRARY OF CONGRESS CATALOGING-IN-PUBLICATION DATA
Shabecoff, Philip.
A fierce green fire: the American environmental movement / Philip
Shabecoff.—1st ed.
p.   cm.
Includes bibliographical references and index.
1. Environmental policy—United States—History. 2. Environmental
protection—United States—History.   I. Title.
HC110.E5S46   1992   363.7'057'0973—dc20   92–14374 CIP

This book has been printed on recycled paper

To Alice, aka Dan'l

Acknowledgments

I wish, first of all, to express my deep appreciation to the Joyce Foundation of Chicago and to Craig Kennedy, Sheila Leahy, and Margaret H. O'Dell for their generous contribution to this book. Their aid made it possible for me to get the help I needed to do the extensive research for this undertaking while working full-time as a newspaper reporter. With the foundation's help, I was able to enlist the energetic assistance of William Maggs and the wisdom and experience of Rice Odell in digging out much of the data I present here.

I am greatly indebted to Clifford Krauss of *The New York Times*, J. Clarence (Terry) Davies, former assistant administrator of the Environmental Protection Agency and executive director of the National Commission on the Environment, and William Clark of Harvard University's John F. Kennedy School of Government for taking the time and effort to read my lengthy manuscript. They all made valuable suggestions and saved me from errors of fact and judgment. Whatever errors remain are mine alone. My wife, Alice Shabecoff, found time from her hectic schedule not only to read and improve my manuscript but to help in a dozen other ways, from collating my printouts to keeping me from kicking my word processor in frustration. I would also like to acknowledge Nancy Breckenridge, who accurately and cheerfully transcribed all of the many tape-recorded interviews gathered for this volume.

Arthur Wang was my patient, persevering editor. In his good-humored but iron-willed fashion, he refused to let me get away with sloppy thinking or fulsome prose. In a very real sense, this book is as much his as mine.

P.S.

Contents

Illustrations follow pages 76, 166, and 250

When I returned to the United States in the fall of 1970 after spending the better part of the 1960s in Europe and Asia as a foreign correspondent for *The New York Times*, one of the changes that first struck me was that the decline of the environment had become a matter of rapidly growing national concern.

Environmental issues were frequently in the news, and the news was almost all bad. A river in Cleveland burst into flame when the chemical wastes oozing into its waters ignited. Beaches and coastal waters were being fouled with sewage and oil. The Great Lakes were dying from fertilizers and detergents. The air over urban and industrial areas was becoming choked with sulfur, carbon, lead, nitrogen, and a poisonous brew of industrial gases. A growing torrent of synthetic chemicals and radioactive materials was toxifying our land, air, and water—even our blood and body tissue and the milk in mothers' breasts. The flow of goods and products churned out for the seemingly insatiable appetite of an affluent consumer society was leaving a suffocating residue that littered our roads and countryside and had created an avalanche of garbage that threatened to bury us. Affluence, the automobile, the interstate highway system, air travel, and uncontrolled development were also transforming the American landscape. Suburbs were increasingly urban; much of the rural landscape disappeared as farms were sold off for subdivisions and woodlands became honeycombed with vacation homes. Mountains were being ripped from the surface of Appalachia to reach the veins of coal beneath the soil. Wetlands were drained for shopping malls and ancient forests were clear-cut to send logs to Japan. Our national parks, the great cathedrals of our New World civilization, were becoming overcrowded and degraded by pollution and development. It would soon become dismayingly evident that even the thin veil of atmosphere that protects this hospitable planet from the radiation of space was threatened by the careless, uncontrolled use of technology that depleted the earth's protective ozone shield and raised the likelihood that the world's temperature would rise with dangerous rapidity because of the accumulation of carbon dioxide and other greenhouse gases.

But something else was happening. Growing numbers of people across the nation not only were becoming increasingly angry and alarmed about the environment but also were becoming aware of what was happening and why, and they were organizing to resist and change the forces leading us down an ecological dead end. The environmental movement was creating a swelling cadre of concerned activists. As demonstrated by the mass outpouring of bodies and emotions on the first Earth Day in 1970, a deep river of concern was running beneath the seemingly heedless materialism of American life.

When I joined the *Times*'s Washington bureau in 1970 I had hoped to write about environmental issues. But the subject was still not considered important enough by *Times* editors to assign a reporter to cover them. I was asked instead to write about the national economy and labor, and later to serve as White House correspondent during the Nixon and Ford presidencies. Only seven years later, in 1977, was I finally given the green light, so to speak, to begin on the environmental beat, at first only on a part-time basis. Very quickly, however, it became a full-time assignment. I soon found myself bearing witness to the emergence of a major social movement, a movement that is becoming one of the most powerful political and cultural forces of our time.

My book is about that movement, its long history, its progress, and its possible future. It is about my conviction that environmentalism, despite its limited successes, offers the best hope that we will be able to save ourselves from the grave dangers we have created by our destructive use of the natural world.

To find the reasons for the emergence of environmentalism, I will first examine how an unspoiled land of great beauty and wonder began to change when Europeans came here five hundred years ago. I shall try to show how our land was settled and tamed by westward expansion, how much of its resources were squandered, how large areas were sullied, disfigured, and degraded, and how our negligent use of the Promethean forces of science and technology has brought us to the verge of disaster.

What this book is chiefly about, however, is how we have at last come fully to recognize the danger and how we are trying to pull ourselves back from the edge of the precipice. We have only slowly accepted individual and collective responsibility for protecting and preserving the natural world and ourselves. It is that hard-earned knowledge and the realization that we must act upon it that forms the basis of the environmental movement.

Environmentalism is a relatively new idea. It was in 1866 that the German Darwinian Ernst Haeckel coined the word "ecology," from the Greek *oikos*—house—to describe the study of how organisms interact with each other in a shared habitat.[1] In 1948, less than a century later, Aldo Leopold, one of the patron saints of American environmentalism, wrote that "all ethics rest upon a single premise: that the individual is a member of a community of interdependent parts."[2] Almost all else in environmentalism proceeds from that premise. Our survival depends on the health of the living world and its component parts—the land, the air, the water, the plants, the animals, the microorganisms. It therefore follows that we are also responsible for the health of the living world for our own well-being and for that of generations to come.

There is a wing of the modern environmental movement that insists that people have an ethical duty to protect nature whether or not it serves human needs. I take a more anthropocentric view. Human welfare is our first priority. But I am deeply sympathetic to those who insist that all nature has a right to exist for its own sake.

I shall also examine the intellectual and institutional foundations of the environmental movement and how knowledge, ethics, aesthetics, fear, anger, communications, and politics have transformed the movement into a mass crusade. That crusade is only now beginning to be recognized for what it is—along with peace and social and economic justice, one of the great causes of our time.

I shall try to demonstrate how the environmental impulse has penetrated our legal system, our economy, our politics, our educational system, our science, our agriculture, our recreation, our mass media, our aesthetics, our religion, and our values. I will look at the grave problems that environmentalism has yet to address and at the forces arrayed against it. Finally, I will take up the crucial question of whether, through environmentalism, we will be able to save ourselves from ourselves.

This is a book about hope, not certain success. Environmentalism is no *deus ex machina*. We have far to travel before we escape the dangers which we have so carelessly created through our abuse of the natural systems that support life.

Just a few words about what my book is not. It is not a work of historical scholarship. I am a journalist, not a historian. I use chiefly secondary sources to describe the settlement of the continent and the Indian societies encountered by the Europeans and to trace the rise of environmentalism and place it in its cultural context. In the early chapters, I draw heavily on the inspired modern scholarship of Richard A. Bartlett, James MacGregor Burns, William Cronon, Stephen Fox, Samuel Hays, Leo Marx, Perry Miller, Roderick Nash, James Oliver Robertson, Henry Nash Smith, and many others. Later chapters rely primarily on my own reporting, particularly from the nearly fifteen years I spent following the issue as environmental correspondent for *The New York Times*. I have also made heavy use of original sources and documents and a large number of interviews conducted specifically for this volume. My task is to present the news—the news of a great emerging social force and how it is likely to affect our time and the future.

Environmentalism does not, of course, begin and end in the United States. The intellectual foundations of modern environmentalism are to be found in Europe and Asia as well as in the United States. I devote one brief chapter to its global ramifications. Environmentalism is becoming a mass movement throughout the world. Grass-roots environmental activists are now at work on every continent. In the 1990s much of the energy and many of the ideas of the environmental movement are emerging outside North America. But this book is chiefly an examination of the movement in this country—how and why it arose and where it may be taking us. A detailed examination of the international environmental movement will have to wait for a later book.

Becket, Massachusetts
March 1992

A

FIERCE

GREEN

FIRE

THE

GARDEN

AND

THE

WILDERNESS

And they shall build houses and inhabit them,
and they shall plant vineyards and eat the fruit of them.
—Isaiah 65:21

We have changed the land and much else.

Only five hundred years, a mere tick of the geological chronometer, have passed since the "Discovery" opened a fresh and verdant new world to the Europeans.

Let us begin by briefly suggesting what North America would have looked like to a late-fifteenth-century European who, through some feat of wizardry, could have soared like an eagle across the continent.

He would fly from the east over millions of acres of dark forest, a long line of wooded mountains behind the coastal plain, a thousand miles of lush, green prairie. He would see long, wide rivers that made their European counterparts look like modest creeks, vast inland seas empty of traffic save for a few solitary canoes. He would pass over a chain of soaring, snowcapped mountains; deserts punctuated by dreamlike pinnacles and deep canyons, a final chain of high mountains, and then a last narrow coastal area, filled with trees in the north and sere in the south. Beyond would be a wide blue ocean, stretching to who knew what fabled lands. Every detail of the landscape below would be vividly etched through the sparkling air.

Wherever our imaginary adventurer went he would see few indications of human occupation. Occasionally, thin plumes of smoke from cooking fires would call attention to an Indian village in a small clearing in the woods. Gliding over the glittering white coastal beaches, he might, from time to time, see a line of women gathering shellfish or the wild grapes that grew in profusion along the coastal marshes. Above the prairie he might spy, if his eyesight was keen, small groups of men stalking herds of bison that covered the plain like a black carpet. He might also see a band of hunters or warriors walking in file along a narrow footpath through the forest.

Alighting, he would certainly be impressed by the great height and girth of the trees surrounding him. He would sniff appreciatively at the crisp, fragrant air and, looking upward from a clearing in the forest, would admire the deep, vivid blue of the sky. Pausing at the bank of a swiftly flowing river, he would notice how clear it was and would stoop for a drink of the clean, sweet water. If it were the proper season, he would be astonished to see streams thick with salmon and shad, or he might gaze with amazement at a thirty-foot-long sturgeon lying motionless in a deep pool next to a shaded bank. If a shadow suddenly passed across the sun, he would look up to stare at an immense flock of passenger pigeons, their noise, as someone would write much later, sounding from a distance like the ringing of bells. He would delight in the abundance of beaver and, being European, might calculate the price their pelts would fetch in London or Amsterdam. Venturing onto the prairie, he would note the great variety of flowers and shoulder-high grasses. He would look with a hunter's eye at the uncountable deer, antelope, elk, bear, and bison, and at the waterfowl that swarmed by the millions to the shallow ponds that dotted the prairie. This game, and the fish he could easily pull from the lakes and streams, along with some corn and beans he might obtain by trade with the Indians he encountered, would make up his diet in this pristine new world.

When the sun fell, our first European would light a fire against the profound darkness of the night. Sitting on the ground, staring into the flames, he would be surrounded by a deep silence, broken, perhaps, by the manic call of a loon, the scream of a panther, or the primal howl of a pack of wolves.

Judging by the records left by European explorers and settlers who would soon follow him to North America, our imaginary adventurer was somewhat overcome by the sheer immensity and, to him, emptiness of the continent. He was frightened by the wild beasts, the tribesmen he could think of only as fierce savages, and the unknown perils of the dark forest. He was lonely, isolated at the edge of an alien realm. But he also had an exhilarating sense of freedom, of openness, of opportunity that contrasted sharply with the sense of limits he had left behind in closed-in, crowded, class-ridden, resource-poor Europe. He was at the threshold of a new life in a fresh, endlessly promising, and abundant new world.

Left to nature—the forces of wind, water, ice, and heat, the evolution of organic life—and to the spare economy of the native Americans, there would have been little perceptible change in the landscape during the brief cosmic moment since the beginning of the mass migration of Europeans to the Western Hemisphere.

But the alien invaders did not attune themselves to the continent's natural rhythms. They sought to subdue the land and its people and, employing enormously powerful tools, to control nature itself.

As a result, the continent has changed almost beyond recognition in those brief five hundred years. The general contours of the continent, the mountains, the great rivers, the plains, are much as they were in the fifteenth century. But virtually all the landscape has been dramatically altered by human activity. The once clear air is opaque from pollution. The magnificent ancient forests have been replaced for the most part by thin, scattered second- and third-growth woods. The wild rivers have turned brown and are tamed by locks and dams. The mountains are scarred by mining and the clear-cutting of their trees. Much of the land is encrusted with cities and wide highways. The natural line of the horizon is broken by skyscrapers, radio and television towers, and smokestacks, and the sky itself is busy with airplanes and helicopters. The economist John Kenneth Galbraith has observed that America has largely become a place of public squalor in the midst of private affluence.[1]

We are increasingly replacing the natural world with what the social ecologist Murray Bookchin calls a "synthetic environment." We have tried, he said, "to bring the laws of the biosphere into accordance with those of the marketplace."[2] We are dependent for our food, our health, our livelihood, the shape of our landscape, and the composition of our air and water on a bewildering array of complex technological, corporate, and governmental systems over which we as individuals have little or no control and which we largely do not even understand. As the ecologist Aldo Leopold pointed out, our civilization is racing far ahead of the slow pace of evolution. The process of evolution tends to elaborate and diversify whereas our technological and economic systems tend to reduce and simplify the biological world. "Man's invention of tools has enabled him to make changes of unprecedented violence, rapidity and scope," Leopold observed.[3]

How have we ourselves changed? How have we reacted to the profoundly altered relationship between ourselves and the natural world? The question is much more difficult to answer in our complex civilization than it was for our fifteenth-century European. However, when we can jet across the country between lunch and dinner or telephone a business associate three thousand miles away in a matter of seconds, the continent no longer seems immense or mysterious. It has been pointed out by Kenneth Boulding, among others, that with the photograph of the small blue Earth against a background of immense space now fixed in our minds, we can no longer think of our planet as anything but finite and vulnerable.

At the end of the nineteenth century, the historian Frederick Jackson Turner advanced the thesis that the American character, indeed, the history of America, was forged by the frontier, the ever advancing line where civilization confronted nature. Each move forward, he argued in his seminal paper *The Significance of the Frontier in American History*, provided a clean slate and free land where the advancing Americans would develop an independent spirit and a democratic society.[4]

While Turner's thesis is challenged by many historians, there is also ample evidence that the closing of the frontier has affected us profoundly—although our profligacy suggests that many Americans delude themselves that the frontier and its vast resources are still there, just beyond the Kmart parking lot.

Over the past century, we Americans appear to have lost much of our faith in the notion of limitless opportunity, much of our optimism and independence. We feel the paradox of a society that is constantly expanding its control over nature while individuals lose ever more control of their own lives in the artificial environment that has replaced nature. "Can any man look at the subway rush and then speak of those jammed midges as 'lords of creation'?" asked the historians Charles and Mary Beard.[5] From the expansive literature of Melville and Whitman, which took up the great themes of human existence in a world of nature, we have moved to the urban, self-obsessed angst in the novels of Philip Roth and the minimalist world of Donald Barthelme from which nature has been evicted. From the inviting, romantic landscapes of Thomas Cole and Asher Durand we have moved to the tortured abstractions of Mark Rothko and Barnett Newman.

Hurtling through the air in the cabin of a jet plane at 30,000 feet, sitting in the dark during a power failure, wheezing from the smog during a temperature inversion, immobilized in our powerful car by gridlock during rush hour, we experience a sharp twinge of anger and helplessness. We sometimes wonder if the machine that now sustains us will someday go permanently out of whack and bring our civilization tumbling down. With Bill McKibben and others, we mourn the end of nature and feel a deep sense of longing for a world with places unspoiled by the works of humanity.

We have, of course, also gained much as we have brought nature under our control. Our labor has been eased, our food and shelter have become more secure. We have reduced the scourge of illness and disease and substantially expanded the number of years we can expect to remain alive. We can communicate and travel over great distances in short periods of time.

But the edifice of civilization we have imposed on our natural landscape is quite obviously in disrepair. We have been acting out the classic cartoon image of a man sitting on the branch of a tree and sawing it off behind him.

Let us trace the path that led us into this dangerous predicament. Then we will describe how a growing number of Americans are uniting in a broad social movement called environmentalism—a movement that is building a potential road out of that predicament.

Geography as well as history began to change when Christopher Columbus anchored his little fleet off the island of San Salvador. The Western Hemisphere, peopled but only lightly touched by human activity, began at that moment to be transfigured. The very fabric of nature on two great continents was to be rewoven by an alien culture.

Like most of those who freely followed them across the Western Ocean, Columbus and his company risked the voyage to the New World for what they could take from it. They came for gold, for a trade route to the spices of India and other riches of Asia, for land, for goods to sell, for glory, for adventure, for religious and personal freedom, to convert the heathen to Christianity. None came for love of the wild new landscape they had stumbled upon.

And yet, from the very first encounter, there was a certain ambiguity about the way the Europeans viewed the New World. Columbus's journal, as abstracted by Bartolomé de Las Casas, records that on November 3, twenty-one days after his first landfall, Columbus climbed a small mountain on Cuba to take the lay of the land. When he returned to his flagship, "he said that all he had seen was so beautiful that his eyes would never tire beholding so much beauty, and the songs of the birds large and small."[6] The bold and ambitious adventurer was clearly touched by the loveliness of the strange landscape.

The entry for the following day, however, revealed that aesthetics was far from Columbus's chief interest. "This people is very gentle and timid, naked as I have said, without arms or law; these lands are very fertile . . . they have beans and kidney beans very different from ours, and much cotton . . . and a thousand other kinds of fruit that I can't describe; and all should be very profitable."[7]

In the first days of Europe's conquest of the Americas, a relationship with the land was established that has endured five centuries. It was beautiful, this exotic New World, but beauty was hardly a consideration when compared with the profit that could be made from it. To the conquistadors of Spain, the gentlemen adventurers of England, the seigneurs of France, and those who followed from the grasping, masculine culture of Europe, America was a virgin land, a land to be admired, even loved, but to be deflowered—forcibly when necessary—to satisfy the passions that drove men westward.

It is half a millennium since Columbus sighted land, but this ambivalent attitude toward America's landscape and its resources still colors our use of the natural world. We still profess our love of the land and its treasures, but our love rarely interferes with our abuse of it.

Although the explorers, adventurers, and settlers came to seize whatever riches and opportunities the land had to offer, it was what they brought with them, far more than what they took, that changed the face of the continent forever. What they brought was Europe—two thousand or more years of Western history, customs, prejudices, and methodology. They brought European agriculture and its alien crops and domestic animals. They brought European technology, philosophy, religion, aesthetics, a market economy, and a talent for political organization. They brought European diseases that decimated the native people. They also brought with them European ideas of what the New World was—and visions of what it should be.

One radiant vision that thoroughly captivated the thoughts of Europeans in the seventeenth century and their American descendants was the image of the garden. The discovery of America offered a miraculous opportunity for restoring the Eden of Genesis, for realizing Virgil's ideal pastoral landscape in a new, unspoiled world. The discovery had opened a wide door, Leo Marx noted, to "a new life in a fresh green landscape . . . Inevitably the European mind was dazzled by the prospect. With an unspoiled hemisphere in view it seemed that mankind actually might realize what had been thought a poetic fantasy."[8]

North America was already inhabited by about four million Indians. Over the centuries the indigenous people had created their own complex cultures. But the European mind saw an empty land that offered a chance to create a quiet, fruitful, bucolic life free of the poverty, turmoil, complexity, and decadence of England and the Continent. It was the ideal of the peaceful shepherd living a life of contemplative plenty in a setting of natural but tamed beauty. If the garden was a myth, it nevertheless exercised a powerful hold on the European mind and continues to this day to color the American perception of our landscape.[9]

This pastoral myth, this vision of an idealized America, remains one of the faintly heard grace notes of the modern environmental movement even as the twentieth century draws to an end. To many of today's environmentalists, the image of what America's true landscape ought to be still continues to inspire.

Reports sent back to Europe by explorers and early settlers provided evidence that the image of the garden was, in some respects at least, a real one, not just the product of religious faith or a literary tradition. Of course, many of these reports were intended to induce settlers to come to the new land to provide the labor that would reap profits for the proprietors of the vast domains granted by kings and companies, such as the charters given in 1606 to the Plymouth and London companies for colonizing New England and Virginia, respectively, the Calverts' charter for Maryland in 1632, and William Penn's charter for Pennsylvania in 1681. Many of those reports strayed considerably from the truth, putting the rosiest possible hue on their descriptions to tempt others to make the dangerous ocean crossing.

In 1562, leading a party of French explorers into Florida, the French Protestant Jean Ribaut was so enraptured with the fragrant green countryside that he pronounced it "the fairest, fruitfullest and pleasantest of all the world."[10]

Arthur Barlowe, captain of a ship sent by Sir Walter Raleigh, described the scene at his first landfall in America in 1584, probably on the Outer Banks of North Carolina: "This island had many goodly woodes and full of deere, conies, hares and fowle even in the middest of summer, in incredible aboundance."[11]

Here is another, related, vision of America—a land of "incredible aboundance." It is a vision that was and is all the more powerful because it is essentially a true one. Here was plenty to satisfy the hungers of the Old World. For land-starved yeomen there was, to European eyes, a vacant continent waiting for the plow. There were beaches covered with grapes, woods crowded with deer, skies filled with fowl, and waters thick with fish. For those who shivered through the long, dark European winters, there was so much timber to burn in the New World, one early English visitor to New England reported, that "a poor servant here that is to possesse but 50 Acres of land may afford to give more wood for timber and fire as good as the world yeelds than many Noble men in *England* can afford to do."[12]

It is probably impossible to exaggerate the importance of this image of America as a land of limitless bounty in shaping the way succeeding generations of Americans thought of and used the resources of their country. The early settlers, the pioneers, and their successors used the soil, the trees, the game, and all the other treasures of the new land with careless profligacy, confident that the supply was inexhaustible.[13]

Peter Kalm, a Swedish naturalist traveling in America in the mid-eighteenth century, was appalled by the Americans' poor stewardship of the land. "In a word, the grain fields, the meadows, the he cattle, etc. are treated with equal carelessness; and the characteristics of the English nation, so well skilled in these branches of husbandry, is scarcely recognizable here. We can hardly be more hostile toward our woods in Sweden and Finland than they are here: their eyes are fixed upon the present gain and they are blind to the future."[14]

With scarcely a word changed, such a judgment could be applied equally to the industrialized, consumer-oriented, high-tech society of America in the closing years of the twentieth century. The belief that the New World is a cornucopia that cannot be emptied continues to dominate our habits and our economic system despite clear evidence to the contrary.

But another, conflicting vision also filled the imagination of the earliest settlers—that of a fierce and frightening wilderness. It was an image strongly buttressed by the immediate reality the early arrivals were forced to confront. America was not a garden. It was the very antithesis of Eden, or so it seemed to the brave but apprehensive early colonists. The explorers and first settlers were faced by a dark, forbidding line of forest behind which was a vast, unmapped continental interior, inhabited, they thought, by savages and filled with ferocious wild beasts.

William Bradford, looking over the water to Cape Cod from the deck of the *Mayflower* in September 1620, gloomily contemplated "a hideous and desolate wilderness full of wilde beasts and wild men."[15]

Even for the intrepid, God-inspired Pilgrims, the prospect was daunting. They thought themselves to be, the historian Perry Miller noted, "alone in America."[16]

In the beginning, mere survival meant conquering the wilderness. The forest had to be cleared to make living space and to provide wood for shelters and fires. Behind the trees lurked the Indians, ready, the settlers suspected, to commit unspeakable atrocities. The forest was filled with wolves, bears, and panthers that would pounce on children and domestic animals—or so they feared. The greater the destruction of the forest, the greater the safety for the tiny communities clinging to the edge of the hostile continent. Removing the trees also opened land for crops and cattle. Killing the wild animals not only filled the pot with meat but eliminated the deer and other grazing animals that stole the settlers' corn and competed with their imported cattle for forage.

To the European settlers, who were largely blind to the values of Indian society, the American natives lived in a state of nature, a state, Thomas Hobbes wrote in his *Leviathan*, published in 1651, where there is "no account of Time, no Letters; no Society; and which is worst of all, continual fear, and danger of violent death; and the life of man solitary, poor, nasty, brutish, and short."[17] In the following century, Jean Jacques Rousseau would praise the beauty and virtue of nature, but to the Europeans coming to the New World in the seventeenth century, Hobbes's view seemed all too appropriate.

In the resonant metaphor of Perry Miller, taken from a sermon given three hundred years earlier by the Reverend Samuel Danforth, the early settlers had an "errand into the wilderness." To the New England Puritan, the biblical injunction to subdue the earth and make it fruitful was at once an imperative of survival and a holy mission. That mission was no less than the planting of a perfect Christian community in the virgin, hostile land.

The New World was a savage place, but, to the Puritan sensibility, at least it was clean of the corruption of England's established church and the other false religions of Europe. The removal of the wilderness would produce an unspoiled site for building the foundation of the new city in which God could be served and his commandments obeyed. To accomplish this errand, the wilderness had to be destroyed, nature itself subdued.

From there it was but a short leap to view the destruction and civilization of the wilderness as the errand itself. Writing in 1653, Edward Johnson, an early colonial historian, counted it "as God's providence that 'a rocky, barren bushy, wild-woody wilderness' was transformed in a generation into 'a second England for fertileness.' "[18]

This belief that destroying the wilderness and taming nature was carrying out the work of God made a deep and lasting imprint on the national character. In 1823, Congressman Francis Baylies stated, "Our national boundary is the Pacific Ocean . . . To diffuse the arts of life, the light of science, and the blessings of the Gospel over a wilderness is no violation of the laws of God."[19]

Thus, two centuries after Plymouth and the Massachusetts Bay colony, was the task of subduing the wilderness transmuted by the congressman into a new concept: Manifest Destiny, as it soon came to be called. The will of God, it was widely believed—or at least professed—now decreed that the new Americans possess the entire continent and convert it from its savage state into a land that could enjoy the blessings of Christian civilization. That meant, of course, that it was God's work to seize the land occupied by Native Americans.

Manifest Destiny, as it came to reflect Americans' impulses, still required the conquest of the wilderness, but increasingly that destiny had to do less with God's will than with the march of secular civilization.

A young, proud, vigorous America had neither time nor patience to reflect on the wonder and beauty of the natural landscape it was replacing. Alexis de Tocqueville, the visitor from France whose perceptive observations continue to astonish us, noted in 1832, "In Europe, people talk a great deal of the wilds of America, but the Americans themselves never think about them; they are insensible to the wonders of inanimate nature and they may be said not to perceive the mighty forests that surround them till they fall beneath the hatchet. Their eyes are fixed upon another sight: The American people view its own march across these wilds, draining swamps, turning the course of rivers, peopling solitudes, and subduing nature."[20]

Translated into the everyday acts and habits of the pioneers and settlers, farmers and townspeople, workers and entrepreneurs, Manifest Destiny became an irresistible force for altering nature. By clearing a patch in the forest, building a home, plowing a field, driving cattle, constructing a road, using and throwing away farm implements, diverting a stream, building a mill, laying track, digging a mine, the Americans who spread across the continent changed the natural environment and they did it with breathtaking speed.

The Western Hemisphere, of course, was not an empty, unpopulated desert when the colonists arrived. The Indians living in North America had long established an astonishing diversity of cultures and had explored and used almost every corner of the land. But as historian Richard Bartlett has pointed out, "regardless of where they lived, the Indians were beautifully attuned to their environment."[21] For the most part, Indian communities lived a mobile existence. In the East, small openings were burnt and cleared in the forest in which the women, who did the farming, could grow corn, beans, and squash. The men hunted deer, moose, and other game, relying on those species that were most plentiful. When game became harder to find, the Indians moved on before the population of any one species declined to dangerous levels. In the West, the Plains Indians followed the buffalo, and satisfied most of their needs for food, clothing, and habitation without making a perceptible dent in the great herds. Indian populations tended to remain relatively low and well within the land's ability to support their nomadic style of life.

Most Indians accumulated few personal possessions. They owned what they could carry with them easily as they moved from camp to camp in the forest or followed the herds over great distances on the plains. The absence of surplus commodities sometimes meant that they suffered through weeks or months of hunger. John Locke described the Indians as poor because of their dearth of possessions and the absence of money and commerce. But as historian William Cronon notes, the Indians did not think of themselves as poor.

There is no need to sentimentalize the Native Americans. Their reverence for human life seldom extended beyond their own tribe. Like the Europeans, they were capable of acts of extreme cruelty. With some notable exceptions, the North American tribes left few permanent reminders of their culture. But their society was in many ways elegant and admirable. Their way of life did not scar the land. Their means of sustaining themselves did not rely on subduing the earth but on using what it offered. The resources of the land were used as a gardener uses a fruit tree, the apples plucked and eaten but the tree itself left unharmed. Indian society was not separate from nature—it was part of it.[22]

The Europeans had no use for this wild garden. Their dreams were very different. They came to take the land, not simply to use it. It was the idea of owning land that brought millions from all stations of life across the great ocean.

Private property—possession—meant permanence. A farm or a plantation was something to be lived on, expanded, and passed on to one's children. To claim the land, boundaries had to be drawn, trees felled, stumps removed, and crops planted. The surrounding forest could provide timber for building houses and barns and for keeping houses warm, but the supply was limited. For other farms nearby also required wood. When demand exceeded local supply, trees had to be felled and hauled from a distance. The surrounding forests provided deer and turkey as a supplemental or even essential source of food—until the disappearance of the trees and overhunting caused their numbers to dwindle. Food crops enabled the land to sustain a much larger population than the hunt-and-gather, slash-and-burn economy of the Indians. But surprisingly quickly in many areas, the European population grew beyond the carrying capacity of the land. Cropland frequently was exhausted by permanent cultivation; cattle, swine, and sheep introduced by the immigrants made far heavier demands on field and forest than wild animals.

The Europeans also brought a technology that contributed to the heavy impact they had on the land. Horses and oxen enabled them to open and cultivate much broader acres. Plows could dig deeply into the soil, exposing far more loam than the pointed sticks used by Indian women. With draft animals, the Europeans could harvest heavier loads and transport them to market. Sailing ships could carry those loads along the coasts or across the ocean. Firearms could more efficiently kill wild animals and birds—not to mention the advantage they gave the Europeans in their unequal contest with the natives for control of the land.

The market economy itself was a European import that helped shape the face of colonial America. Whereas the aboriginal people took from the land only what they could consume, the colonists and their successors sought to grow surpluses, which they could sell for cash or trade for manufactured goods and other commodities. That meant clearing more land, cutting more timber, planting more crops, raising more cattle. All these activities changed nature's subtle rhythms that had been at play without interruption for hundreds of generations.

The market demand for crops, as well as for fish, timber, furs, and other commodities, was "a causal agent of ecological change."[23] To satisfy the demand, these commodities were harvested at a rate that could be sustained only at the cost of permanent damage to the land. In the southern colonies, the market encouraged the development of a monoculture in tobacco, leading to a steady decline in the fertility of the soil. To pay the taxes imposed on them, the settlers often were forced to increase production, thus accelerating soil depletion. Even the Indians were drawn into this "alien commercial economy"[24] through the fur trade and their increasing dependence on guns, metal, cloth, and other European manufactures.

The Indians attuned their lives to the surrounding environment; the Europeans' economy was based on fragmenting it. Instead of treating their surroundings as an interdependent ecological system, colonists tended over the long run to break their holdings into ever smaller economic units.

The production of surpluses led to the accumulation of capital and the creation of wealth, largely in the towns that served as market centers. The land itself soon became a commodity to be bought and sold—an object of speculation.

The political skills of the Europeans, fueled by capital, made it possible for their market economy to be expanded and protected and, to an extent, regulated. The resources of North America became commodities of transatlantic trade with surprising rapidity. The deforestation of New England and the disappearance of the beaver in the East are but two dramatic examples of how the demands of the market could deplete abundant resources in short order. Finally, the European concept of individual and social progress, of changing and improving the conditions of life, encouraged alteration of the landscape.

From the very beginning, therefore, the colonists were a force for both change and environmental degradation.

Among the European imports that had the quickest, most significant, and lasting impact were the diseases that decimated the Indian populations. Even in the early days of the Massachusetts Bay colony, John Winthrop noted that smallpox was "thinning" the ranks of the nearby tribes.[25] There was little pity for the horrible effect on the natives. According to historians Bruce and William Catton, "most Englishmen already had a highly developed sense of their own racial and ethnic superiority, and the Indian was simply in the way. He must move, stand aside or be eliminated."[26]

The immigrant culture was able to conquer the continent in the space of a few short centuries. Americans created a brash, expansive, open-hearted democracy that became an inspiration for the rest of the world. The United States offered a haven for the persecuted, a fresh start for the poor, new opportunities for the daring. In time it also became an international granary, mill, foundry, and factory that helped satisfy much of the material needs of other countries around the globe.

While the new Americans were generally heedless of what they did to their surroundings, from the earliest days there were those who loved the land for itself. A handful—the *coureurs de bois*, the frontiersmen who were the living counterparts of James Fenimore Cooper's fictional Natty Bumppo, and the mountain men—cherished the untamed forest through which they roamed with as light a tread as the aboriginal inhabitants. Sharp-eyed observers saw the waste and thought of the price that would someday have to be paid for it. There were some who expressed regret over the felling of the trees and the slaughter of the birds.

The rudiments of conservation were evident even in the early colonial days. New England town meetings drafted regulations governing the cutting of timber and where and when cattle could graze.[27] In northern Virginia, farmers faced with worn-out soil at the end of the eighteenth century began to plant clover and apply gypsum to the land to restore fertility. Jefferson, among others, experimented with contour plowing to retard erosion.[28]

The frontiersmen, the intrepid woodsmen who served as the advance scouts of civilization, became folk heroes and then the mythic protagonists of American literature.

In Cooper's *The Pioneers*, the seventy-year-old Natty Bumppo, trapped by the laws and restrictions of a new frontier town after a lifetime of freedom in the forest, pleads, "The meanest of God's creaters be made for some use, and I'm formed for the wilderness; if ye love me, let me go where my soul craves to be ag'in!"[29]

As Henry Nash Smith pointed out, Bumppo's plaint reflects the conflict between the need of a new community, a new civilization, to establish permanence and inculcate the concept of property rights on the frontier on one hand and "the old forest freedom" on the other. It was a question of free access to the bounty of nature—whether in the form of game or of land—versus individual appropriation and the whole notion of inviolable property rights. Smith notes that Bumppo's creator, James Fenimore Cooper, had a "genuine ambivalence toward all of these issues."[30] This ambivalence remains as strong in the national psyche today as it was then and is reflected in the fierce and unremitting battles between conservationists and corporate interests for control over the remaining public domain.

Of course, Cooper wrote *The Pioneers* early in the nineteenth century and the romanticism of that era undoubtedly contributed to his portrait of the Leatherstocking. But Daniel Boone—the real thing—expressed similar if somewhat conflicted thoughts about the untamed land. In his autobiography, which, it seems, was largely written by John Filson, another Kentuckian, Boone described himself as "an instrument ordained to settle the wilderness." But Boone also expressed his "astonishing delight" in primitive scenery and declared,

"No populous city, with all the varieties of commerce and stately structures, could afford so much pleasure to my mind, as the beauties of nature I found here."[31]

The strong, brave, self-reliant frontiersmen and pioneers, uneducated perhaps, but with a deep appreciation for the natural beauty of the land, are not only prototypes of American fiction but also a reflection of our self-image. Even today, we think of the American character as shaped by the experience of civilizing the wilderness. Even today, in the face of wholesale destruction of the landscape for development, we still take it as a given that Americans have a deep and abiding love of the land.

It is easy to be cynical about this image, but it cannot be lightly explained away. It persists in American thought and in present-day conservation and environmental movements. Only in the past century have we begun to talk of an ethical duty to preserve the land. Such an obligation has yet to affect our actions deeply. But as we have seen, from earliest times there were the rudiments of a tradition to protect and conserve nature.

By the time of the American Revolution, the wilderness along the eastern seaboard had been pretty much tamed. While some pockets of forest remained, the thirteen colonies were largely covered with farms, dotted with villages, and punctuated by a few substantial cities, notably Boston, New York, Philadelphia, and Charleston, which served as centers of commerce, learning, and art. Boone was already opening up Kentucky, piercing the dark forest of the interior.

At least part of the New World had been transformed into what Leo Marx has called "the middle landscape," a compromise between the primeval wilderness and the urbanized, crowded, deforested surface of much of the Old World. The garden yearned for by the first settlers had in large measure come to pass, or so it seemed.

To Thomas Jefferson and many of his contemporaries, this middle landscape was the natural and proper condition of the new nation. Jefferson believed strongly that the United States was and should continue to be a nation of yeoman farmers. "Those who labor on the earth are the chosen people of God," he contended in his *Notes on Virginia*, published in 1785.[32] This agrarian ideal was, in fact, the way most Americans at the time thought the natural environment should be managed.

Americans today still feel a deep sense of need for that idealized countryside. Even I, the city-bred grandchild of immigrants from the ghettos of Russia and Poland who did not arrive on these shores until more than half a century after Jefferson died, feel a strong desire to find a place in that vanished American landscape. Its memory is a deep well of longing among many people in today's busy society, a well from which the environmental movement has only begun to draw.

The agrarian dream proved to be ephemeral even in Jefferson's time. The golden age, if it was one, passed quickly. At the opening of the nineteenth century, the young nation was poised to strike across the continent to the Pacific. The Native Americans would be ruthlessly pushed aside. President James Monroe wrote in 1817, "The hunter of the savage state requires a greater extent of territory to sustain it, than is compatible with the progress and just claims of civilized life . . . and must yield to it."[33] Gardens would be created along the way, but so would cities, factories, mines, dams, canals, and other works of Western civilization that threatened and in time would bury the pastoral ideal.

Early in the nineteenth century, an awesome new force, industrialization, was gathering strength in Europe. Soon exported to the United States, the industrial revolution swept away Jefferson's vision of America as an agrarian land. The steam engine, the railroad, the mechanical thresher, and hundreds of other ingenious artifacts that increased man's ability to transform the natural world and put it to use were puffing and clattering and roaring in all corners of the land.

In Leo Marx's powerful metaphor, a machine suddenly appeared in the garden, shattering the stillness of the pastoral landscape and changing forever the balance of forces between human beings and the rest of nature.

SUBDUING

NATURE

As we grow older
The world becomes stranger,
the pattern more complicated . . .
                    T. S. Eliot

By July 4, 1804, the expedition commanded by Captains Meriwether Lewis and William Clark had been laboriously making its way up the Missouri River from St. Louis for nearly two months. Lewis and Clark had been dispatched by President Jefferson to explore the lands acquired in 1803 from France by the Louisiana Purchase and to seek a route to the Pacific Ocean.

Each day on the river had brought them exhilarating new sights previously familiar only to Indians and a few white trappers and traders. Clark, a tall redheaded man famous for his bravery in battle in the fierce Indian wars that followed the Revolution, was not given to poetic outbursts. But the entry in his journal for that evening suggests his enthusiasm for the landscape through which the expedition was passing.

> The plains of this country are covered with a leek green grass, well calculated for the sweetest and most nourishing hay—interspersed with copses of trees, spreading their lofty branches over pools, springs or brooks of fine water. Groups

of shrubs covered with the most delicious fruit is to be seen in every direction, and nature appears to have exerted herself to beautify the scenery by the variety of flowers, delicately and highly flavored, raised above the grass, which strikes and perfumes the sensations and amuses the mind, throws it into conjecturing the cause of so magnificent a scenery . . . in a country far removed from the civilized world.[1]

The valley of the Missouri was indeed far removed from the civilized world that Clark knew. Although the population of the United States in 1804 had reached six million, almost all of it was confined in a narrow strip along the eastern seaboard. Daniel Boone and other pioneers, however, were already leading the way through the passes of the Appalachians and the Ohio Valley, and other areas of the old Northwest Territories were starting to attract adventurous settlers.

But the interior of the continent was still largely empty of Europeans. Save for the changes in the Indians' way of life brought about by the guns, horses, metals, and other European imports, which may have had some slight impact on the environment, the plains remained as they had been in pre-Columbian days. And when the awestruck members of the Lewis and Clark expedition came to the towering, snowy Rocky Mountains and then to the Coast ranges with their ancient, soaring trees, they found those, too, unchanged by humans. America at the start of the nineteenth century was still a garden and a wilderness. The great prairie stretched more than a thousand miles from the Appalachians to the Rockies. Although much of New England had been stripped of trees, the country still contained more than 700 million acres of dense primeval forest. Rivers flowed freely from the mountains to the sea, their surfaces empty save for an occasional canoe or bateau. Indian tribes still followed the bison and hunted the deer and elk, assured in many cases by solemn treaty that the land that sustained them would be theirs forever.

But the tiny band of soldiers and boatmen commanded by Lewis and Clark, a mere speck beneath the immense arch of the sky as day by day they poled and dragged their boats up the river, was the thin wedge of a relentless civilization that would tame, transform, and, with innocent ferocity, transmute the landscape that both men found so enchanting.

Jefferson intended that Lewis and Clark prepare the way for settlement of the continental interior. They were to study the land and its resources carefully to determine where it was suitable for farming, what mineral resources could be exploited, and what plants and animals could serve commercial purposes. They were also to identify and name the species they found, a process of scientific classification that itself represented the beginning of the long process of confining, dominating, and altering nature.

Seventy-two years after Lewis and Clark set off on their great adventure, the span of a single lifetime, the United States celebrated the hundredth anniversary of its independence. A centerpiece of that celebration was the Centennial Exhibition in Philadelphia, which brought together the artifacts of the nation's progress over the previous century. The exhibition has been re-created and, prior to the bicentennial celebration in 1976, put on permanent display by the Smithsonian Institution in Washington, D.C. It offers a vivid tableau of how the Americans of 1876 viewed themselves and the pride they took in the accomplishments of their still young country.

To stroll through the exhibits with Lewis and Clark's descriptions of the landscape still fresh in mind is to be astounded by the extent and rapidity of change.

Here were Samuel Morse's telegraph and Alexander Graham Bell's telephone—inventions that enabled Americans to communicate across great distances with the speed of light. Here was the locomotive Jupiter, a shining iron horse that hurtled through the countryside Lewis and Clark had crossed with so much effort so few years before. Here were machine tools and industrial equipment powered by steam engines with flywheels ten feet in diameter. Here were electric arc lights, mechanical threshers and harvesters, seed drills, and a hundred other artifacts attesting to man's technological dominion over the earth and its resources. Here were the repeating rifles that helped drive the Indians into ever smaller, more remote, and less desirable pockets of the country. Intricately carved and inlaid furniture, luxurious carriages, grand pianos, elegant tableware electroplated with silver, and objets d'art imported from Europe and Asia testified that many Americans had attained a life of affluence and leisure in a safe and settled landscape.

The natural world was represented at the Centennial Exhibition by a few cases of stuffed birds and animals.

How did it happen? How did an unspoiled, undeveloped continent come to be placed so completely under the yoke of Europeans in so few short years?

The answer, of course, originates with the land.

Land was the great magnet that attracted immigrants. Albert Gallatin, Jefferson's Secretary of the Treasury, stated it simply: "The happiness of my country arises from the great plenty of land."[2]

To make use of this latent wealth and power, the newly independent nation had to establish dominion over it. At the end of the Revolution, virtually all real estate was owned privately or by the states. The states, through their historic charters, owned not only the lands within their colonial borders but also most of the "western territories," which included most of the land drained by the Ohio River to the Mississippi.

On October 29, 1782, the Continental Congress accepted the land owned by New York State outside its boundaries. Virginia, Massachusetts, Connecticut, the Carolinas, and Georgia soon followed New York's example by ceding their frontier holdings to the Congress. In this way the national government acquired title to some 233 million acres.[3] It thus became the nation's greatest landholder and has remained so ever since.

The Louisiana Purchase was made in 1803, followed by the purchase of Florida from Spain in 1819 and then the acquisition of Texas and other lands in the Southwest from Mexico in 1848 in settlement of a war that, most historians agree, was fomented by the United States for that purpose. Additional land in the Southwest was later obtained from Mexico through the Gadsden Purchase of 1853. Earlier, in 1846, the compromise settlement of a boundary dispute with Britain had given the United States the territory that now comprises Washington, Oregon, Idaho, and some abutting lands. The last major land acquisition came in 1867, when Andrew Johnson's Secretary of State, William Seward, in a transaction called "Seward's Folly" at the time, purchased Alaska and its 378 million acres from Russia for $7 million.[4] Thus by purchase, treaty, and war, the United States government obtained some 1.8 billion acres.

The United States comprises over 2.3 billion acres of some of the most varied terrain in the world.[5] Land was held by the national government in the name of all its citizens. It belonged to no king, no feudal lord, no great corporation; it was the people's land. Even the states were to have no claim to the lands within their borders except for those specifically granted to them by the national government, a principle that has been conveniently ignored by the "Sagebrush Rebels" of the late twentieth century.

Having acquired almost 2 billion acres, the federal government confronted one of the most difficult and controversial questions in its history: how to dispose of it. It is a question that the government has never answered to the satisfaction of all its citizens, and the struggle for control of the public domain remains intense to this day.

Jefferson, inspired by the vision of an agrarian nation built by the labor of the small freeholder, wanted the land to be given or sold cheaply in small but sustainable allotments to independent farmers. Alexander Hamilton argued that the best use of the land would be to sell it in large blocks to corporations and speculators. Bernard Shanks contends that this conflict over "aristocratic" as opposed to "democratic" uses of land has been a persistent element in decision making over the disposal of federal lands and that "the basic argument remains today: corporations versus the public as a whole."[6]

Before disposing of property, the federal government first sought to impose a geometric discipline on the untamed heartland. Under the Land Ordinance of 1785, all the public domain was to be surveyed and laid out in regular plots, each a mile square, or 640 acres. There may be no straight lines in nature, but the new lords of the land shaped nature to meet their needs and desires. The ordinance adopted more than two hundred years ago has left an indelible imprint on the countryside, permanently framing the native landscape. The checkerboard of fields and the grid of straight roads that demarcate the nation's heartland today are the legacy of that law. The meandering lines and disorderly contours of the native landscape were, over time, substantially obliterated.

Thus, not just with rifle, plow, and ax but also with compass and plumb line did the new Americans impose their will on nature.

Eager to start disposing of land to raise cash for the huge debt remaining from the Revolution and to begin the process of nation building, the fledgling government started in 1795 to offer land in the public domain for sale in sections of 640 acres and quarter sections of 160 acres at relatively affordable prices.[7] From the beginning, however, there were demands for free land by the pioneers who were opening the new country and by the swelling tide of Germans, Irish, and other immigrants from Europe. Not until 1862, however, during the Civil War, did Congress pass the Homestead Act, which enabled settlers to obtain title to a quarter section of public land after five years of living on and improving it. The act also permitted land to be purchased by homesteaders for $1.25 an acre.

Horace Greeley, newspaper publisher and avid promoter of western settlement ("Go West, young man . . .") called the Homestead Act "a magnificent national democratic triumph—a bold but noble promise."[8] But historians have pointed to the failings and abuses of the law. Henry Nash Smith contended that the act "almost wholly failed to have the results that had been predicted," because it played into the hands of unscrupulous developers who used the law to obtain large holdings, which were then resold, often for substantial profit.[9]

From the outset, speculators and developers or "boomers" arrived with or sometimes ahead of the pioneers, grabbed choice lands by hook or by crook, and once again made the natural environment a commodity to be bought and sold for the sake of accumulating wealth.

Land speculators and developers undoubtedly played a significant role in opening the West by attracting settlers with their dreams and their hyperbolic promises. The speculator, wrote the historians Bruce and William Catton, "was composed of varying quantities of dreamer, salesman, patriot, and con artist, on a scale that ranged from penny ante pitchman to continental empire builder."[10] Charles and Mary Beard found that the transfer of the public domain to private hands was "effected by fraud and chicane so daring and so colossal as to exceed the imagination of the innocent . . ."[11]

With possibly unmatched largesse, the government feverishly continued to transfer lands to private, corporate, and state hands. Nearly 160 million acres were given to the railroads as incentives to lay track across empty land, of which about 42 million acres were subsequently forfeited when the companies failed to meet the conditions of their grants. The theory was that the railroads would offer land to the settlers to induce them to put down roots along the right-of-way, thus creating profitable traffic for their lines. And that is what in fact happened. Extraordinarily generous grants of land inevitably enabled the railroads to join the ranks of the major land speculators.

Land grants were made to the states to support schools and other institutions and to build canals and roads. They were made to war veterans and to timber and mining companies. In all, the national government gave away or sold at a nominal sum well over a billion acres in what the Beards described as a "saturnalia"[12] of land disposal. During the nineteenth century, this disposal was presided over by the government's General Land Office, which was widely recognized at the time as "notoriously corrupt and inefficient."[13]

Whether they staked their claims under the Homestead Act or bought their farms from the railroads or speculators, the settlers quickly flowed into the newly opened land, first in a trickle and then, after the Civil War, in a torrent that was to spread across much of the continent before the end of the nineteenth century. They cut and burned the trees, tore stumps from the soil, plowed and planted their fields, built cabins and sawmills, and founded their towns and cities. The Native Americans who occupied the land were simply forced onto reservations, out of the way of the onrushing white horde. Efforts by the Indians to slow the conquest of their lands by war and by negotiation were, in the end, a relatively minor impediment pushed out of the way by the growing tide of settlers. Drought, locusts, freezing winters, range wars, and the Civil War had virtually no effect in slowing this astonishing mass movement of human beings over the ocean and across the continent. By the time of the Centennial, the population of the United States, swollen by immigration, was 46 million, nearly eight times the number who lived here when Lewis and Clark ventured into the virgin heartland. By 1890, the director of the Census Bureau declared that a frontier no longer existed.

Population growth and geographic expansion, however, were only two facets of one of history's most sweeping cultural transformations, which took place at uncontrollable speed and would soon not only create a new society and new economic relationships but also radically shift the balance between nature and humanity in North America.

The term "industrial revolution" was coined in France in 1810 "as a metaphor of the affinity between technology and the great political revolution of modern times."[14] Nowhere in the world did the revolution take place as quickly and completely as it did in the United States during the nineteenth century. Nowhere did the landscape more quickly become degraded as a result of that revolution.

The new machines swiftly accelerated the consumption of raw materials from the nation's farms, forests, and mines. Standardized parts enabled consumer products to be turned out in mass quantities cheaply as well as quickly, placing items ranging from clocks to sewing machines within the reach of millions. As the huge casualties of the Civil War demonstrated, even warfare became industrialized, increasing the efficiency with which soldiers could slaughter one another.

Timberlands were distributed just like any other part of the federal domain. They were fair game for the same kind of cheating and manipulating that characterized the land rush. Even before independence, choice timber had been stolen from the British rulers of the thirteen colonies, who had reserved the tallest and straightest pine trees to be used as masts for the Royal Navy. These trees were marked with a broad arrow to show that they belonged to the king. But in the dark forests there was no one to enforce the law and the colonists, with pragmatic lèse-majesté, stole and used these superb trees as a matter of course. Stealing public timber was a practice that continued throughout the nineteenth-century settlement and many conservationists maintain that it persists to this day.

Lumbering became the nation's most important industry in the late eighteenth and early nineteenth centuries. In demand for heating, for building houses, barns, and shops, for ships, furniture, farm implements, and later for railroad ties, for factories and paper making, wood was the young country's most widely used raw material. The supply, of course, seemed inexhaustible. Forests darkened huge swaths of the continent. By 1840, however, most of the forests of New England and New York had been cleared and the timber industry moved on to the woodlands of the Great Lakes region. Soon those, too, were exhausted and the axmen moved on to the Northwest. The last extensive stands of these woodland leviathans are now being cut down as the timber industry removes the remaining major forests of redwoods and Douglas firs on the West Coast.

The forests melted away before the axes of the advancing Americans. Not only was the wood needed but clearing the trees was, as we have seen, almost universally viewed as an act of civilization— God's work. Moreover, conservation did not emerge as a popular ideal until the end of the nineteenth century. While a few prescient voices called for the creation of forest reserves as early as the 1790s, it was an idea whose time would not come until the latter part of the nineteenth century. The settlers never thought of their ax work as " 'deforestation' but as 'the progress of cultivation.' "[15]

Over much of the continent, the soil that had been shaded by trees since the retreat of the glaciers was opened to the sun. In many areas, the land was spiked with stumps, like stubble in a harvested cornfield, from horizon to horizon. Brush and brambles choked what had recently been woodland glades sheltering deer and other forest creatures, many of which were rapidly disappearing from the country-side.

Even at the beginning of the nineteenth century, it had been apparent to many that the destruction of the forests was having a profound effect on the environment, although they would not have used that word. Soon after the tree cover was removed, the forest soil began to lose nutrients such as organic matter and minerals. The soil began to be washed away, turning clear streams into slow, muddy ditches, filling lakes, and killing fish.

Naturalists had long recognized that removal of the forests and the replacement of trees with crops changed the climate. The soil appeared to be drier; the surface of the land was hotter in the summer and in the winter it was colder without the moderating influence of the tree cover. Because the ground froze to a greater depth, it was unable to absorb as much of the snowmelt in the spring. Watersheds emptied more quickly and flooding became more prevalent. Once forested areas turned into swamps that bred mosquitoes and other disease vectors.

The ecological changes worked by deforestation in the eighteenth and nineteenth centuries were local, occasionally regional. Not until the twentieth century did we begin to change natural systems on a continental and global scale. But by the beginning of this century, the continent had been profoundly changed by the extensive removal of the trees. The wilderness, with all its dangers, its mystery, its promise, was largely gone. The few fragments of remaining wild land were no longer places to be feared and civilized but, to a growing number of Americans, reminders of an earlier era that were to be preserved and cherished. In many areas the great abundance of wood that so impressed the first settlers had given way to scarcity. Soil erosion, loss of watersheds, and disappearance of game had by the latter part of the nineteenth century become national problems as the once seemingly endless forests were methodically leveled.

As wasteful as rapid deforestation was the style of agriculture practiced by the settlers in the new country. Eastern farmers tired of doing eternal battle with New England's rocky terrain or coaxing crops from the played-out soil of the South, and land-hungry recent immigrants from Europe, swarmed to the heartland, drawn irresistibly by the thick, black loam of the prairies. That tough soil, armored since the retreat of the glaciers by a thick shield of grasses and their root systems, was pierced by the sharp edges of steel plows being turned out in rapidly increasing numbers by John Deere and exposed to sun, wind, and rain.

In the mid-nineteenth century, three-quarters of the nation's 24 million people lived in rural areas.[16] Farming was still the occupation of the majority. Inevitably, the way the hardworking, often long-suffering farmers went about their business affected not only the land but the ecology of the continent. Each new field that was planted displaced an age-old, interdependent world of plants, animals, insects, and microorganisms that had been aeons in evolving. With each crop harvested, the chemical, mineral, and biological nature of the soil itself was altered. The native flora and fauna were quickly replaced by the plants and animals brought from Europe.

With some exceptions, notably the Pennsylvania Dutch, the new settlers had neither the knowledge nor the inclination to conserve the soil they tilled. As Bernard Bailyn noted: "They tended to look on land as a temporary and expendable resource that could be mined as rapidly as possible."[17] As early as 1818, James Madison, writing on "Intelligent Husbandry," commented, "With so many consumers of the fertility of the earth, and so little attention to the means of repairing the ravages, no one can be surprised at the impoverished face of the country."[18]

Meanwhile, the big cities and growing wealth of the East were creating a rapidly expanding market for wheat, corn, beef, and other cash crops. In the heartland, bustling, ambitious new cities, particularly Chicago, seemed to spring up overnight, offering additional outlets for food crops and other products of the land and serving as hubs of trade. New roads and canals, the steamboat and the locomotive, made domestic and foreign markets increasingly accessible to farmers in the center of the continent. Eli Whitney's cotton gin, Cyrus McCormick's reaper, Benjamin Holt's combine, and all the other ingenious inventions encouraged the development of a highly productive, efficient agriculture that was economically rewarding but sharply reduced the biological diversity of the land. Single crops such as cotton and tobacco grown for a distant market had long been the basis of the South's slave-powered agriculture. After the Civil War, King Cotton was succeeded by King Wheat, King Corn, King Cattle, and the lesser royalty of what was already a great agricultural nation as farmers produced crops not simply to sustain themselves and their families but to sell surpluses to a national and world market. In 1830 it was estimated that it took three hours of human labor to produce a bushel of wheat. By the end of the century, with mechanical aids widely in use, a bushel was produced in less than ten minutes.[19]

Even the semi-arid lands of the high plains seemed to be no obstacle to farming by the westward-flowing tide of settlers. Rivers were tapped and deep wells dug for irrigation. Agronomists and botanists developed other methods of farming the dry land. Where science had no answers, eager settlers placed their faith in promoters and prophets who promised that rain would come to the dry country once the land had been cultivated and trees planted. Cattle and sheep soon dotted the open range which previously had provided forage and water for the vast herds of bison, deer, elk, and antelope. The cowboys and their longhorns took over public grasslands, but in keeping with a practice that ranchers defend to this day, they paid little or nothing to the government and the public for the privilege.

The country had turned into a garden, indeed; some, in fact, described the United States as "the Garden of the World."

This garden, however, was something less than Eden. It was crawling with not one but many serpents. Single-crop farming impoverished the soil and encouraged the proliferation of insect and weed pests. Farmers producing commodities for distant markets were vulnerable to exploitation by local merchants, banks, railroads, and commodity brokers. Increasingly marginal lands came under the plow. Droughts made a mockery of efforts at "dry farming" the land west of the 100th meridian. Territories that later became states— Wyoming, Montana, Colorado, Utah, New Mexico, and Nevada—

were occupied by more tillers of the soil than they could sustain. Too many cattle overgrazed the range, causing severe soil erosion and the degradation of streams and pools at which they drank. The abuse of the range continues in many areas today, despite laws and rules designed to protect the public lands.

Producing commodities rather than living off the plants and animals of nature's bounty, as the predominantly hunter-gatherer Indians had done, the new Americans were separating themselves from nature. They became powerful manipulators of the natural world rather than occupying a niche within it. Moreover, American agriculture progressively alienated workers from the land by substituting capital-intensive machinery, energy, and other technology for expensive labor. Here was another trend that would accelerate dramatically in the twentieth century. Over time, agricultural practices were increasingly dictated by the demands of capital and markets rather than by the relationship of people with the land they lived on.

Mining both preceded and quickly followed settlement of the interior and left deep and permanent scars on the continent's land and waters. Gold in California, copper in Montana, coal and oil in Pennsylvania, iron ore in Minnesota, and lead in Illinois attracted fortune hunters and job seekers. Mining was a boom-and-bust industry. Reports of a strike would draw thousands of prospectors and workers and those who lived off them; tent and shanty towns appeared like fungi on the landscape, usually to be deserted when the veins played out. But as the first industry in many areas, mining had a key role in opening the new country.

"Ephemeral as it was," Henry Steele Commager and Samuel Eliot Morison noted, "the mining frontier played an important part in the development of the West and of the nation. The miners familiarized the American people with the country between the Missouri and the Pacific and advertised its magnificent resources. They forced a solution to the Indian problem, emphasized the need for railroads, and laid the foundations for the later permanent farming populations."[20] Mining also created wealth and power for many in the United States and attracted substantial amounts of investment from abroad. It was one of the most important bases of the industrial strength that made the young nation a world power by the end of the nineteenth century.

The federal government received little or nothing in the way of direct payment for minerals taken from the public lands that ostensibly belonged to all the people. Bernard Shanks has estimated that if the government had demanded royalties on minerals from its domain, it would have received more than $1 billion in nineteenth-century dollars from the iron and copper mines of the Great Lakes region alone.[21]

Mines were operated without care for the surrounding countryside—the idea that such concern was important would simply not have occurred to most nineteenth-century Americans. As a result, mining produced more than wealth. The picks and shovels, the hoses and dredges, and the smelter fires of the miners created the nation's first widespread pollution and environmental health problems. "Mining left behind gutted mountains, dredged-out streams, despoiled vegetation, open pits, polluted creeks, barren hillsides and meadows, a littered landscape, abandoned camps, and burned-out miners and entrepreneurs who came to mine the miners," wrote historian Duane Smith.[22]

Some of the most pervasive and devastating damage to the landscape was caused by California gold miners who employed ever more destructive methods to wash away the soil that covered the treasure they so eagerly coveted. Starting with pans shaken over a stream, the forty-niners developed powerful hydraulic technology, finally fixing on a system that channeled a rushing stream through canvas sheeting into a large metal nozzle which shot the water with tremendous force against the stream banks and hillsides, washing away soil, gravel, and rocks. Trees, grass, entire hills were carried off by "hydraulicking," as it was called, leaving behind moonscapes similar to those created by strip mining for coal in the twentieth century. The massive amounts of debris thus washed away clogged streams and covered fields and meadows, sometimes seriously interfering with local farming. Marysville, a California town downstream from large-scale "hydraulicking" operations, was forced to build levees to keep the debris from the choked Mary River from covering its streets. The levees were built higher and higher until they formed a wall taller than the rooftops. Even then, when the river flooded, the spoil from the mining operations cascaded over the levees into the town.

Enraged farmers banded together to form what can be regarded as a rudimentary environmental group. But for a long time they could make no progress against a mining industry that was protected by the boomer mentality of the West and by the devotion to laissez-faire that permitted property owners to do with their land as they chose.

Mining contributed to the deforestation of the countryside. Woodlands were often cleared for mining operations; enormous amounts of timber were needed for the posts and beams that supported mine shafts and to fuel smelter operations. One contemporary observer of the silver-mining operations at the Comstock mine in Virginia City, Nevada, quoted by Duane Smith, said, "The Comstock lode may truthfully be said to be the tomb of the forests of the Sierras. Millions on millions of feet of lumber are annually buried in the mines, nevermore to be resurrected."[23]

Butte, Montana, which was built starting in the 1870s on and around one of the world's biggest open-faced copper mines, was a victim of reckless mining in an era when there was little awareness of or thought given to its consequences for health or aesthetics. As described by Richard Bartlett: "Sterile yellow and gray slag dumps stretched out across gulches like lava from the mines, and noxious fumes from the great smelters killed all the vegetation in Butte for miles around, to say nothing of its effect on the populace . . . everything about Butte reeked of the worst of 19th century despoilment and people put up with it without asking why."[24]

One contemporary resident insisted that Butte was healthier than other cities because the fumes from the smelters acted as a disinfectant, killing the microbes that caused diphtheria and other disease. This sanguine observer also contended that ladies were "very fond" of the city because "there is just enough arsenic there to give them a beautiful complexion and that is the reason the ladies of Butte are renowned wherever they go for their beautiful complexions."[25]

Steam shovels came into use in the 1880s, enabling the coal operators of Pennsylvania and the iron ore producers of Minnesota's Mesabi Range to peel away the very crust of the earth to extract raw materials for industry and wealth for themselves. Spoil from the coal mines was starting to turn streams acid. The discovery of oil in Titusville, Pennsylvania, in 1859, brought drilling rigs that poked into the skyline; large areas of soil were soaked with black ooze.

In the nineteenth century, railroad trains crisscrossing the continent and steamboats spewing smoke along the rivers and across the oceans opened new markets and increased the mobility of an already footloose people. In the latter half of the century, as roads became covered with macadam and iron bridges spanned the great rivers, there were few places in the country that were not easily accessible —or exploitable. Starting in 1839, the tap of the telegrapher's key enabled people to communicate even when they were thousands of miles apart. Photography allowed people to gaze upon places or faces they might never otherwise look upon. All of these inventions tended to lessen the mystery and power of nature. The scale of the continent was being reduced to human dimensions.

"The wide air and deep waters, the tall mountains, the outstretched plains and the earth's deep caverns, are become parcel of his [man's] domain and yield freely to his researches and toils," exulted the *Democratic Review* magazine in its issue for March 1845.[26]

The new machines and new industries created an often insatiable demand for labor. From the cotton mills of Lowell to the steel mills south of Chicago, millions of new jobs were available to immigrants, who doubled the nation's population every twenty years. Americans began a love affair with machinery, an obsessive relationship that continues to this day. The machine represented progress, abundance, opportunity, equality, freedom. A right-minded but excessively optimistic writer for the *United States Review* predicted in 1853 that within fifty years "machinery will perform all work—automata will direct them. The only tasks of the human race will be to make love, study and be happy."[27]

The power of the new machines reinforced the power of aggressive capital in its heedless assault on the environment. Impersonal corporations, often enjoying monopoly positions in the marketplace, sought to accumulate profits without concern for the niceties of how it was done. Morison and Commager thought that "America, where success had always been its own justification, was the land first destined for complete conquest by the industrial Moloch."[28]

Perhaps the most dramatic transformation after the Civil War was the growth of the cities. The big markets and accumulation of wealth concentrated in cities by the industrial revolution created new economic opportunities that attracted people to urban areas as irresistibly as salmon are drawn to their spawning streams. In the nineteenth century the population of New York City increased from 1 million to 3.5 million, Philadelphia's from 500,000 to 1.3 million, Boston's from 170,000 to over 500,000. Chicago, which grew from a shanty town on the swampy edge of Lake Michigan to a metropolis of nearly 1.7 million, was the biggest of the many new cities that extruded on the previously empty landscape.

By the latter part of the nineteenth century the city had replaced the open land as the locus of opportunity. Young people gladly deserted their family farms—and their numbing, interminable servitude to the land—and flocked to the cities for jobs, adventure, and the exciting promise of modern urban living. As the frontier began to close, the cities rather than the countryside—where size of land-holdings increasingly determined social status—became the places where equality and democracy could be found.

But it was in the cities that environmental pollution and its effects were most pervasive. A survey by a citizens' group in New York City in the middle of the nineteenth century found that "domestic garbage and filth of every kind is thrown into the streets, covering their surface, filling the gutters, obstructing the sewer culverts and sending forth perennial emanations which must generate pestiferous disease. In winter the filth and garbage, etc. accumulate in the streets to the depth of sometimes two or three feet."[29]

Most cities undergoing explosive growth were nightmares of primitive sanitation and waste disposal systems. Privies for sewage and private wells for water were still widely used in the metropolitan areas until the end of the century—and the former increasingly contaminated the latter. Cholera, typhoid, diphtheria, and other diseases carried by water and filth were rampant.[30] In 1881, the mayor of Cleveland called the Cuyahoga River "an open sewer through the center of the city." It remained so until passage of the Clean Water Act in 1972.

While cities offered excitement and opportunity, the metropolises of the nineteenth century were often barren, ugly places cut off from nature. Frederick Law Olmsted, a talented, visionary landscape architect, helped to persuade New York City to reserve land in the heart of Manhattan Island to create Central Park. For the most part, however, the burghers and civic leaders of nineteenth-century cities were much too wrapped up in development, expansion, and profit making to give thought and valuable real estate to the creation of green, open spaces. Young people from the country must have had a sinking feeling when upon entering a big city for the first time they found themselves hemmed in by dirty streets filled with crowds of hurrying, indifferent passersby.

In his autobiography, Frank Lloyd Wright gave a vivid account of his first impression of Chicago when he arrived there as a young man in 1887:

> Chicago! Immense gridiron of noisy streets. Dirty ... Heavy traffic crossing both ways at once, managing somehow: torrential noise . . . A stupid thing, that gridiron: crosscurrents of horses, trucks, street cars grinding on hard rails mingling with streams of human beings in seeming confusion and clamor. But habit was in the movement making it expert, and so safe enough. Drear—dim—smoked.

Smoked dim and smoking. A wide desolate vacant strip
ran along the waterfront over which the Illinois Central
trains puffed, shrieked and ground incessantly, cutting the
city off from the lake.[31]

Perhaps there was a fleeting moment in the nation's past when
the industrial and rural landscapes were in balance; when industry
and urban expansion may have complemented the dominant pastoralism. In the beginning, the power of the machine and the freedom
of the city may have enriched the garden. But like Jefferson's golden
age of yeoman farmers, that moment quickly passed. There was a
price to pay for all the new power and wealth made possible by the
industrial revolution. The price was the degradation of the environment, the squandering of resources.

Some of the nation's wildlife was quickly overwhelmed by the
technology of an advancing civilization. The passenger pigeon is often
cited as a tragic example of humanity's skill in annihilating life.
Elimination of bison from the plains is an even more powerful example of how the technology and economy of the expanding nation
reduced the richness of the continent's wildlife. Pigeons, bison, and
other animals—not to mention the Native Americans, who by the
end of the nineteenth century had been reduced by disease and destruction of their culture to about a third of their pre-Columbian
population—were the first casualties of the new and careless civilization that swept across the continent.

There is, of course, no gainsaying the benefits of the industrial
revolution to the nation and the world. Many nineteenth-century
accomplishments constitute a great breakthrough for the human race.
In the United States they meant abundance and growing equality
and equity. The enormously increased cultivation and productivity
of the land ended hunger, or would have save for flaws in the structure
of the economy and in people's hearts. Many of the technical and
scientific achievements of the century would eventually make everyday life safer, cleaner, healthier, and more convenient. Machinery and
new sources of energy eased the burden of work and provided leisure

for the creation and enjoyment of arts and for the appreciation of the natural world, or what was left of it. Transportation and communications shrank distances and eased the loneliness of human existence.

Some middle ground could have been found, perhaps, between Jefferson's pastoral ideal and the modern industrial state. Our grandfathers and great-grandfathers left their descendants what we, with the wisdom of hindsight, can regard as a diminished natural heritage.

But to make moral judgments about ecological misdeeds of our nineteenth-century ancestors would be largely an exercise in anachronism. How can we call them to account for crimes against the environment when they did not even know the word and the very concept was only beginning to be discussed by scientists in the latter part of that century?

There were indeed greedy developers and entrepreneurs and ruthless empire builders. But the great majority of pioneers and settlers who took and used the land were seeking to survive and prosper in the most direct and simple way they could. As we have seen, land and natural resources were in such abundance that they could not have envisaged the end of nature's bounty. Then, too, they were so hard-pressed in wresting a living from the land that they did not have the time or energy to show concern for it. Subduing, changing, and using the land was progress; it was the natural order of things. It was an age of optimism, when the new Americans could do no wrong as they swept across the continent building a new nation.

We can deplore the greed and avarice of the speculators and robber barons who looted the continent. That, too, however, was the spirit of the time. John D. Rockefeller proclaimed his goal in life was to become rich and when oil and monopoly made him so he was held up as an exemplar of his generation. When Andrew Carnegie explained his great accumulation of riches as a fulfillment of the Calvinist stewardship of wealth under God, he was hailed as a thinker, captain of industry, and philanthropist.

The national government, perhaps, could have done more to protect the land and its resources as well as public health. But for most of the century the government was still a weak presence in most areas of the country. There was, moreover, no body of laws with which the government could assert its authority. Laissez-faire was the order of the day.

There were, of course, individuals who lamented the passing of the bison, the waste of the land, who complained of the filth and noise of the cities. But love of nature in the first hundred years after independence was largely romantic. By the end of the century, however, there was a growing body of information about the harm that was being done the natural world and some new ideas about how to set things right. But even that little knowledge was not widely disseminated. There was as yet no accepted ethic that would impel people to treat the land, air, and water with wisdom and care. To a large extent, they did not know what they were doing.

Today, however, another century has come and almost gone and we no longer have that excuse.

THE

AWAKENING

Heaven is under our feet as well as over our heads.
—*Henry David Thoreau*

In 1815, toward the end of his long life, Daniel Boone left his home in Missouri for one last visit to his beloved Kentucky. He had become an almost mythic figure—the pathfinder who had opened the savage wilderness to settlement but who relished the free life of the forest and was as comfortable on its dark trails as the Indians he had helped drive out.

Still vigorous although already in his eighties, Boone once again roamed the Kentucky woods with his long rifle. On several occasions, he crossed paths with a young Haitian-born Frenchman who spent his mornings in the forests armed with a gun and with a sketchbook as well. John James Audubon was a recently married shopkeeper whose business in Louisville was failing, probably because he was much more interested in painting birds and other wildlife of the young country than he was in earning a living for his family.

Boone and Audubon! It is startling and pleasant to think of them together. According to an account of their meetings given by Van Wyck Brooks, the old pathfinder and the gregarious young painter and naturalist took to each other, sitting down for long conversations and, on one occasion, spending the night together in a woodland cabin, with Boone sleeping on the floor and letting the less hardened Audubon have the only bed. Boone regaled Audubon with tales of his adventures on the wild frontier and showed him how to shoot squirrels from trees.[1] One likes to think they also talked about the birds and animals they had seen and about how they enjoyed the freedom and wildness of the forests.

Audubon was not a conservationist or environmentalist as we would define them today. He generally shot the birds that were his subjects so he could sketch them at leisure. But he was something of a naturalist as well as an artist. His paintings in *The Birds of America* and *The Viviparous Quadrupeds of North America* called the attention of his contemporaries to the wonders of nature in his adopted country. He combined a frontiersman's ardor for travel and adventure with an almost scientific keenness of observation and an artist's aesthetic appreciation of the beautiful wildlife he painted. Often penniless, he was forced to go to England in 1826 to get his great work on North American birds published. While he did not condemn the juggernaut of westward settlement, he did express deep regret over the destruction of the forests: "The greedy mills," he wrote in an essay, "told the sad tale, that in a century the noble forests . . . should exist no more."[2]

More affluent in later years after the highly successful publication of *The Birds of America*, Audubon eventually bought an estate on the Upper West Side of Manhattan in New York. It was a large wooded area through which deer and elk still sometimes passed, and after he died in 1851 his widow, Lucy, to help provide for herself and her children, subdivided the property and built several houses upon it. On New Year's Day 1857, a businessman from Weehawken, New Jersey, named George Blake Grinnell moved his family, including his young son George Bird Grinnell, into one of the houses of Audubon Park. While he was growing up, the Audubon house was a second home to young Grinnell. He called Lucy "Grandma" and joined her grandchildren in taking reading and writing lessons with her in her bedroom, on a wall of which hung Audubon's painting "The Eagle and the Lamb." The painting fascinated him, Grinnell wrote years later. It was at Audubon Park, he also said, that he came to relish the out-of-doors.³

George Bird Grinnell eventually disappointed his father by giving up the family business to study paleontology and to become a scientist, sportsman, and writer. He once accompanied a military expedition commanded by General George Armstrong Custer to help classify plants and animals in the West. He acquired and became publisher of *Forest and Stream* magazine. Having watched the systematic slaughter of the bison on his expeditions in the West, Grinnell wrote frequently and movingly of the need to preserve wildlife and of the wanton destruction of the nation's forests. In 1886 he wrote an editorial in *Forest and Stream* proposing a society for the protection of the nation's birds, many species of which were in danger of being wiped out by hunters who collected them for their feathers or just for sport. The idea immediately attracted wide attention and support and it became the origin of today's Audubon Societies. In 1887 he proposed an organization dedicated to conserving game species and joined with a rising young politician named Theodore Roosevelt and several other wellborn sportsmen to form the Boone and Crockett Club, an elite organization that had as its goal ending the relentless, wasteful slaughter of big game animals, including the nearly exterminated bison.

Now barely remembered, Grinnell was one of the crucial early figures in mainstream American conservation, active and influential even before the term came into common use.

"Appreciation of wilderness began in the cities," says historian Roderick Nash.⁴ As we have seen, that is not entirely true. Boone acquired his love of wilderness and solitude while roaming the forests. Audubon did not remain in the cities with his sketchbook; he shot the birds in the forests and took them home to paint. There were many other wanderers of the plains, forests, and mountains who discovered, described, and helped create a broad appreciation for the natural wonders of North America. Two of particular interest are John and William Bartram, father and son, naturalists who roved the countryside indefatigably in the eighteenth and early nineteenth centuries, discovering and classifying plants and animals and rhapsodizing in print over the beauty and wonder of nature's gifts.

Nash is essentially correct, however. It is undeniable that the articulation of the joys of nature and the first calls for its protection did not come from the settlers struggling to wrest a livelihood from the wild frontier but from the scholars, poets, philosophers, scientists, writers, painters, clerics, and even the politicians of the settled, increasingly urbanized East. Out of the Enlightenment sprang the early suggestions for preserving resources on utilitarian grounds. The flowering of transcendentalism and romanticism in this country in the first half of the nineteenth century contributed to what was essentially a cult of nature that worshipped its beauty and primitiveness. This cult was, at once, contradictory and complementary to the utilitarian calls for wiser stewardship of the land. The growth of scientific knowledge in the same century produced sobering data about the consequences of human exploitation of the environment, although, as Keith Thomas has noted, science also tended to place man apart from and above the natural world.[5]

In the second half of the century, more Americans began to awaken to what their country was losing and to the costs of that loss. But the awakening was painfully slow. Many who raised their voices did so to lament the ruthless destruction of nature rather than to urge reform. Systematic efforts to preserve the land and its resources did not get under way until the end of the century. Although some progress was made in preserving public lands, the early conservation and preservation movements were not greatly successful. It would not be until the last third of the twentieth century that environmentalism would explode into a mass movement.

Many of the first calls for what we would now term environmental action were stimulated by pragmatic concerns. As early as 1793, the Reverend Nicholas Collins called on the American Philosophical Society to help protect birds from extinction until such time as it was learned what role they played in the "oeconomy of nature"—in effect what ecological niche they filled.[6] Almost identical arguments are made today by scientists and conservationists who plead for the preservation of the world's biological diversity.

Several attempts were made to reserve forests for timber to be used by the Navy. President John Quincy Adams tried to set aside live oak forests along the Gulf Coast for shipbuilding and repairs but he was reversed when Andrew Jackson became President and insisted on the rights of the "people" to the nation's resources. The people, of course, included the timber companies that were rapidly destroying the nation's forests and accumulating huge profits. Adams, noted Richard Bartlett, was "the first President to manifest any real interest in conservation and was ahead of his time in comprehension of the problem."[7]

In the early part of the nineteenth century, however, there were less tangible, less anthropocentric stirrings of environmental conscience. Travelers were coming back from the frontier to tell of the great beauty they had seen and the awe they had experienced in the wild country to the west and to express regret over its inevitable passing. Even then there were farsighted individuals asking if some of the unspoiled land could not be saved.

George Catlin roamed across the then truly wild West in the 1830s, painting the Plains Indians and the wildlife he saw there. He was one of the first Americans to call for saving at least some portions of the wild land and its inhabitants: "Many are the rudenesses and wilds in Nature's works which are destined to fall before the deadly axe and desolating hands of cultivating man," he wrote later. To preserve some of that vanishing beauty, Catlin proposed that the government create a *"magnificent park"* (italics in original) where "the world could see for ages to come, the native Indian in his classic attire, galloping his wild horse, with sinewy bow, and shield and lance, amid the fleeting herds of elks and buffaloes. What a beautiful and thrilling specimen for America to preserve and hold up to the view of her refined citizens and the world, in future ages! *A nation's park* [italics in original], containing man and beast, in all the wild and freshness of their nature's beauty."[8]

This was nearly forty years before the designation of the first national park. Of course, when the national park system was adopted it failed to include Indians among the protected species. Native Americans tend not to regard themselves as tourist attractions.

We have already seen how the popular Leatherstocking novels, written over three decades starting in the 1820s, lamented the passing of the wilderness and the waste of its wildlife. Among those enamored of Cooper's works was Francis Parkman, Boston Brahmin, historian, crafter of some of the most elegant prose ever produced in this country, and eulogist of the wilderness. As a young man, Parkman traveled to the far reaches of the West, guided by old mountain men and, for a time, living with a band of Sioux. His book *The Oregon Trail*, published in 1849, emerged from this trip. But so, too, did his deep feeling for the land, the forests, the people, and the spirit of the raw, unsettled continent. This feeling shines through almost every page of his masterwork, the monumental *France and England in North America*. A fine example is this passage from Part 4 of that work, *The Old Régime in Canada*, explaining why the coureurs de bois were "spoiled for civilization" after a year or two of bush ranging.

> Perhaps he could sometimes feel, without knowing that he felt them, the charms of the savage nature that had adopted him. Rude as he was, her voice may not always have been meaningless for one who knew her haunts so well,—deep recesses, where, veiled in foliage, some wild shy rivulet steals with timid music through breathless caves of verdure; gulfs where feathered crags rise like castle walls, where the noonday sun pierces with keen rays athwart the torrent, and the mossed arms of fallen pines cast wavering shadows on the illumined foam; pools of liquid crystal turned emerald in the reflected green of the impending woods.[9]

Parkman did not applaud the triumphant march of civilization across the country. Like James Fenimore Cooper, he "despised commerce and businessmen, industrialism and all its works."[10]

As the century progressed, this distaste grew intense in some quarters. John Orvis, a resident of the Brook Farm commune, observing the industrialization of Vermont, warned that the "beautiful pastoral life of the inhabitants will give place to oppressive factory life—quiet rural pursuits will be absorbed in the din, conflict and degradation of mechanical and manufacturing business."[11] Brook Farm, one of a number of rural communes formed in the mid-nineteenth century, purported to offer a lifestyle of freedom and harmony with nature as an alternative to the constraints of urban industrialism. Distrust of business and industry and the kind of progress they represent is a strain that can still be found running through some sectors of the modern environmental movement, but it is much less pervasive than opponents of the movement claim.

By the middle of the nineteenth century, romanticism held sway in the more settled areas of the United States. Rousseau had now won his argument with Hobbes on both sides of the Atlantic. Life in a state of nature was no longer perceived as mean, brutish, and short but, in some ways, more fulfilling and desirable than civilization. "The earth left to its own natural fertility and covered with immense woods, that no hatchet ever disfigured, offers at every step food and shelter to every species of animals" including humans, Rousseau taught.[12] Men are freer, happier, and more honest the closer they are to nature, he argued. By cutting down the forests, men created fields which they "had to water by the sweat of their brow . . . it was iron and corn which first civilized man and ruined humanity."[13] The English romantics, particularly William Wordsworth (1770–1850), were an important source of the veneration of nature that swept this country.

American writers and painters, enthusiastically embracing romanticism, turned often to the landscape for inspiration. The notion that nature is inherently more honest, innocent, and virtuous than civilization was welcomed because Americans assumed as a matter of course that their young country was "in perpetual touch with nature," not debauched and artificial like ancient, weary Europe.[14] This view is gloriously reflected in the paintings of Thomas Cole, Asher Durand, and other members of the Hudson River School with their scenes of dark forest glens, rocky crags, and lush valleys. The poet William Cullen Bryant told his friends Cole and Cole's fellow painter Henry Inman to "go forth . . . and list to Nature's teachings."[15]

Some of these same artists, however, also prophesied the death of nature in the face of America's advancing industrialism. Cole, who also dabbled in poetry, made this dire forecast in his "Lament of the Forest," written in 1841:

> Our doom is near; behold from east to west
> The skies are darkened by ascending smoke;
> Each hill and every valley is become
> An altar unto Mammon, and the gods
> Of man's idolatry—the victims we. . . .
> A few short years!—these valleys, greenly clad,
> These slumbering mountains, resting in our
>   arms,
> Shall naked glare beneath the scorching sun,
> And all the wimpling rivulets be dry.[16]

The most influential articulation of the importance of nature and the relationship of humans to the natural world came from the transcendentalists of New England, particularly from two who are part of the bedrock of American literature and American thought—Ralph Waldo Emerson and Henry David Thoreau.

The New England interpretation of Immanuel Kant's transcendental concepts gave primacy to the spiritual aspects of life over the material. All humans, to the transcendentalists, have within them the divine spirit, which Emerson called the "Over-Soul." This spirit was present throughout nature, and humans could become close to the wisdom, power, and beauty of nature through love and through ridding themselves of the artifices of civilization. Writing about sources of knowledge in *The American Scholar*, Emerson declared, "The first in time and the first in importance of the influences on the mind is that of Nature . . . There is never a beginning, there is never an end, to the inexplicable continuity of this web of God."[17]

Emerson's veneration of nature did not lead him to dismiss industrialism or technology out of hand. Writing in 1856 of his visit to England, he said that "the wise, versatile, all-giving machinery" had earned "bounteous" wealth for the British. But he also saw the consequences of reliance on the machine and warned of overdoing technology. "The only drawback on this industrial conveniency is the darkness of its sky. The night and day are too nearly of a color . . . In the manufacturing towns, the fine soot or *blacks* darken the day, give white sheep the color of black sheep, discolor the human saliva, contaminate the air, poison many plants, and corrode the monuments and buildings."[18] Inventions such as the locomotive and the hot-air balloon would bring many changes, some of them beneficial, but "Nature cannot be cheated," he cautioned.[19]

This blend of reverence for nature and acceptance of technology, provided it is limited and controlled, is reflected in the ideology of today's mainstream environmentalism. But Emerson, and many others of his time, also believed that sacred nature had the ability to heal itself and therefore could recover from any of the ills inflicted on it by human activity. Modern environmentalism knows all too painfully that human activity can inflict mortal damage on natural systems. John Passmore argues that Emerson's view of an eternal nature interferes with our willingness to take ecological crises seriously. To save fragile nature, he insists, it is necessary to recognize "that neither man nor nature is sacred or quasi-divine."[20]

Emerson appreciated nature largely from the sanctuary of his library; his anti-materialism was most pronounced on the lecture platform. A very different species, however, was his neighbor, friend, and student Henry David Thoreau.

Thoreau, truly an American original, walked firmly through his short life to the cadence of a distinctly offbeat drummer. He did not just talk about nature, he lived in and with it. "Henry talks about nature as if she'd been born and grew up in Concord," a neighbor said.[21] Thoreau rarely left the borders of his native village. He was born in Concord on July 12, 1817, and died there in 1862. He lived virtually all his life among its woods, fields, ponds, and streams.

Unlike Emerson, Thoreau did not look complacently on the increasing dominance of industrialism and technology. He watched the shadow of locomotive smoke fall over Walden Pond and knew full well what that shadow portended—nothing less than the death of pastoralism in the United States. He was saddened by the foreknowledge that the machine would soon dominate the landscape and men's lives.

Many of the leitmotifs of modern environmentalism were sounded in Thoreau's prose. He was a sharp critic of the dehumanizing effects of industrial practices and the kind of economy they supported. "I cannot believe," he said in *Walden*, "that our factory system is the best mode by which men may get clothing. The condition of the operatives is becoming every day more like that of the English; and it cannot be wondered at, since, as I have heard or observed, the principal object is not that mankind may be well and honestly clad, but, unquestionably, that the corporations may be enriched."[22]

He also saw clearly the waste and despoilment of economic development and foresaw that much worse was to come. Observing the forests of the Northeast being gobbled up by the timber companies, he said, "Thank God, men cannot yet fly and lay waste the sky as well as the earth."[23]

Thoreau can be regarded as the spiritual founder of the modern crusade to preserve what is left of our wilderness. "In wilderness is the preservation of the world," he proclaimed, and to many of today's environmental militants his dictum is still a call to battle. To Thoreau, wilderness was the counterbalance to the heavy burdens placed on the human soul by labor and the cares of living in an increasingly materialistic, urbanized society. The errand into the wilderness prescribed by Thoreau was far different from that of the fearful, God-driven Puritans of two centuries earlier. Humanity would save itself and plant the spirit of God, not by destroying wilderness, but by becoming one with it.

While he constantly returned to the theme of the refreshing, redemptive values of the wilderness, he also was among the first to admonish his fellow citizens that the natural world was not created for the benefit of human beings but existed for its own sake. Struck by the utter savagery of the landscape on a camping trip through the wild woods of Maine, he saw "that earth of which we had heard, made out of chaos and old night. Here was no man's garden . . . It was the fresh and natural surface of the planet earth, as it was made for ever and ever . . . so nature made it and man may use it if he can."[24]

Thoreau even anticipated some of the causes and methods of today's radical environmentalists. He raised the question of the rights of animals, for example, expressing sympathy for the plight of the shad whose migratory path along the Merrimack River is interrupted by a dam and by fishermen. "Who hears the fishes when they cry?" he asked in *A Week on the Concord and Merrimack Rivers*.[25]

This passage also contains what may be the first reference to the possibility of ecosabotage—acts of violence against property to protect animals and other parts of nature. Addressing the oppressed shad, he says, "I for one am with thee, and who knows what may avail a crow-bar against that Billerica Dam?"[26] There is no evidence that Thoreau ever took up that crowbar to tear down the dam to save the fish. Ecosabotage as a weapon against the destruction of nature would not emerge again until a century and a half later with the novels of Edward Abbey and the militant wing of the "deep ecologists." Going to jail rather than comply with government tax laws imposed to finance the war with Mexico, which he opposed, Thoreau set a precedent of civil disobedience, which some of today's militants employ to protect animals, old forests, and other of nature's creations.

Like many of today's environmentalists, Thoreau appreciated the value of nature even when it was not beautiful or useful to human beings. "Shall I not rejoice also at the abundance of the weeds whose seeds are the granary of the birds?"[27] He preferred to study the habits of birds rather than to shoot them for sport—although he was not against hunting; he thought the sport introduced young men to the forests. With his profoundly holistic view of nature, he even anticipated the controversial "Gaia" theory, named after the Greek goddess of the earth and propounded by James Lovelock in 1979, that the earth is a single, living organic being.[28] "The earth I tread on," wrote Thoreau, "is not a dead, inert mass; it is a body, has a spirit, is organic and fluid to the influence of its spirit."[29]

The central issue addressed by Thoreau, however, was embodied in the questions of how life ought to be lived and what gives meaning to life. These are fundamental themes of environmentalism, although today's environmental leaders tend to shunt them aside in the heat and tumult of their endless trench warfare against the powerful forces that threaten both human health and the natural world.

Explaining why he spent two years living alone in a cabin at the edge of Walden Pond, Thoreau had this to say:

> I went to the woods because I wished to live deliberately, to front only the essential facts of life, and see if I could not learn what it had to teach, and not, when I came to die, discover I had not lived. I did not wish to live what was not life, living is so dear; nor did I wish to practice resignation, unless it was quite necessary. I wanted to live deep and suck out all of the marrow of life, to live so sturdily and spartan-like as to put to rout all that was not life, to cut a broad swath and a close shave, to drive life into a corner and reduce it to its lowest terms.[30]

One must be "neighbor to the birds," not to crowds of other human beings. "The most alive is the wildest." The full, rich flavor of life can only come directly from nature. "It is a vulgar error to suppose that you have tasted huckleberries who have never plucked them."

It is not a bad argument against the urbanized, overcivilized materialism that is engulfing-late twentieth-century America.

Like Emerson and others who praised and defended nature in the nineteenth century, Thoreau was not free of ambivalence. He left his cabin on Walden Pond after two years and returned to live in his mother's home, where he remained for the rest of his life. He liked nature wild, but not too wild. The savagery of the Maine forests overawed him somewhat. He loved the woods around Concord, with human neighbors not too far away. Because of his distrust of government, he never proposed that laws be created to preserve the wilderness and prevent other threats to nature. Many of his contemporaries who knew his work dismissed him as an impractical dreamer or an elitist who was indifferent to what people must do to survive and to get on in the world. He was little heeded in his lifetime.

To us today, however, living in the America that he feared was coming, Thoreau's passionate voice rings with clear intensity and relevance. The skies have become dirty, the fish have disappeared from many of our befouled streams, our chemically treated blueberries are tasteless, our days are consumed with getting and spending, and rarely do we touch the raw surface of nature. That we know how far we have strayed and what we must do if we are to return to real life, we owe in large measure to the hermit of Walden Pond.

The values that Thoreau and the transcendentalists saw in the natural world were those of the soul and spirit. To them, the ills afflicting the natural world grew out of personal actions, and salvation could come through personal choice. But they made no systematic analysis of what was happening to the world around them. Nor did they see the magnitude of the dangers created by our abuse of the land and its resources. They offered no plans, no prescriptions for saving the natural environment. It remained for another Yankee, from the Green Mountains of Vermont, to recognize the pervasive, inexorable harm that human activity was inflicting on the natural systems and resources that sustain life and to call attention to that harm in what is, without doubt, the seminal book of American environmentalism.

His name was George Perkins Marsh. Born in 1801 in Woodstock, Vermont, he became a lawyer, a teacher, a naturalist; he bred sheep, ran a woolen mill and a marble quarry, edited a newspaper, dabbled in real estate, served as his state's fish commissioner, was elected to Congress as a member of the Whig Party, and for many years served as United States ambassador to Turkey and then to Italy. He was a tireless scholar, spoke and read twenty languages, traveled widely in Europe and the Near East, and had an early and abiding interest in and love for nature.

Having witnessed the exhaustion of the soil as a result of poor farming practices and the destruction of the forests in his native Vermont, Marsh then observed the barren, degraded environment of much of the Mediterranean basin and studied the history of land and resource use in Europe and Asia. From this background and scholarship Marsh produced, in 1864, *Man and Nature; or, Physical Geography as Modified by Human Action*.[31] More than a century and a quarter after its first publication, his book still carries the force of revelation.

Marsh looked at nature from neither a broad romantic or transcendental perspective nor a narrow, utilitarian point of view. He studied the historical and scientific record then available and reached the conclusion that human activity was having a very destructive effect on much of the world.

Marsh's argument was simple. Nature, if left undisturbed, is basically stable. The damage natural forces such as storms do to the land is usually superficial and heals quickly. But human activity, abetted by human technology, can permanently transform the earth. Destroying the forests, plowing the soil, draining the bogs, channeling the streams had already devastated much of the Old World. Deforestation, in particular, Marsh felt, had led to soil erosion, the drying up of watersheds, and the loss of many plant and animal species. It also caused greater fluctuations in temperatures and may have changed annual rainfall patterns, he believed. Intensive cultivation and overgrazing had transformed fertile areas into deserts, he said.

Ernst Haeckel had not yet coined the word "ecology" when Marsh wrote *Man and Nature*. But Marsh was essentially describing the destructive effect of human activity on ecological systems—rending the "web of life," to use a term that had been long in use by his time. Acting largely in ignorance, humans were harming themselves by destroying the balance of nature that made life possible.

There are parts of Asia Minor, of Northern Africa, of Greece and even of Alpine Europe, where the operation of causes set in action by man has brought the face of earth to a desolation almost as complete as that of the moon; and though, within that brief space of time we call "the historical period," they are known to have been covered with luxuriant woods, verdant pastures and fertile meadows, they are now too far deteriorated to be reclaimable by man, nor can they again become fitted for human use . . .[32]

Even more bluntly: "But man is everywhere a disturbing agent. Wherever he plants his foot, the harmonies of nature are turned to discord."[33]

Marsh offered many examples of how heedless destruction of nature can have adverse consequences for humans. In one he described how insect pests can proliferate when humans kill off the birds that eat the pests. "Hence, in his wanton destruction of the robin and other insectivorous birds, the *bipes implumis*, the featherless biped, man, is not only exchanging the vocal orchestra which greets the rising sun for the drowsy beetle's evening drone, and depriving his groves and his fields of their fairest ornament, but he is waging a treacherous warfare on his natural allies."[34]

The idea that human activity can cause major and irreversible damage to the earth was new. In his introduction to the centennial edition of *Man and Nature* in 1965, David Lowenthal noted that "a century ago, man's power was generally thought to be either negligible or benign."[35] Marsh was the first to demonstrate that the cumulative impact of human activity was not negligible and, far from benign, could wreak widespread, permanent destruction on the face of the earth.

Primitive human societies that live by hunting and gathering cause relatively minor damage to nature, Marsh contended. But the cultivated garden, in Marsh's revolutionary view, far from being the re-creation of Eden, was in fact an agent of destruction.

When Europeans first arrived in North America, Marsh noted, the continent was covered with forests and nature was in harmony. The nation was still young and large portions of the country were still relatively untouched. "The industry and folly of man have as yet produced little appreciable change."[36] Even so, irreparable damage was already being done. "But we are, even now, breaking up the floor and wainscoting and doors and window frames of our dwelling, for fuel to warm our bodies and seethe our pottage . . ."[37] And, he warned, the worst could be yet to come as humans acquired greater power to alter the physical world.

Yet Marsh was no Cassandra. He believed in the power of knowledge and science to redress the balance between humans and nature. He called for intense study of the impact of human activity on the natural world, particularly in those places where the destruction was already great. But he also insisted, in words that would be appropriate in today's newspaper, that "the world cannot afford to wait till the slow and sure progress of exact science has taught it a better economy."[38]

In the mid-nineteenth century, coal was just beginning to be widely used and oil was coming on the market. Marsh could not have known about acid rain, the greenhouse effect, or other environmental problems caused by the large-scale combustion of fossil fuels. But neither would he have had patience with today's government officials and industrialists who insist that no action be taken to deal with threats to the environment until all the scientific evidence was collected and reviewed.

Man and Nature was successful and influential from the time of its publication, both in the United States and in Europe. Gifford Pinchot, who would play so large a role in the fledgling conservation movement, called it "epoch-making"[39] and made liberal use of its ideas. Pinchot's sometime ally and frequent rival, John Muir, was also influenced by the book. Lewis Mumford in our time called it the "fountainhead of the conservation movement." Its perspective and ideas continue to permeate the modern environmental agenda, an agenda followed even by those leaders who have never read it. There have been at least two academic conferences in the United States in the past thirty years devoted to the central themes of the book. It remains as fresh, relevant, and audacious as it was in 1864.

Marsh's great work, however, had virtually no immediate impact on environmental policies or environmental practices in the United States. The post-Civil War period was an age of explosive geographical expansion and industrial and economic growth. The country was on the move and on the make. The Americans' boundless energy and bubbling optimism did not leave much room for gloomy thoughts about what was happening to Mother Nature. Even those who spoke for nature were torn by the ambivalence that characterized American attitudes from the very beginning. A telling illustration of the ambiguity of American attitudes toward nature and civilization is provided by Walt Whitman's poem "Give Me the Splendid Silent Sun." Here are a few lines from its first stanza:

> Give me the splendid silent sun with all his beams full-dazzling,
> Give me juicy autumnal fruit ripe and red from the orchard,
> Give me a field where the unmow'd grass grows, . . .
> Give me solitude, give me Nature, give me again O Nature
>   your primal sanities.

Now here are some lines from the second stanza:

> Keep your splendid silent sun,
> Keep your woods O Nature, and the quiet places by the
>   woods . . .
> Give me Broadway, with the soldiers marching—give me the
>   sound of trumpets and drums! . . .
> Give me the shores and wharves heavy-fringed with black ships!
> O such for me! O an intense life, full to repletion and varied.
> The life of the theatre, bar-room, huge hotel for me!

For most of the nineteenth century, the ebullient young country was still not ready to take a sober look at the environmental consequences of its long binge of expansion and development. Those who raised their voices to complain about the waste and destruction, or tried to do something about it, were usually accorded the same degree of respect and attention with which a temperance preacher was welcomed in a frontier saloon—or Walt Whitman's Manhattan barroom for that matter. Nevertheless, isolated acts of conservation and efforts to preserve the environment multiplied as the century progressed, and set a pattern for the years to follow.

In the 1850s, New York City hired Frederick Law Olmsted, a landscape architect, gentleman farmer, and writer to help create a park on 770 acres in the middle of Manhattan Island. Central Park was not Olmsted's idea. It had been championed for years by a number of influential citizens, including William Cullen Bryant and a respected landscape gardener, Andrew Jackson Downing. Nor did Olmsted single-handedly design Central Park. He had a number of collaborators, notably Calvert Vaux. But it was Olmsted's superb administrative abilities that were instrumental in bringing the park project to fruition. He left a legacy of his vision across the country, not just with urban parks but by helping preserve open space. He was one of the first to propose that the glorious Yosemite Valley be protected by California as a park and he played a leading role in the preservation of Niagara Falls.[40] Yosemite was granted to California, which did reserve it for the public. David Brower, a leading environmentalist of our time, contends that the preservation of Yosemite as a park in 1864, eight years before the creation of Yellowstone National Park, was not only the beginning of the national park system but also a key starting point for environmentalism in the United States.

Charles Capen McLaughlin, the editor of Olmsted's collected papers, wrote, "We can still look to his work for guidance in controlling urban sprawl . . . Olmsted fought selfish and shortsighted thinking with imaginative proposals to enhance the life of his own times and that of future generations."[41]

In 1872, Congress set aside the first major reservation of federal land when it created the 2-million-acre Yellowstone National Park to be a "pleasuring ground for the people" in perpetuity. This farsighted legislation is all the more astonishing in that it took place during the presidency of Ulysses S. Grant, whose administration is infamous for pandering to corrupt business interests that exploited the public domain. But at the time, creating Yellowstone Park was an isolated event rather than a reversal of what was by then the time-honored practice of giving away federal resources to private interests at the expense of the public weal.[42] Even Yellowstone is not a clear-cut example of those in high office demonstrating zeal or visionaries fighting to preserve the area in behalf of future generations. There is some evidence that the Northern Pacific Railroad backed the creation of the park as a means of stimulating traffic in the West.[43] If the evidence is correct, the nation owes the railroad industry a debt of gratitude, whatever its motives.

A milestone of quite a different kind was created in 1872 when Congress passed a mining law that allowed individuals or companies to stake a claim to public land which they could then patent for a nominal fee if they could demonstrate the possibility of a mineral strike. The law remains in force to this day and is considered a bane by environmentalists, who contend that it is used by industry and private parties to obtain title to valuable public land at virtually no cost except at the expense of the American people.

The government in Washington was by the 1870s starting to exhibit some concern over the consequences of unthinking land use and resource exploitation. At that time, Arnold Hague of the U.S. Geological Survey warned that deforestation would cause streams to overflow their banks and produce floods. In 1874, Dr. Franklin B. Hough, in a report to President Grant's Secretary of Agriculture, noted that the nation's forests were being illegally harvested by profiteers and were rapidly disappearing. He recommended that the federal government adopt European-style forest management.

Carl Schurz was a German immigrant who brought a knowledge of forestry and a love of trees to this country. A politician, Civil War general, and campaigner for civil service reform, Schurz became President Rutherford B. Hayes's Secretary of the Interior in 1877. He tried to stop the ruthless theft of timber from the nation's forests and to punish the thieves. He also tried to institute professional management of the forests in the careful Prussian manner.

The time was not yet ripe. "The timber barons and their congressional allies" ran "roughshod" over Schurz, with Congress withholding appropriations for his forest program.[44] Small fines were imposed on a few timber thieves and that was that. Reform in the public forests was decades away.

In 1889, in a speech to the newly formed American Forestry Association, which would be a significant force in protecting the nation's public forests, Schurz described his experience as Interior Secretary:

> I observed enterprising timber thieves not merely stealing trees, but stealing whole forests. I observed hundreds of sawmills in full blast, devoted exclusively to the sawing up of timber from the public lands . . . immense tracts being devastated that some robbers might fill their pockets . . . We succeeded in limiting somewhat the extent of depredations upon the public forests and in bringing some of the guilty parties to justice . . . but the recommendations of rational forest planning went for nothing. Some laws were indeed passed but they appeared rather to favor the taking of timber from the public land rather than to stop it . . . Deaf was Congress and deaf the people seemed to be. Only a few still voices rose up here and there in the press in favor of the policy I pursued.[45]

In 1878 Schurz received a report from another pioneer of scientific, rational land use who also was far ahead of the temper of the age and of its political establishment. Major John Wesley Powell, a one-armed veteran of the Civil War, explorer, and daring runner of the Colorado River, had intensively studied the soil, rainfall, water resources, and flora and fauna of the region west of the 100th meridian. His *Report on the Lands of the Arid Region*, written for the Interior Department, warned that the prevailing methods of land distribution and agriculture would not work in the dry West. Available water, not the number of acres cultivated, was the key to survival in the dry region, he explained. The land was suitable for grazing sheep and cattle, not for crops, and therefore the old quarter section was not the way to parcel out the land. Holdings must be big, 2,500 acres or more, to support a single ranching family. He warned, however, that the dry range could support far fewer cattle than stockmen were raising.

If the dry land was to be farmed, as opposed to grazed, Powell insisted, irrigation would be vital and that would require the building of dams and the diversion of rivers and streams. Each farmer would have to be assured of rights to water. But irrigated farming required smaller acreages, so water rights ought to be given to farms of no more than 80 acres.

The government ignored Powell's report. Its failure, contended Henry Nash Smith, was due at least in part to the fact that it contradicted the long-held vision of the West as a fertile garden. Powell demanded that this myth be scientifically assessed, but Americans could not yet accept that the land was more of a desert than a garden.[46] Eventually, however, Powell was vindicated. In 1902 (the year he died), Congress passed the Reclamation Act, and the hundreds of dams and irrigation systems created as a result of that landmark legislation transformed the West into an approximation of Powell's vision for the area. It is ironic that by the end of the next century the reclamation projects themselves would be recognized as a threat to the ecological health of the West.

The first faint tremors of public response to the degradation of the environment began to be felt in the last third of the nineteenth century. Anti-smoke leagues were formed in New York and other cities to call for control of the dense clouds of soot spewed into the air by coal-fired furnaces. Anti-smoke ordinances were duly passed in a number of cities in response to citizen agitation.

A challenge to giving away publicly owned natural resources to individuals or corporations seeking to enrich themselves was made by the journalist Henry George in his widely read *Progress and Poverty*, published in 1879. People have a right to what they produce themselves, he wrote, "but man has another right, declared by the fact of his existence—the right to use of so much of the free gifts of nature as may be necessary to supply all the wants of that existence, and which he may use without interfering with the equal rights of anyone else; and to this he has a title as against all the world."[47] George was lionized by the eastern establishment, but his argument for preserving the resources of the public domain for use by all of the people was ignored by policy makers. His ideas lingered, however, and were absorbed by the progressive movement at the end of the century.

The first systematic effort to permanently protect federal lands was embodied in the Forest Reserve Act of 1891, which was passed by Congress in the closing hours of its term. A last-minute change in the legislation gave President Benjamin Harrison authority to set aside portions of the federal domain. The provision was added at the insistence of the President's Secretary of the Interior, John W. Noble. According to several historians, members of Congress who voted for the legislation, many of them hostile to the concept of conservation, did not understand the implications of what they were doing.[48] But at Noble's urging, President Harrison quickly withdrew 13 million acres to set up fifteen forest reserves, what we know today as national forests. Unlike the national parks, the forests were not to be shut off from all exploitation, but their use was to be controlled by the federal government. Six years later, lame-duck President Grover Cleveland created another thirteen reserves totaling over 21 million acres. Thus was the country's national forest system, which now includes 160 million acres of useful and beautiful land, called into being by an absentminded Congress.

Other than the forest reserve law, however, it was still business as usual. There was as yet no broad national policy for the protection of the land and its resources, no moral or ethical or even rational approach to the way the country lived within its own natural body.

As the nineteenth century was drawing to a close, three talented, idiosyncratic, charismatic, and driven men were making their entrance on the national stage. Gifford Pinchot, John Muir, and Theodore Roosevelt were to write the first pages of modern environmental history in the United States.

Roosevelt, of course, is remembered as the first and greatest of our conservation-minded Presidents. TR appointed the redoubtable Gifford Pinchot as his chief forester and relied heavily on his counsel to formulate vigorous policies in order to preserve public lands and resources. Pinchot was the leader and chief publicizer of the creed of conservation. Roosevelt was also greatly influenced by John Muir, the naturalist and writer and eloquent spokesman for the preservation of nature and the wilderness. After camping with him in the Sierras in the spring of 1903, Roosevelt came under Muir's spell and was his ally in many but, as we shall see, not all battles Muir fought to protect the land. A founder of the Sierra Club in 1892, Muir was the inspiration for much of the present-day effort to preserve wild and open places.

Pinchot is often described as the "father of conservation" and he considered himself to be so. The term had actually been used in its modern sense by George Perkins Marsh many years before Pinchot appropriated it to describe his own approach to managing the nation's natural resources. However, Pinchot apparently did not recall Marsh's use of the term and adopted the word from the British government's "conservancies" in India.

Born in 1865 and growing up in an affluent French-American family in Milford, Pennsylvania, Pinchot, like many other environmental activists, was an ardent outdoorsman. At his father's suggestion, he decided to become a forester, a profession then virtually unknown in the United States, and went to Europe to study scientific forestry and forest management. There he became convinced that government control of the forests was necessary to stop the wanton destruction of trees by those interested only in the immediate wealth they could take from the land. But he was also taught that scientific management of the forests would not be possible unless it was demonstrated that commercial profits could be assured over the long run by such measures.[49]

Pinchot's view of the forests was that they should be made to serve the future of the nation as well as the present. This would require forestry practices that would assure a sustained yield of timber over the years. The forests should be used, but they should be used wisely and efficiently. To do so, however, the forests would have to be protected from the exploiters and destroyers.

After working as a private forestry consultant—he managed George W. Vanderbilt's Biltmore Forest near Ashville, North Carolina—and serving on a forest commission set up by President Cleveland, Pinchot was appointed by President William McKinley in 1898 to head the Agriculture Department's Forestry Division. But at Agriculture he was a forester without forests. All forest reserves came under the jurisdiction of the Interior Department. Pinchot spent years trying to have the reserves transferred out of the Interior Department and away from the corrupt General Land Office. He finally succeeded in 1905 during Roosevelt's second term in the White House. While the transfer to the Agriculture Department led to the creation of the Forest Service and to a new professionalism in the management of the public forests, it also caused a split in the administration of federal lands that has been a source of problems ever since.

While horseback riding through Washington's Rock Creek Park one morning in 1907, Pinchot had a flash of insight. The importance of using the forests wisely was not an isolated issue; all the nation's resources were linked and vital for the country. "Seen in this new light," he wrote, "all these separate questions fitted into and made up the one great central problem of the use of the earth for the good of man."[50]

Former Interior Secretary Stewart L. Udall, in his book *The Quiet Crisis*, describes Pinchot's revelation as the starting point of organized political resistance to the "exploitation and misuse of the continent's resources" that had been taking place since the Europeans arrived four hundred years earlier.[51] Pinchot's ideas were adopted with such fervor by Roosevelt, among others, that in a short time they achieved the status of what Samuel P. Hays calls the "gospel of efficiency" and Charles Cushman Coyle describes as the "gospel of prudent use." As we shall soon see, however, an entirely different sort of land gospel was simmering in the national consciousness.

In his 1910 book *The Fight for Conservation*, Pinchot stated:

The central thing for which Conservation stands is to make this country the best possible place to live in, both for us and for our descendants . . . Conservation is the most democratic movement this country has known for a generation. It holds that people have not only the right, but the duty to control the use of the natural resources, which are the great sources of prosperity. And it regards the absorption of these resources by the special interests, unless their operations are under effective public control, as a moral wrong. Conservation is the application of common-sense to the common problems for the common good . . .[52]

When Roosevelt ascended to the presidency in 1901 after the assassination of William McKinley, he moved conservation to the center of the national agenda. With Pinchot, who had advised him when he was governor of New York State, serving as his right hand on conservation issues, Roosevelt moved aggressively to assert public primacy over the nation's resources. Conservation, under Roosevelt, was a major weapon of the progressive movement, a movement aimed at redressing the social, economic, and political imbalances caused by industrialization, urbanization, and the concentration of economic power within the hitherto unrestrained corporations.

A rancher, big-game hunter, camper, amateur entomologist, and co-founder of the Boone and Crockett Club, Roosevelt was a lifelong nature lover. He had, his biographer Edmund Morris noted, an "almost Indian veneration for trees, particularly the giant conifers he encountered in the Rockies. Walking on silent, moccasined feet down a luminous nave of pines, listening to invisible choirs of birds, he came close to religious rapture, as many passages in his books and letters attest."[53] Thus he came to the Oval Office as a true believer and practicing environmentalist. That he became President was a great fortunate accident of our environmental history. He was regarded as an outrageous maverick by many in the Republican Party who were aghast when he succeeded President McKinley.

Their fears were soon justified, particularly the fears of those

Republicans who were growing fatter on public resources. But "for a country returning to nature on many levels, T.R. was the right president at the right time,"[54] wrote Stephen Fox. He made protection of the federal lands a centerpiece of his presidency. He brought the size of the national forest system to nearly its present level. He approved the reversion of Yosemite from California to the federal government in order to make it a national park. Ignoring his somewhat shaky statutory authority, he multiplied the number of national parks. Starting with tiny Pelican Island in Florida's Indian River, he launched the nation's system of wildlife refuges. Following Pinchot's suggestion, he appointed an Inland Waterways Commission to investigate the condition of the nation's navigable waterways and to recommend measures for their protection and improvement. He persuaded Congress to pass the Reclamation Act of 1902, which helped develop water and power for much of the West while, by limiting federal water rights to farms of 160 acres or less, also dealt "the first broad blow for land reform since the Homestead Act of 1862."[55] The Reclamation Act was often abused in the years to come and is regarded by environmental groups today as a mixed blessing. But at the time it was an important step toward democratization of western lands.

TR also made full use of the "bully pulpit" of the presidency to spread the message of conservation. In 1908, he called the governors of all the states to a White House Conference on Conservation, now often regarded as the beginning of a true national conservation movement. One breakthrough of that historic conference was to establish the protection of human health as a legitimate goal of conservation. Today, safeguarding people from the dangers of pollution is the engine that gives much of the thrust to the environmental movement, but at the turn of the century it was a startling new direction.

"The spirit and vigor of our people are the chief glory of the republic," said the commission's report. "Yet even as we have neglected our natural resources, so have we been thoughtless of life and health. Too long have we overlooked that grandest of our resources, human life."[56]

Conservation also challenged the prevailing notion, a relic by the end of the nineteenth century, that America's resources were inexhaustible. The great abundance described by the first explorers to draw settlers to the New World could no longer be taken for granted. Henceforth, abundance would require planning and prudent management. Samuel Hays contends that "conservation, above all, was a scientific movement, and its role in history arises from the implications of science and technology." Its most important contribution, he believes, was the introduction of applied science and professional management to the development of natural resources.

Perhaps the greatest legacy of the Pinchot/Roosevelt collaboration, however, was its emphasis on conservation as an issue of democracy. The resources of the public domain were to be used for the benefit of all the people, not just the powerful. While economic interests would continue to skim the resources of the public lands for self-enrichment, such practices would never again be regarded as a morally acceptable norm. Thereafter, the exploitation of the nation's resources would have to be justified under the guise of spurring economic growth, protecting jobs, safeguarding national security, or some other subterfuge.

Pinchot and Roosevelt preached more than they practiced a democratic approach to the distribution of resources. Their methods of setting and administering policy were more or less autocratic. But the democratic principle had been established and would never be surrendered by those who cared about the land. Today, every decision involving disposal or use of the public lands is scrutinized and often contested by grass-roots organizations.

While the policies of Pinchot and Roosevelt opened a new era of wiser use of the public domain, their policies contained what today are recognized by environmentalists as significant flaws. Pinchot wanted the forests managed for their usefulness, not for their beauty; aesthetics meant little to him, at least professionally. He was not interested in preserving the natural landscape for its own sake. He cared little for protecting wildlife and less for providing recreational opportunities in the public lands. Roosevelt was moved by the spiritual qualities of nature and was more ambivalent about the uses of the land. But he tended, in the end, to follow the lead of Pinchot, his good friend and adviser.

In those years, the cause of wild nature was being eloquently and effectively sounded by another remarkable man whom Roosevelt had befriended: John Muir. He was a bearded, mystical Scotsman who pursued a career as a naturalist, writer, publicist, and lobbyist and who can lay legitimate claim to fathering one major wing of the contemporary environmental movement.

Muir was born on April 21, 1838, in Dunbar, Scotland, where as a young child he was strongly attracted to the natural world. When he was eleven, the Muir family emigrated to Wisconsin. He spent a boyhood of endless toil forced on him by his dour father.[57] One afternoon in 1864, while wandering through a swamp in Canada, where he had gone to dodge the Civil War draft (he had no special feelings of allegiance to the United States, according to historian Stephen Fox, and did not even become a citizen until he was sixty-five), the lonely Muir came across two wild white orchids growing against a bank of yellow moss. As he described it, the encounter was an apotheosis that fixed the course of his life. "I never before saw a plant so full of life; so perfectly spiritual, it seemed pure enough for the throne of its Creator. I felt as if I were in the presence of superior beings who loved me and beckoned me to come. I sat down beside them and wept for joy."[58] It sounds much like Thoreau's transcendental rapture with nature, but Muir was converted by his wild orchids years before he read *Walden*.

Three years later, walking across Florida on another of his anabases from civilization, Muir was entranced by the palm trees and other tropical vegetation and wildlife. He was led to question the Christian belief that "plants are not like man immortal, but are perishable—soul-less." Alligators might appear fierce and cruel to humans but "beautiful in the eyes of God . . . How narrow we selfish, conceited creatures are in our sympathies! How blind to the rights of all the rest of creation! . . . Well, I have precious little sympathy for the selfish propriety of civilized man, and if a war of races should occur between the wild beasts and Lord Man, I would be tempted to sympathize with the bears."[59]

Muir's view of the relationship between humans and nature was very different from the Puritan mission into the wilderness. The wilderness should not be destroyed to make way for Christian civilization. On the contrary, the Creator gave all life an equal right to exist, and to destroy plants and animals was ungodly. To use a word that was not coined until later, Muir took a biocentric view of the world as opposed to the almost universally held anthropocentric view that the world was created for the use of humans to do with what they will. Today, a substantial body of environmental, philosophic, and even religious thought shares Muir's redefinition of the relationship between humans and nature.

By the late 1860s Muir made his way to California's Sierra Nevada and into the breathtaking Yosemite Valley. He had found his habitat. For five years he immersed himself in the wilderness. He slept under the stars until the California rains drove him indoors, and then took a job as a shepherd to earn the minimum amount of money on which he needed to live—he once bragged he needed only three dollars a week. He studied the glaciers of the high passes and once climbed to the top of a conifer during a storm to enjoy the sensation of riding the wind.

Through his writing and his proselytizing of all who crossed his path, Muir soon became the nation's archpriest of wild nature. Sometimes his pronouncements sounded like Thoreau calling wilderness the preservation of the world. "Thousands of tired, nerve-shaken, over-civilized people are beginning to find out that going to the mountains is going home; that wilderness is a necessity; and that mountain parks and reservations are useful not only as fountains of timber and irrigating rivers but as fountains of life."[60] But his chief tenet was that wilderness, like all of nature, existed for its own sake and its existence must be honored and safeguarded by a human community that humbled itself before the marvelous works of the Creator. In tune with the new science of ecology, he believed that everything in the universe was "hitched" to everything else and there-fore was of value.

Muir was angered and disturbed by the degradation of Yosemite by lumbermen and stockmen, particularly by the damage done by sheep—"hoofed locusts" he called them. He and the editor of the *Century Magazine*, Robert Underwood Johnson, decided when camp-ing along the Tuolumne River that the only way to protect Yosemite was to have the federal government take the land back from California and make it a national park.[61] The two men undertook a spirited lobbying campaign kicked off by a series of articles to win support among the new conservation establishment in the East. He won a formidable ally when, in 1903, he took President Roosevelt camping in the mountains. The two men talked around the campfire late into the night, and when they awoke in the morning under a blanket of newly fallen snow, Muir had a friend and a convert. As he rode back from the excursion, Roosevelt shouted to waiting aides that it had been "the grandest day of my life."[62] Three years later, Roosevelt signed the bill making Yosemite a national park.

During the course of the Yosemite campaign, Johnson had pro-posed to Muir the creation of a permanent society to protect Cali-fornia's natural areas. At first Muir was skeptical. But when Henry Senger, a professor of philology at Berkeley, approached him in 1892 with a proposal for creating an alpine club, Muir gave him his blessing. Together with other California academics, including William D. Armes and Joseph LeConte, who were college teachers, and Warren Olney, a San Francisco lawyer, they formed the Sierra Club that same year. Muir became its first president. Among the goals of the new organization was "to enlist the support and cooperation of the people and the government in preserving the forests and other natural fea-tures of the Sierra Nevada Mountains."[63]

With the Sierra Club was born the organized amateur crusade to preserve what was left of the unspoiled American landscape. Pres-ervationism soon became one of the deepest currents of the environ-mental movement, and for several periods the Sierra Club was one of its most powerful forces. As the new century progressed, the preservation movement would grow into what others have called a "cult of the wilderness." While the Boone and Crockett Club and the Audubon movement were already trying to slow the slaughter of wildlife, the preservationists now sought to protect *places* for their wildness and beauty. The movement soon became entwined with the emerging science of ecology, with its emphasis on the interrelationship of living organisms and the systems that support them. Out of the preservationist impulse also arose an intellectual and moral perspective on the relationship between humans and nature that is loosely called "the land ethic."

Up to a point, Pinchot and Muir could make common cause. Heedless, selfish destruction of the land was anathema to both of them. Both called for government efforts to preserve the country's resources. Both were concerned about future generations. For a time they regarded each other as colleagues and even spent a night together camping out on the rim of the Grand Canyon.

But the point of accommodation was quickly passed. Pinchot, a politician as well as a forester (he later became governor of Pennsylvania), insisted that the land and its riches should be used by people both wisely and efficiently. Muir, the mystic and naturalist, demanded that the land and its wild occupants be protected from human assault, although he continued to recommend that men and women look to the wilderness for their spiritual salvation. The fox and the eagle could not occupy the same territory. Their relationship deteriorated to the point where—probably because of Pinchot's intervention—Muir was not invited to the White House Conference on Conservation in 1908.

The clash between their divergent philosophies came to a climax in what is perhaps still the most famous dispute in the history of American conservation, the fight over the Hetch Hetchy Valley. Called a "twin" of the Yosemite, the beautiful Hetch Hetchy was a few miles to the north, along the course of the Tuolumne River. San Francisco wanted to dam the river and flood the valley in order to provide water and, later, electric power for its growing population. Pinchot, true to his utilitarian faith, strongly supported the project. Muir, with the fervor of an Old Testament prophet, opposed it.

"These temple destroyers," he wrote of those who wanted to flood the valley, "devotees of ravaging commercialism, seem to have a perfect contempt for Nature, and instead of lifting their eyes to the God of the mountains, lift them to the Almighty Dollar. Dam Hetch Hetchy! As well dam for water tanks the people's cathedrals and churches, for no holier temple has ever been consecrated by the heart of man."[64]

Both sides marshaled formidable allies; both sought to enlist the support of the President. Roosevelt, uncharacteristically indecisive, finally came down on the side of the dam. Congress eventually approved of the Hetch Hetchy project in 1913. Muir died the following year.

Much has been made of this deep and probably inevitable cleavage in the American conservation movement at the moment of its birth. It was, of course, to have a lasting influence on ideas and policies pertaining to the use of natural resources. To this day the Forest Service, the Bureau of Land Management, and other federal land and resource management agencies do homage at the altar of "multiple use" of the federal estate, which in practice tends to come out as maximum sustainable development of resources. But the conservation movement itself—that is to say, the modern environmental movement—has long since united behind the preservationist crusade as conceived by Muir and others. While today's environmental organizations give lip service to multiple use, they do so basically as a fallback position. They know that the public, while increasingly sympathetic to protecting open space and wilderness, would not accept shutting out economic activity on all those parts of the federal domain that would otherwise be worthy of preserving in their pristine state. Today's environmentalists, or many of them, accept the exploitation of some public lands only to put themselves in a position to save others.

Here, then, are great bridges across American environmental history. From Daniel Boone, born in the first half of the eighteenth century, to John James Audubon, to Grinnell, Teddy Roosevelt, Pinchot, and Muir, to the National Audubon Society and the Sierra Club, two of the national organizations leading today's struggle to preserve and protect our land, our resources, our health, and the natural systems upon which life depends. The nineteenth century produced many other thinkers and activists who helped lay the intellectual, aesthetic, moral, scientific, and political foundations of modern environmentalism, among them George Catlin, Henry David Thoreau, Ralph Waldo Emerson, George Perkins Marsh, Frederick Law Olmsted, Francis Parkman, Carl Schurz, and John Wesley Powell. They were the first to teach us that to save ourselves, we must slow the destruction of nature.

Environmental history does not flow in an unbroken channel from colonial woodsmen to today's environmental leaders. Environmentalism is formed of many tributaries. But from earliest times, even before Boone, many Americans understood and appreciated the beauty of their wild country. There have always been ambivalent emotions among at least some Americans about the disfigurement of a virgin land and sporadic concern about squandering the patrimony of natural resources.

This chapter has traced the emergence of environmentalism from native American soil. Obviously there were European and Asian roots as well. We have seen how Rousseau, Wordsworth, and the romantics made an impression on thought in this country. Thoreau and other American thinkers were influenced by the great English naturalist Gilbert White of Selborne. Buddhism and Eastern pantheism also had an impact on the transcendentalists and others who thought about nature. Charles Darwin and natural selection had a major impact on issues involving the land and its resources, although that impact was mixed. To many, Darwin's *On the Origin of Species*, published in 1859, showed that man was part of nature, not something apart as the Judeo-Christian tradition and the Enlightenment had led people to believe. Some drew from that the conclusion that nature must be protected. But others took the concept of survival of the fittest to mean that nature should be ruthlessly exploited.

Even Karl Marx contributed to the slowly growing body of political writing that addressed environmental issues, although there is no evidence that his ideas were much heeded by early environmental leaders here. Under capitalism, Marx wrote, "nature becomes for the first time simply an object for mankind, purely a matter of utility" and turns nature, like labor, into a mere commodity to be bought and sold.[65]

But the emerging environmental movement was essentially made in America. It was a response to the sudden transformation of what had been a country untouched and unspoiled by Western civilization—the retreat of the wilderness and the startling intrusion of the machine into the garden. It reflected the dismay of Americans who were discovering that, contrary to long-held belief, resources and opportunity were not limitless, even on the vast North American continent. In one of its aspects, environmentalism was scientific rationalism applied to the relationship of humans and nature; it was the realization that the freewheeling, anything-goes approach to land and resources that had spurred the building of a new nation was no longer acceptable. In another, it was a quasi-religious cult of the land.

Conservation was something new in the world. It fit none of the existing political categories—it was neither right nor left, but had its own set of unique and conflicting values.

At the beginning, conservation was dominated chiefly by rich, white, male Protestants. As Stephen Fox so aptly put it, the movement was never so elitist as at its conception. Women played a vital role at many levels of conservation, including the revival of the Audubon Society after George Bird Grinnell let it drop. But they were essentially shut out of leadership in the early days.

Those organizations were first staffed and run by committed amateurs, and the amateur tradition in environmentalism was to continue for many years. But amateurism would prove to be inadequate for meeting the escalating threats to the natural world and to human well-being that would be generated by technology and economic expansion and population growth over the next century. In the nineteenth century, population growth, industrialization, urbanization, and the market economy had transformed the American landscape. In the next century they would threaten to overwhelm it. The Promethean fires let loose by the technology and the energy that fueled it would present human beings, for the first time, with the ability to make the world uninhabitable for their own species.

George Perkins Marsh
ARTIST UNKNOWN   THE NEW YORK TIMES

George Bird Grinnell
NATIONAL PARK SERVICE

John Muir

Gifford Pinchot
THE NEW YORK TIMES

Harold Ickes
THE NEW YORK TIMES

Bob Marshall
THE WILDERNESS SOCIETY

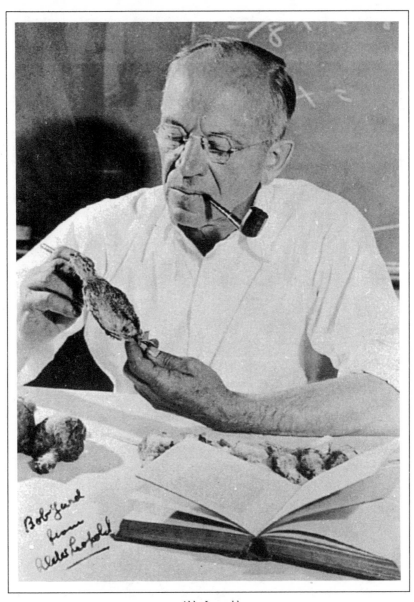

Aldo Leopold
THE WILDERNESS SOCIETY

KEEPERS

OF

THE

HOUSE

. . . the early mornings are strangely silent
where once they were filled with the beauty of bird song.
—Rachel Carson

Henry Adams, a clear-eyed historian as well as the grandson and great-grandson of Presidents, was born in 1838, the same year as John Muir and almost exactly at the time, he once noted, that the steam locomotive first came into use. Living into the twentieth century, Adams was much bemused in his later years by the astonishing leaps that were being made in science, technology, and the development of new sources of energy.

Adams was not pleased by everything about the new America emerging in the early years of the twentieth century. Accompanying his old friend John Hay, then Theodore Roosevelt's Secretary of State, on a railroad trip to the St. Louis World's Fair of 1904, he observed that "agriculture had made way for steam; tall chimneys reeked smoke on every horizon, and dirty suburbs filled with scrap-iron, scrap-paper and cinders, formed the setting of every town."[1]

On the whole, however, Adams was more awed by than critical of the explosive acceleration of technology, science, and industrialism. The new American born since 1900, he wrote, "the child of incalculable coal-power, chemical power, electric power, and radiating energy, as well as new forces as yet undetermined—must be a sort of God compared with any former creation of nature. At the rate of progress since 1800, every American who lived into the year 2000 would know how to control unlimited power. He would think in complexities unimaginable to an earlier mind."[2] Some of the prospects fascinated Adams. Perhaps, he conjectured, even time travel would be mastered and his late-twentieth-century counterpart would be able to go back, sit on the steps of Rome, and discuss history with Edward Gibbon.

Of course, science and technology had limits, Adams pointed out. "All the steam in the world could not, like the Virgin, build Chartres."[3] Moreover, the new forces at the disposal of humanity were bound to create new problems that society had never faced. Already in the early years of the twentieth century, he found that "prosperity never before imagined, power never yet wielded by man, speed never reached by anything but a meteor, had made the world irritable, nervous, querulous, unreasonable and afraid."[4]

Adams also predicted that the accelerated change would produce sharp discontinuity with the past—a new world where the rules of living would have to be learned afresh. "The movement from unity into multiplicity, between 1200 and 1900, was unbroken in sequence, and rapid in acceleration. Prolonged one generation longer, it would require a new social mind. As though thought were common salt in indefinite solution it must enter a new phase subject to new laws. Thus far, since five or ten thousand years, the mind had successfully reacted, and nothing yet proved that it would fail to react—but it would need to jump."[5]

We have not mastered time travel. But Adams's prophecies are pretty much on target. The America he grew up in has vanished.

Muscle, animal, and steam power have given way to electricity, internal-combustion engines, and nuclear reactors. The horse and the locomotive have been subordinated to today's automobiles, jetliners, and interplanetary spacecraft.

Industry has made increasing use of synthetic substances. At the same time, industry consumed natural resources at an ever expanding rate. The population of the country has more than tripled since 1900. A rural people has become thoroughly urbanized and much of the open countryside has been lost to development. Production of goods and services has doubled every ten years or so. The national market is becoming globalized; the national economy a vast magic barrel that pours out a torrent of consumer goods and services. The torrent accelerated at an exponential rate, particularly after World War II.

This dramatic growth has had side effects now considered to be unfortunate—some would say tragic. The land itself was broken, paved over, subdivided, and sullied. The wastes and effluents of industrial technology and supercharged economic activity—many deadly to human health and the natural environment—were spewed into the air, dumped into the waters, and buried in the earth. The residues of industrial activity began to turn up in the shells of bird's eggs, in the flesh of animals, in mothers' milk, in the blood of children, and in the body fat of almost all Americans. Before the century was over, human activity was seriously altering the very physical, chemical, and biological systems that regulate life on the planet. Nature was being replaced.

Only toward the end of the twentieth century, however, did significant numbers of Americans begin to make the intellectual "jump" that Henry Adams warned would be required to confront the forces let loose by energy and technology and the consequent loss of continuity with the past. For most of this century, few people paid much attention to what was happening. We were fouling our own nest but, as former Environmental Protection Agency official Milton Russell noted, "the stench was overpowered by the stronger perfume of money."[6]

Progressivism ebbed with the departure of the energetic Theodore Roosevelt from the White House and with him federal leadership of the young conservation movement. Some of the spirit of the movement died with John Muir. Gifford Pinchot soon ran afoul of President William Howard Taft and his Interior Secretary, Richard A. Ballinger, who busily went about trying to reverse many of TR's conservation policies. After Pinchot accused Ballinger of attempting to "turn over the government lands to the power trust,"[7] Taft dismissed him as chief of the Forest Service. With the exception of the administration of President Woodrow Wilson, which was distracted by World War I, conservatives, not conservationists, were in control of the federal government until Franklin D. Roosevelt gained the presidency. As President Calvin Coolidge complacently noted in 1925, the business of America was business. Conserving the nation's lands and resources was not considered an important part of that business by the government and many of its citizens.

This century's most tainted stewardship of public resources—until the Reagan administration in the 1980s—occurred during the Presidency of Warren Gamaliel Harding, an administration slavishly subservient to business.

The federal government finally got back into the conservation business in a significant fashion when Teddy Roosevelt's second cousin Franklin entered the White House in 1933. Born in 1882 and raised on a beautiful, expansive estate on a bluff overlooking the Hudson River, the young FDR explored the neighboring countryside on foot and on horseback, swam in the still-clean river in the summer and skated and sailed his iceboat on it in winter. Throughout his life he cared deeply about trees and devoted much thought to his plantings in Hyde Park even while beset by government crises during his presidency. It was his political creed, however, as much as his love of nature, that led Roosevelt to make major conservation projects central to his New Deal reforms.

Roosevelt believed, James MacGregor Burns wrote, "that government could be used as a means of human betterment. He preached the need to make government efficient and honest. He wanted to help the underdog, although not necessarily at the expense of the top dog. He believed that private special interests must be subordinated to the general interest. He sought to conserve both the natural resources and the moral values of America."[8]

The Civilian Conservation Corps, the Soil Conservation Service, and the Tennessee Valley Authority were among the many New Deal programs designed to serve both the land and the people. The CCC was a public works program that eventually put nearly 3 million jobless young men to work. That work included planting trees, preventing soil erosion, building roads and structures in national parks, constructing small dams for flood control, and other projects intended to heal and improve the land. Among other things, the CCC demonstrated that there need be no conflict between preservation of the environment and the creation of jobs.

The Soil Conservation Service was born out of the terrible drought and erosion that was tearing the topsoil away from large areas of the Dust Bowl and sending it swirling across the skies. Earth from the Dust Bowl, which included 50 million acres stretching over parts of fifteen Great Plains and southwestern states, darkened the heavens across the country. Hugh Bennett, the first head of the SCS, was testifying before a Senate committee seeking additional funds when he pointed out the window to a dark cloud moving rapidly past the Capitol and said, "There, gentlemen, goes part of Oklahoma now."[9] The service was a strong affirmation of the federal government's responsibility to care for the country's physical landscape. Another such affirmation was the Taylor Grazing Act of 1934, which, for the first time, set rules on the use of the public range intended to limit the abuses that were causing severe degradation of the land.

Few New Deal programs were more controversial than the Tennessee Valley Authority. The TVA was a government body created to develop resources that previously had been placed solely in private hands. Its opponents branded it as socialist or worse. But unfettered capitalism had turned the Tennessee basin into what was essentially an ecologically devastated rural slum. The river and its tributaries were filled with silt and prone to flooding, their potential for hydropower untapped. The region was deforested and badly eroded. Most of its valuable minerals had been taken. As Stewart Udall noted: "The raiders had come and gone, leaving a demoralized people to pick up the pieces."[10]

The TVA planned for the entire basin: it transformed the rivers into sources of cheap power and made them navigable once more, created jobs, helped restore the soil, and brought scientific agriculture to the region for the first time.

It is ironic that the TVA is now criticized by some environmentalists who believe that the air pollution from its coal-fired power plants, its damming of the region's few remaining stretches of free-running rivers, and its foray into nuclear power make it an enemy of the environment. There is a good deal of justice to their complaints. But the TVA brought hope and even a touch of prosperity to a despairing people and set an example of government planning for the protection and use of the land and its resources for the benefit of the broad public instead of a few wealthy and powerful special interests.

FDR and his Interior Secretary, Harold L. Ickes, aggressively added lands to the public domain. They acquired hundreds of thousands of acres of private property in the East and amalgamated them with existing national forests or created new forests. They asserted claim to millions of acres in the West, including land that by 1950 would comprise the Grand Teton National Park.[11] Roosevelt tried to introduce scientific planning in the use of public lands and resources by creating the Natural Resources Planning Board, a proposal that abruptly died when Congress, then digging in its heels against New Deal spending, cut off all funding.

Ickes, a Republican progressive in the tradition of Theodore Roosevelt and a self-styled "curmudgeon," believed that conservation was one of the most important functions of the federal government. He campaigned strenuously but unsuccessfully to place all administration of federal lands and resources in a "Department of Conservation," a goal still on the agenda of many environmentalists. He was also a strong advocate of minority rights, particularly the rights of Native Americans to retain their own lands and culture. He was instrumental in setting up major programs to reclaim arid lands and to construct big hydroelectric projects in the West, opening large new areas to settlement and providing cheap electric power to people who previously did without it. Under Ickes, wrote historian Douglas H. Strong, "the much-maligned Interior Department had gained a prestige and respectability it had never known."[12]

The New Deal environmental programs were pushed into the background by World War II. But the conservation ethic introduced as a central feature of federal policy by Theodore Roosevelt was carried a giant step forward by his cousin Franklin.

The nation's attention to conservation was diverted primarily by the two great wars and the Roaring Twenties. For many years, with few exceptions in this century until the 1960s, efforts to preserve the land and its resources had a low priority on the nation's public agenda.

A spark had been ignited, however, and it was not extinguished. Nurtured and fed at first by a small coterie of visionary individuals and the voluntary organizations they formed, by a few pioneering public servants, by passionate hunters and fishing enthusiasts, and then by a growing number of scientists, public health professionals, scholars, a number of enlightened business leaders, and a band of concerned activists, that deep concern for the fate of the natural world smoldered below the surface of the nation's affairs until a generation after World War II, when it emerged, reinvigorated, as the social movement we call environmentalism.

The conservation movement in the early years of the twentieth century was woven of several different and not always mutually reinforcing strands. One was the romantic-transcendental love of nature. A second was the gospel of efficient use of resources. A third was the democratic principle that the public land and its resources belong to all the people. And a fourth was the rising concern over the environmental and occupational threats to human health from dreadful sanitary conditions, tainted food, and the smoke, soot, and other effluents of a supercharged industrial economy.

While it was founded on the premise of scientific utilitarianism, the conservation movement, along with the broader environmental movement with which it later converged, has often enveloped itself in a mantle of almost religious self-righteousness.

The early conservation movement developed, in the spirit of progressivism, the concept that the public domain was a commons, with land, wildlife, and other resources to be used with the welfare of the general public in mind. This concept was later extended to include air and water as well.[13]

Conservation, as practiced with varying degrees of enthusiasm by the federal government after Pinchot's time, also stressed the efficient use of the public domain. The Forest Service took and continues to take as its mission extracting the maximum sustainable yield from the national forests. The Army Corps of Engineers and the Bureau of Reclamation, which was created by the Reclamation Act of 1902, devoted their energies to the development of the nation's river systems for navigation, irrigation, and electric power. The Commerce Department's Bureau of Fisheries and the Agriculture Department's Biological Survey, which merged and were absorbed by the Interior Department in 1940 as the Fish and Wildlife Service, for many years devoted much of its manpower to enhancing the population of game fish, ducks, geese, and other species popular with hunters and fishermen. The New Deal's Soil Conservation Service concentrated on saving the land for agriculture and silviculture but often produced environmental damage by channeling free-flowing streams.

The private voluntary organizations were more concerned with preserving the land in its natural state, although some of them did seek to exploit the land for their own purposes. The hunters and fishermen wanted to save the habitat of their quarry. Many national park enthusiasts were interested in recreation rather than wilderness as such. But the Hetch Hetchy battle had set a precedent for "radical amateurs" ready to defend the land, wildlife, and other public resources out of idealism and conviction.[14] If there was a quasi-religious strain to the "cult of conservation," preservationism, which evolved into what has been called the "cult of the wilderness," at times took on an almost mystical intensity worthy of its prophet, John Muir.

After Muir's death, the Sierra Club lost its militant edge and spiritual conscience for many years, evolving into a social club that stressed mountain climbing, wilderness hiking, and river trips and largely avoided public policy debates. But new champions arose to protect the public domain.

The environmental army was gathering strength. In the first half of this century its ranks included dozens of organizations and hundreds of leaders. It would be numbing to list them all and I will only try to call attention to a very few of the key groups and figures that provided many of the intellectual, scientific, political, and moral underpinnings of modern environmentalism.

Although the federal land agencies remained committed to the efficient exploitation of public lands and resources, the National Park Service, organized in 1916, aligned itself from the beginning with the preservationists. In large part the policies of the service were the creation of its first director, Stephen T. Mather, and his assistant, Horace M. Albright, who succeeded him. The law creating the service included language drafted by Frederick Law Olmsted, Jr., that would require that the parks, their scenery, wildlife, and natural resources be preserved "unimpaired for the enjoyment of future generations."[15] Mather, a successful businessman and charismatic leader, was instrumental in developing a broad national constituency for the parks, which, in turn, made possible their continual expansion and the exclusion of commercial interests that wanted to exploit the resources within their borders.

Albright, who developed the goals and programs of the park service, also worked hard to preserve the parks in their natural state. Upon retiring as director in 1933, he wrote a letter to the members of the service urging them to "oppose with all your strength and power all proposals to penetrate your wilderness regions with motorways and other symbols of modern mechanization. Keep large sections of primitive country free from the influence of destructive civilization. Keep these bits of primitive America for those who seek peace and rest in the silent places . . ."[16]

In the first half of the century, hunting and fishing organizations were the most politically effective environmental activists. In 1922 a group of midwestern sportsmen formed a new conservation group called the Izaak Walton League in honor of the seventeenth century Englishman who wrote *the* book on the pleasures and techniques of sport fishing: *The Compleat Angler*. Under the leadership of Will H. Dilg, an advertising executive and bass fisherman turned ardent wildlife advocate, the league took on fights, such as reducing water pollution and ending the drainage of marshes, that were later to emerge as issues of mainstream environmentalism. During the Coolidge administration, while leading a battle to block a project that would drain huge stretches of river bottoms on the upper Mississippi, Dilg organized and directed what may have been the first modern environmental lobbying campaign in Washington, employing a full-time staff of assistants and enlisting the support of a wide range of groups, including the General Federation of Women's Clubs. Against the betting of smart money, the league won the battle.

Hunters, fishermen, and sportsmen also formed the core of another major conservation group, the National Wildlife Federation, organized in 1936. Its founding father was a free-spirited duck hunter and popular editorial cartoonist, Jay N. "Ding" Darling. Dismayed by the plummeting duck population, Darling produced cartoons that reflected his disgust with greedy hunters and with the drainage of wetlands, the vital feeding and nesting areas for waterfowl. The federation was intended to be a clearinghouse for conservation issues. But it was backed by gun industry money and often took positions that reflected industry concerns on key issues. Darling "lost interest in the group because it functioned too often as a lobby for the gun industry."[17] Membership in the federation continued to swell until the organization grew so big it was called "the General Motors of the conservation movement." In time, however, the federation evolved into a major force in the campaign for environmental reform.

John Muir's mantle as the passionate voice for the wilderness fell on unlikely shoulders. Robert Marshall, born in 1901, grew up in New York City, the son of Louis Marshall, a well-to-do civil liberties lawyer and co-founder of the American Jewish Committee.

However, the Marshalls spent their summers at a camp in the Adirondack Mountains and there young Bob fell deeply in love with the wild forests, the swift mountain streams, and the remote peaks. An enthusiastic climber, he regarded every mountain in the Adirondacks as a personal challenge. In his short life—he died at age thirty-eight—Marshall earned a doctorate in plant pathology at Johns Hopkins University and became a professional forester and director of the Forest Service's Division of Recreation and Lands. He was a tireless mountaineer, backpacker, and explorer; he was a writer and chief founder and financial supporter of the Wilderness Society, an organization formed in 1935 to fight for the preservation of his beloved primitive areas.

Lanky, with a lively face and a wry smile, and by all accounts a humorous, witty, and gregarious young man, Marshall nevertheless devoted his life to saving the nation's rapidly dwindling wilderness with the single-minded devotion of cloistered monk. "We want no straddlers," he said when describing the kind of dedicated members his Wilderness Society should seek.[18] Marshall argued that wilderness areas were needed for aesthetic reasons and for the psychological health of the American people as an antidote to the "drabness" and "horrible banality" of modern civilization.[19] He warned that time was running out for saving what little remained of a landscape untamed by human activity. "Just a few years more of hesitation," he said in the 1930s, "and the only trace of that wilderness which has exerted such a fundamental influence in molding American character will lie in the musty pages of pioneer books and the mumbled memories of tottering antiquarians."[20]

T. H. Watkins, editor of *Wilderness*, the society's magazine, contended that before Marshall and his society there was "no true movement" for the preservation of the nation's remaining roadless primitive areas. "One could comfortably argue," Watkins wrote in 1985 on the occasion of the society's fiftieth anniversary, "that Robert Marshall was personally responsible for the preservation of more wilderness than any individual in history."[21]

Marshall died in 1939, long before the creation of a federal wilderness system. But his society—led by a core of talented, inspired, and now storied conservationists, including Robert Sterling Yard, who had helped Stephen Mather build popular support for the national park system; Benton MacKaye; Olaus Murie, a wildlife biologist who had spent years trekking across Alaska to study its elk and other species, accompanied by his wife, Margaret Murie, who wrote eloquently of their adventures in the wild; Sigurd Olson, a naturalist and writer whose prose celebrated the glories of the lakes and boreal forests of northern Minnesota; and Howard Zahniser, a brilliant, persistent lobbyist and tactician—played a central role in winning passage of the landmark Wilderness Act of 1964. The Bob Marshall Wilderness in Montana, one of the glories of the wilderness system, is named in his honor.

Aldo Leopold was another founder of the Wilderness Society who died before the Wilderness Act was passed. Born in 1887 in Burlington, Iowa, Leopold trained at the Yale School of Forestry and worked under Pinchot in the Forest Service. He was one of the first to suggest that parts of the forests be set aside as wilderness areas. But Leopold, a disciple of the emerging science of ecology, had a much larger vision of conservation than simply preserving wild land. It was a vision that called for humanity to adopt an entirely new set of rules to govern its behavior toward nature.

A passionate hunter, like so many of the early conservationists, Leopold had long believed that good game management required killing predators that preyed on deer and other species sought by hunters. But two experiences, one scientific, one quasi-religious, changed his view completely.

Leopold's spiritual revelation came, probably in 1909,[22] when he and some companions, hunting on a mountain in New Mexico, spied a mother wolf and her cubs and opened fire on them. Here is his account of what happened next: "We reached the old wolf in time to watch a fierce green fire dying in her eyes. I realized then, and have known ever since, that there was something new to me in those eyes—something known only to her and to the mountain. I was young then, and full of trigger-itch; I thought that because fewer wolves meant more deer, no wolves would mean a hunters' paradise. But after seeing the green fire die, I sensed that neither the wolf nor the mountain agreed with such a view."[23]

When wolves and mountain lions were killed as part of a game management program on Arizona's Kaibab Plateau in the 1920s, the deer herds in that isolated area at first expanded dramatically. But, no longer culled by predators, the herd's growth soon exceeded the capacity of the plateau to sustain it. With the range on the plateau ravaged by starving animals, forage was eliminated and the deer herd perished. From this experience, Leopold drew several lessons: a species cannot be understood or protected in isolation from its habitat, including other animals that prey on it; in an environment already dominated by human beings, humans had no choice but to assure that ecological systems remain in balance. If that meant the active management of game, including culling of game herds, then so be it.

Human beings, Leopold stressed, are only one part of the great "pyramid of life,"[24] but they had acquired the power to destroy other parts of the pyramid. Doing so threatened the entire structure, including humanity itself. Well-meaning efforts to conserve land and the life it sustains would be futile, he contended, in the absence of a scientific understanding of how the pyramid is held together.

In his *Sand County Almanac*, first published in 1949, Leopold quoted Thoreau's affirmation that "in wilderness is the preservation of the world." But unlike Thoreau, he meant biological as well as spiritual preservation, stressing that wild areas were storehouses of genetic diversity. As Wallace Stegner, the writer and environmentalist, has pointed out, Leopold was "one who made us begin to understand that wilderness is indispensable for science and survival."[25]

Science alone, Leopold concluded, could not preserve this chain of life in a complex world where humans hold the power of life and death over entire ecological systems. What is necessary, he insisted, is a new "land ethic," adopted by society as a whole, based on science but also on love of and respect and reverence for the natural world.

"The land ethic," Leopold explained, "simply enlarges the boundaries of the community to include soils, waters, plants, and animals, or collectively: the land."

While most people professed a love of the land, they behaved as ruthless conquerors, Leopold observed. "Just what and whom do we love?" he asked, and answered:

> Certainly not the soil, which we are sending helter-skelter downriver. Certainly not the waters, which we assume have no function except to turn turbines, float barges, and carry off sewage. Certainly not the plants, of which we exterminate whole communities without batting an eye. Certainly not the animals, of which we have already extirpated many of the largest and most beautiful species . . .[26]

A true land ethic, Leopold concluded, "changes the role of *Homo sapiens* from conqueror of the land-community to plain member and citizen of it."

These concepts, merging science and ethics, are now the commonplace working principles at the heart of the environmental movement. But at the time they were new ideas to most conservationists and preservationists, whose horizons were often confined to one piece of land or one species or one set of issues at a time. For much of the public at large, they are lessons still to be learned. *Sand County Almanac*, published a year after Leopold's death, became one of environmentalism's sacred texts. Its simple, powerful prose outlined many of the basic goals of today's conservation and environmental organizations. Historian Donald Fleming described Leopold as "the Moses of the New Conservation impulse of the 1960's and 70's, who handed down the Tablets of the Law but did not live to enter the promised land."[27] Wallace Stegner called him "an American Isaiah."[28]

The dark pall of World War II and the careless optimism and materialism of the immediate postwar years pretty much drove conservation issues off the national agenda. Public health officials continued to press for improved sanitation and control of disease vectors.

Pioneering investigations by Abel Wolman of Johns Hopkins University in the 1930s, 1940s, and 1950s stimulated concern about the dangers posed by municipal water and sewage systems. But the broad agenda we now call environmentalism was largely ignored.

The generally conservationist policies of the New Deal era of the 1930s and 1940s suffered under the Eisenhower administration, which sought to revert to the nineteenth-century tradition of turning over federal lands and resources to the highest bidder or those with the right political connections. Eisenhower's Secretary of the Interior, a former Chevrolet dealer from Oregon, Douglas McKay, attempted to block public power projects and turn energy resources over to private companies. He also tried to abolish a number of federal Fish and Wildlife Service areas and to transfer Nevada's big Desert Game Reserve to the state's fish and game department. So assiduous was McKay in seeking to get rid of federal property that he was dubbed "Giveaway McKay."[29] But as Stephen Fox noted, McKay was only one manifestation of the "Rotarian sensibility of the Eisenhower Administration" and of the homage being paid by most Americans of that era to the gods of unrestrained economic growth.[30] The giveaways of land and resources during the Eisenhower years, however, were not nearly as ambitious as those sought by the Reagan administration.

Government slowly began to respond to public alarm over the environment during the 1960s. For many federal officials, the issue was new and strange. Stewart Udall, a congressman from Arizona who was Secretary of the Interior in the Kennedy and Johnson administrations, recalled that when he first became secretary "people would say, 'Udall, what are you going to do about ecology?' And I would answer, 'What's ecology?' "[31] Originally a proponent of building dams, Udall gradually became converted to the cause of protecting the environment. During Udall's tenure at Interior, President Kennedy proposed the creation of the Land and Water Conservation Fund, which took federal revenues from offshore oil drilling and used them to acquire land for national and state parks and recreation areas. The fund was set up by Congress in 1965. A year earlier,

Congress had adopted, after many years of debate, the landmark Wilderness Preservation Act. The National Wild and Scenic Rivers Act and the National Trails Act were both passed in 1968. During the 1960s clean air and clean water legislation was enacted and, while relatively toothless, those statutes did set the stage for much stronger laws in the next decade. In that period, the Public Health Service had eleven environmental divisions with missions that included lead control, rat control, and water pollution control.

In all those years there were those who watched, worried, and warned their countrymen of the folly of their indifference to their misuse and destruction of nature.

Prominent among the prophets was Lewis Mumford. Inspired by the work of Patrick Geddes, a Scotsman who had coined the word "megalopolis" earlier in the century, Mumford warned in several books that the swelling size and power of the cities was overwhelming the countryside. Western civilization, he complained, had taken a wrong turn since the science of Bacon, Newton, and Galileo had reduced the universe to a set of discrete parts and principles. Such a mechanistic view led society to believe it could subjugate and rule nature with science and technology. As a result, modern civilization was being overwhelmed by the megalopolis and the "megamachine," artificial creations that enslaved humans instead of serving them. To Mumford, as one commentator pointed out, the automobile filled in the last open spaces and was "the true Frankenstein's monster of the 20th century, only surpassed in its destructive potential by the Hydrogen Bomb, but more dangerous because more complacently indulged."[32]

The natural world was not a machine that could be easily manipulated by men—it was whole, interdependent, ecological, Mumford argued. Human values could be achieved in a crowded modern world only by abandoning the "megamachine," which gives excessive power to humans, and adopting a technology that was suited to this holistic world, he insisted. "What is the use of conquering nature," he asked, "if we fall prey to nature in the form of unbridled men?"[33]

Mumford was among the first of a growing number of scientists and scholars to warn of the ecological dangers of excessive human growth and power. Another eloquent voice was raised by René Dubos, an ecologist and microbiologist, who, while on the faculty of Rockefeller University, pioneered in the development of antibiotic drugs during the World War II era. At a time when these "wonder drugs" were universally praised as a great gift to mankind, Dubos began to question the wisdom of using them to wipe out the microorganisms that were the very foundation of the chain of life. He feared that humans, acting out of arrogance and ignorance, could cause incalculable damage to the ecological systems they inhabited by seeking to eradicate some species that were responsible for limited harm to them.

Humanity would best serve itself, Dubos believed, not by seeking complete mastery over nature, but by exercising self-restraint toward the natural world. The loneliness and alienation of contemporary life, he insisted, was caused not only by the breakdown in relationships between human beings but also by "the chaos in the relationships between man and his environment."[34]

Dubos did not suggest that humans leave nature alone. He was not urging a return to the primitive. He praised the cultivated landscapes of the British countryside, the Ile de France, and New England, which, he found, had not been "conquered" but gradually humanized over time through a subtle "wooing" of nature.[35] Neither did Dubos believe that technology must be abandoned. In fact, he said, there are grounds for optimism that Western civilization could reverse the trend toward self-destruction if "science, technology, and social organization can be made to serve the fundamental needs and urges of mankind, instead of being allowed to distort human life."[36] The belief that science, technology, and social institutions will play a crucial role in rescuing us from the ecological crisis they helped create is a central article of faith among mainstream environmentalists today.

Dubos's concept of the human environment was the central theme of the 1972 United Nations Conference in Stockholm and, twenty years later, was at the heart of what the nations of the world were trying to achieve at the United Nations Conference on Environment and Development in Rio de Janeiro. His admonition to "think globally, act locally," is now part of the catechism of the environmental movement. A habitually smiling, self-described "despairing optimist" (the title of a column he wrote for *The American Scholar* magazine for a decade),[37] Dubos was born in 1900 and died eighty-two years later. He is recognized as a philosopher-scientist in the great tradition and one of the sages of modern environmentalism.

One of the most controversial issues of modern environmentalism was raised by a group of neo-Malthusian scientists and sociologists who warned that an exploding world population was placing an unsustainable burden on food and other natural resources. Uncontrolled growth, they contended, would lead to social collapse, even the destruction of many of the ecological systems that support life. Science and technology had so far averted the catastrophe predicted by Thomas Robert Malthus, the English cleric who warned at the end of the eighteenth century that geometrically expanding population would outstrip food supplies and lead to mass starvation. Thus with world population now doubling every thirty-five years, the impact of millions of hungry, desperate people on the world's life-support systems is viewed by some ecologists as the key issue of our time.

In *Our Plundered Planet*, published in 1948, Fairfield Osborn warned that scientific marvels that had continued to produce enough food to keep a world fed could not be expected to do so indefinitely. Osborn, a lifelong conservationist, was president of the New York Zoological Garden. His father, the biologist Henry Fairfield Osborn, had been president of the American Museum of Natural History in New York. "The miraculous succession of modern inventions has so profoundly affected our thinking as well as our everyday life that it is difficult for us to conceive that the ingenuity of man will not be able to solve the final riddle—that of gaining subsistence from the earth," he wrote in *Our Plundered Planet*, and added, "The grand and ultimate illusion would be that man could provide a substitute for the elemental workings of nature."[38]

An essay entitled "Tragedy of the Commons," by the ecologist Garrett Hardin, published in 1968 in *Science*, made an influential if hotly debated case for social intervention to limit population growth and resource consumption. The essay offered a parable which purported to show how a commons, a publicly owned pasture, would inevitably be destroyed by its users. Any individual user of the pasture, he noted, stood to profit by grazing as many of his or her own cattle as possible, because the grass was free. But if all members of the community did the same thing, the commons would quickly be overgrazed, eroded, and useless for feeding animals—and humans—in the future.

A "Social Darwinian,"[39] Hardin argued that society should not assist the impoverished and undernourished through welfare programs or send food to starving people in other countries. Or, Hardin insisted, if these people accepted social help they should be required to agree to limits on their rights to procreate.

While Hardin's precepts were assailed as unnecessarily harsh, even within the growing environmental community, the notion that population control was a key to the ecological health of the planet and the well-being and possibly the survival of humanity continued to gain wide, although by no means universal currency. Some radical environmentalists continue to urge draconian measures to curb population growth.

The most widely known proponent of the view that overpopulation is a catastrophic ecological problem is Paul R. Ehrlich, a biologist and tireless speaker and writer whose book *The Population Bomb*[40] became a best-seller in 1968. In it he predicted that overpopulation would inevitably lead to massive famines and epidemics in the near future. Ehrlich and others founded the organization Zero Population Growth, which proposed an imperative social goal for the United States and other relatively affluent countries. It was their duty to set an example of population restraint that could be emulated throughout the world.

In a subsequent book, *How to Be a Survivor*, Ehrlich used the "spaceship earth" metaphor coined earlier by Kenneth Boulding to suggest that the world was a closed system that could sustain only so many people and that exponentially growing population and con-

sumption of resources assured misery for all but the "first-class passengers" aboard the ship and they, too, would be in jeopardy over
the long run.[41]

For the United States, the country of limitless horizons, nurtured
on what Stewart Udall called "the myth of superabundance," the idea
that there could be boundaries to growth and that the carrying capacity
of the land itself was finite was difficult to accept. But the evidence
kept coming in. In 1972, the Club of Rome, a group of influential
businessmen and scientists, published a slim volume called *The Limits
to Growth*, which presented statistics showing that the world was
running out of resources with which to sustain economic growth and
an exploding population. It was also running out of time.

Using mathematical models developed at the Massachusetts Institute of Technology, *Limits* projected population trends, resource
depletion, food supplies, capital investment, and pollution. Its sobering
conclusions were threefold:

1. If the present growth trends in world population, industrialization, pollution, food production and resource
   depletion continue unchanged, the limits to growth on
   this planet will be reached sometime within the next one
   hundred years. The most probable result will be a rather
   sudden and uncontrollable decline in both population
   and industrial capacity.
2. It is possible to alter these growth trends and to establish
   a condition of ecological and economic stability that is
   sustainable far into the future . . .
3. If the world's people decide to strive for this second
   outcome rather than the first, the sooner they begin
   working to attain it, the greater will be their chances of
   success.[42]

The data and the models used in *Limits* were widely challenged.
But the possibility that humanity might exceed the earth's carrying
capacity gained worldwide recognition and a prominent place on the

American environmental movement's list of impending catastrophes.

Some environmental thinkers, however, rejected the notion of overpopulation and resource depletion as the sole or even chief cause of our environmental ills. They pointed instead at wasteful consumption, destructive technology, poor social and economic organization, and the power and privilege of corporations as the source of pollution and other strains on natural systems.

In *Our Synthetic Environment*, published in 1962, the social ecologist Murray Bookchin described the ecological horrors and deterioration of human health caused by technological giantism and the poisons and other destructive pollutants dumped by industry into the land, air, and water. Bookchin did not reject technology but insisted that a sane society required "a reordering and redevelopment of technologies according to ecologically sound principles . . . based on non-polluting energy sources such as solar and wind power, methane generators, and possibly liquid hydrogen that will harmonize with the natural world."[43] Changing technology would not be enough, however. Bookchin concluded that "there can be no sound environment without a sound, ecologically oriented social environment," and called for a decentralization of society, into compact, biologically rational regions where the economy would serve the needs of humans rather than corporations and their massive technology.[44] Bookchin's views have attracted a small but intense following.

Barry Commoner, who also took issue with the neo-Malthusians, had an enormous impact in alerting the American people to the environmental dangers that threatened them and their world. Commoner, who was born in Brooklyn in 1917, is a scientist and self-described political radical who ran for President in 1980 as the candidate of the Citizens Party. He was one of the first and most prominent scientists to call attention to the threats to the environment posed by technological excesses that followed World War II. His books *Science and Survival* and particularly *The Closing Circle*, which combined the discipline of science with a stinging moral sensibility, form an important part of the literature of modern environmentalism.

Alarmed by reports circulating within the scientific community about radioactive fallout from aboveground testing of atomic bombs in the 1950s, Commoner, then teaching at Washington University in St. Louis, helped form an organization of scientists and civic leaders called the St. Louis Committee for Nuclear Information. The committee, through its public education efforts, played a significant role in the successful campaign by scientists, initially led by Linus Pauling and Herman J. Muller, to persuade the United States and the Soviet Union to ban aboveground testing. The atmospheric testing of atomic devices was one of the newer issues around which the modern environmental movement rallied.

One of the committee's projects, a study of baby teeth, found that radioactive strontium 90 from the tests was being taken up through the food chain into human bones and, contrary to the claims of the Atomic Energy Commission, posed a serious threat to human health. Dr. Pauling's scientists' petition demanding an end to testing was circulated by Commoner's office.[45] The 1963 Nuclear Test Ban Treaty, Commoner later wrote, should be considered "the first victorious battle in the campaign to save the environment."[46]

A biologist with a sharp and eloquent tongue, and a fierce sense of political engagement, Commoner applied rigorous scientific analysis to his examination of the broad causes of the widening environmental degradation. His view of biology was ecological and holistic. He criticized the molecular biologists for reducing living systems to ever smaller component parts, an approach, he said, that ignores the interrelationships within a system and between systems. Such an approach, passed on by scientists to engineers, had produced a technology that did not consider feedbacks, such as pollution, but only the narrow purpose for which its products were designed.[47]

It was destructive, inappropriate technology, not excess population or affluence, that was chiefly responsible for the pollution that most threatened the earth's biological systems, Commoner insisted in *The Closing Circle*. Particularly in the postwar years, he argued, the market economy created products, such as high-compression automotive engines, nitrogen fertilizers, plastics, and pesticides such as DDT, which by their synthetic nature created pollution that remained outside the natural cycles of the ecosphere and threatened to over-whelm it.

> Human beings have broken out of the circle of life, driven
> not by biological need, but by the social organization which
> they have devised to "conquer" nature: means of gaining
> wealth that are governed by requirements conflicting with
> those which govern nature. The end result is the environ-
> mental crisis, a crisis of survival. Once more, to survive,
> we must close the circle. We must learn how to restore to
> nature the wealth that we borrow from it.[48]

The solution, he said, was not "barbaric" measures to limit population growth or to set levels of permissible pollution and then regulate industry to try to make it meet those limits. What was required was to change technology so that it did not pollute and break the cycle of life. This could only happen, he contended, if the pro-duction system were taken out of the hands of private corporations and turned over to social governance.

Commoner's insistence that socialism—or the "S-word," as he mockingly called it—was the road to ecological salvation opened a wide gulf between him and the mainstream national environmental groups, to whom he was a perpetual gadfly. For his part, Commoner was convinced that the established environmentalists were only nib-bling at the edges of the problem rather than working at its roots. He had even less respect for the efforts of the federal, state, and local regulatory agencies to address the toxification of the environment. But *The Closing Circle*, along with his other writings and many lectures and often acerbic speeches, did as much to awaken the country to the rapidly worsening environmental crisis as any other effort by a contemporary writer or scientist—save Rachel Carson. Across the country there are many men and women who will recall that they first began to march in the environmental crusade when they heard the sharp tattoo of Barry Commoner's drum.

After World War II, alarm and anger over the despoliation of the nation's environment slowly began to simmer toward a boiling point. Attempted raids on the minerals, timber, grass, and other resources of the national parks and other parts of the public domain by profiteers rekindled some of the activism that had been dormant among the old-line preservationist groups. The Sierra Club, in particular, sprang to aggressive life after the war when it was taken over by a group of "young Turks" led by the legendary photographer Ansel Adams and by David Brower, an imaginative, forceful, strong-willed, charming, and difficult man who would later be dubbed the "archdruid" of the conservation movement by the writer John McPhee. Now regarded as one of the most militant of the old preservationist groups, John Muir's club had subsided in the 1920s and 1930s into a somewhat passive social organization that sponsored hikes and stayed out of public issues until the Turks took over. Michael McClosky, who came along a generation after the Turks and later succeeded Brower as executive director of the club after a bitter internal brawl in 1969, recalled that in the 1950s no one could join the club without being recommended by two sponsors. Since then, the club, like many other environmental groups, has sought a broad national membership to serve as foot soldiers in its fight to preserve nature and protect human health.

With Brower as its dynamic leader, the Sierra Club once again became a potent force. In the 1960s and 1970s it lobbied actively to block dams in Dinosaur National Monument and the Grand Canyon and to save California's Mineral King Valley and its redwood groves and other natural treasures from the hands of commercial interests. Under Brower, the club began for the first time to turn to the law courts to protect the environment. He helped set up the environmental movement's first organization for influencing electoral politics. He made extensive use of the mass media to put across the message of environmentalism and the club; during his tenure, he published many books that brought the beauty and the plight of the American landscape to the public. Brower contends that one of these books, *This Is the American Earth*, featuring magnificent photographs by Ansel Adams and others and a poetic text by Nancy Newhall, played a major role in building wide public support for protecting the land and in linking the old preservationist impulse to the powerful emerging drive to stop pollution.[49] Brower was tireless in leading the club into new issues and in speaking, writing, and testifying to generate concrete action on those issues.

In time, club directors came to feel that Brower was becoming a one-man show, leading the club in directions not all of them wanted to go—for example, launching without discussion within the club an international advertising and fund-raising campaign for an "Earth National Park."[50] They complained that he was a poor manager who had dragged the club into serious financial difficulties. Led by Adams, the club board forced Brower to resign in 1969. He then formed a rival environmental group he called Friends of the Earth, the name taken from a quotation from Muir: "The earth can do all right without friends, but men, if they are to survive, must learn to be friends of the earth."[51] His new group was even more militant and took on a wider range of issues. Friends of the Earth organizations formed in several countries in Europe and Asia, making it one of the first international environmental organizations. By the 1980s, Brower ran afoul of his new associates and once again had to move on. Undaunted, he formed still another organization, the Earth Island Institute, which soon became active in publishing books on environmentalism and ecology and in fighting no-holds-barred battles to protect wildlife and other natural resources.

While varying judgments have been made about David Brower, there can be no doubt that he led several victorious campaigns to save the land, helped rekindle the transcendental flame lit by Thoreau and Muir, and played a major role in pulling the old preservationist movement out of the comfortable leather armchairs of its clubrooms and into the down-and-dirty arena of local and national policy making.

A number of new organizations formed in the postwar years in response to the slowly widening perception that some drastically bad things were beginning to happen to the natural world because of human activity.

Immediately after the war, Fairfield Osborn formed a group

called the Conservation Foundation to examine and publicize broad ecological issues, including the effect of pesticides on the environment. In 1965, he persuaded a U.S. Tax Court judge, Russell Train, to resign from the bench and take over as president of the foundation. Train, who had become interested in wildlife during a safari to Africa and had founded the African Wildlife Foundation, was also a founder and vice president of the United States wing of the World Wildlife Fund.[52] He went on to become Under Secretary of the Interior and then the first chairman of the Council on Environmental Quality during the Nixon administration and, under President Ford, the second administrator of the Environmental Protection Agency. Train combined concern for and involvement in protecting the environment with political, administrative, and social skills unmatched in the movement since Gifford Pinchot. Although a lifelong Republican, he publicly condemned the environmental misdeeds of the Reagan administration. In 1991, late in his career, concerned that the United States had fallen off the track of environmentally sound policy making, he organized a "national commission on the environment" to provide guidance and support for a new agenda for sustainable economic and social growth.

Another significant postwar force for saving land and wildlife was not an environmental organization or a leader of one but a Supreme Court justice—William O. Douglas. Born in Washington's Yakima Valley, Douglas was a hiker, camper, and lover of the out-of-doors throughout his life. In his younger days an adherent of the Pinchot school of utilitarian conservation, he was converted to the Muirist faith of preserving rather than exploiting the natural world by an exposure to Buddhist reverence for life during a trek in the Himalayas.[53] As a justice and as a writer of books on conservation, he insisted that "wilderness values" must be protected because they are "a passionate cause for millions" even if those millions are a minority of the population.[54] He played a leading role in the successful effort to preserve the Chesapeake and Ohio Canal and its towpath, which runs from Washington, D.C., to western Maryland: the canal was designated a national historical park in 1971. In a famous dissent in the case of *Sierra Club* v. *Morton* in 1972, he wrote that parts of nature are entitled to be represented in court, and that before "priceless bits of Americana (such as a valley, an alpine meadow, river, or a lake) are forever lost or are transformed as to be reduced to the eventual rubble of our urban environment, the voice of the existing beneficiaries of these environmental wonders should be heard."[55]

The issue of whether the courts of law could be used to block harm to the aesthetic values of the environment—as opposed to damage to persons or property—was first raised in the early 1960s. Plans by Consolidated Edison to build a pumping station at Storm King Mountain in the lower Hudson Valley had provoked intense protests by residents of the area and by hikers and campers who used the mountain and who objected that the project would destroy the beauty of the area. Forming an organization called the Scenic Hudson Preservation Conference, these citizens filed suit against the Federal Power Commission, which had denied their petition to withhold permission for the project. David Sive, a New York lawyer, was a leading attorney for the group.

The commission asked the court to dismiss the suit on the ground that the citizens group had suffered no financial or personal injury. "But in a landmark decision, the Court of Appeals for the Second Circuit ruled that Scenic Hudson should be allowed to bring suit owing to its 'aesthetic, conservational and recreational' interest in the area," recalled the writer Tom Turner.[56] Among other things, the decision required that Consolidated Edison consider alternatives to building a pumping station at the site, including the alternative of building no facility at all.

The importance of that decision to the emerging environmental movement is hard to exaggerate, according to David Sive. With the Storm King precedent, the cause was given a powerful new weapon against the onslaught of corporate might and the inertia of government. Sive observed that "environmentalism has used litigation as no other social movement has before or since."[57]

Sive went on to become one of the founders of the Natural Resources Defense Council, an environmental group that has made particularly effective use of the law courts. Little known to the public, he played a key role in arming the environmental movement for the great battles ahead.

The opening to the courts was quickly exploited. In 1966, a lawyer on Long Island, Victor Yannacone, sued to prevent the spraying of DDT on the fields and wetlands of the island. The following year, Yannacone joined forces with Charles Wurster and other scientists of the State University of New York at Stony Brook to form the Environmental Defense Fund in New York City, the first of the new-style national environmental groups. This combination of law and science would be an effective force for the environment in the coming years. The Environmental Defense Fund, the Natural Resources Defense Council, and other new groups that adopted similar techniques took on many issues, such as toxic wastes and air and noise pollution, that had largely been ignored by the older conservation groups.

In the early 1960s, a time of general social unrest, the mood of the country with regard to environmental issues was clearly shifting. A widely noticed television commercial aired by the Advertising Council, an arm of the advertising industry, showed an American Indian wandering through a landscape littered with garbage, a tear trickling down his cheek. The message was clear: the beautiful land inhabited by the Native Americans when Columbus arrived in the New World had been besmirched by subsequent generations and the time had come to start cleaning it up. While one could question the motives of the commercial—the corporations that are the major advertisers are often the biggest polluters and an advertising campaign was simpler and less expensive than changing their manufacturing processes—the ad was an effective one. It confronted the television-viewing public with the uncomfortable truth that we were becoming a nation of nest-fouling, wasteful overconsumers.

Changes in the way people chose to live also reflected, at least in part, a growing acceptance of new environmental values. The migration to the suburbs was, for many if not most of the families who moved, an environmental choice for open space, greenery, cleaner air, less noise, and a generally healthier place to live. (Of course, the move to the suburbs also was for much of the white middle class a flight from the swelling minority populations in many of the major cities.) The demand for vacation homes at the seashore or in the mountains was another manifestation of environmental values as well as of the postwar affluence of a growing fraction of the population. People were becoming more alert to the food they ate and the environmental hazards that over time might make them ill. Two periodicals put out by J. I. Rodale—and later his son Robert—from their farm in Emmaus, Pennsylvania, *Organic Gardening and Farming* and *Prevention*, which stressed the avoidance of foods grown with synthetic chemicals and exposure to toxic and artificial products, attracted wide readership. Rodale took particular issue with the food processors who put dangerous additives in their products and with the government regulators who let them get away with it.[58] A new "health food" industry sprang up, although some products that were sold in these stores represented little if any improvement from a health standpoint over those sold in the regular food chains.

Emerging environmental interest was also reflected in the boom in outdoor recreation—camping, hiking, boating, skiing, even birding. Roger Tory Peterson's bird guides became best-sellers. Television programs about nature and wildlife, many of them based on the science of ethology, drew substantial audiences. A number of young people influenced by the counterculture of the 1960s sought to return to nature by forming rural communes. While almost all of these groups failed, the impulse in large part reflected the young people's rejection of materialistic lifestyles that either ignored or harmed the environment.

Samuel Hays has contended that modern environmental values are largely a result of a search for new, nonmaterial "amenities" by the increasingly affluent Americans of the postwar era. These amenities—clean air and water, better health, open space, recreation—were consumer items that many Americans now had the leisure and security to demand. "Environmental quality," Hays wrote, was an integral part of a "new search for a higher standard of living."[59]

The swelling environmental impulse in this country has many dimensions to it. But consumerism undoubtedly is one of them. It is no accident that Ralph Nader, the country's leading consumer advocate, has also been a strong voice for environmental protection. The crusade for safe automobiles, which brought Nader wide public recognition, was also a crusade against pollution. *Unsafe at Any Speed*, the book that indicted the automotive industry, included a chapter on air pollution from motor vehicles. Looking into the abuses of the industry, Nader found that their products "were using the air as a sewer and it was free of charge. They denied it was harmful at all."[60]

Nader, born in 1934, grew up in Winsted, Massachusetts, where local industries poured pollution into the air and into the town's two rivers. While attending Princeton he came across a dead blue jay on the campus killed by DDT sprayed on the trees. When he took the bird to the school newspaper and urged its editors to write about the dangers of pesticides, he could not get the editors interested. From his early experiences, however, he concluded that pollution was "a cumulative form of violence that is different than street crime only in that the cause and effect is not immediate . . . it is deferred battery."[61] Among the advocacy organizations Nader formed, with the help of money won in a lawsuit against the General Motors Corporation, were state and national Public Interest Research Groups with an agenda that included lobbying for environmental protection. The tall, saturnine, and ascetic Nader, single-mindedly dedicated to the general weal, became a symbol of a public probity that many Americans believed was lacking in their political and corporate leaders.

In 1980, Stephen Fox found Nader to be "the most effective single influence in mobilizing public opinion against pollution."[62] While this conclusion could be challenged by the many Americans who were brought to awareness of the issues by Barry Commoner, Rachel Carson, and others, there is no doubt that Nader, an incorruptible voice speaking for the American consumer, helped bring industrial pollution into the full glare of national attention.

For many years, environmentalism was a disjointed, inchoate

impulse; a revolution waiting for a manifesto; citizens' anger seeking a Bastille to storm. Was the cause love of nature or fear of pollution? Do we need to protect wildlife or is it human beings that are at risk? Were there any villains to attack? Was there any hope of salvation?

The answers came in a remarkable book by a remarkable woman. *Silent Spring* by Rachel Carson, excerpts of which were first published in *The New Yorker* in 1962, is now recognized as one of the truly important books of this century.[63] More than any other, it changed the way Americans, and people around the world, looked at the reckless way we live on this planet. Focusing on a specific problem—the poisoning of the earth by chemical pesticides—*Silent Spring* was a broad examination of how carelessly applied science and technology were destroying nature and threatening life, including human life. Beautifully written and a best-seller, it sounded a deep chord which affected people emotionally and moved them to act. It may be the basic book of America's environmental revolution.

Born in 1907, Carson grew up in Pennsylvania, developed a deep love of the sea, and became a marine biologist. By all accounts a gentle, loving, somewhat reclusive but tough-minded woman, she was strongly influenced by the physician and humanitarian Albert Schweitzer's "reverence for life." The dedication of *Silent Spring* is: "To Albert Schweitzer who said 'Man has lost the capacity to foresee and to forestall. He will end up by destroying the earth.' "[64] She worked for many years as a biologist for the Fish and Wildlife Service's experimental station in Patuxent, Maryland, before the success of *The Sea Around Us* and *The Edge of the Sea*, both best-sellers, enabled her to resign and devote full time to writing. Long alarmed by the dangers of DDT and other pesticides, she tried to sell an article to magazines on the subject but was turned down because the publishers feared loss of advertising from food and chemical companies. So she decided to write a book instead.[65] *The New Yorker*, apparently not to be intimidated, condensed large portions of the book.

Silent Spring begins with two lines from John Keats's poem "La Belle Dame Sans Merci":

> *The sedge is withr'd from the lake,*
> *And no birds sing.*

Carson then goes on to describe "a town in the heart of America" surrounded by prosperous farms, fields of grain, green hillsides, trees and wildflowers, foxes and deer, pools filled with trout, and "countless birds." But then a "strange blight crept over the area," silencing the voices of the birds, causing the cattle to die and the chickens to lay eggs that would not hatch. Adults and children developed unexplained illnesses and some of them died. The only clue was a white powder that had "fallen like snow upon the roofs and the lawns, the fields and streams."

That town did not exist, Carson explained, but all of the things that she described had happened in towns around the country. "A grim specter has crept upon us almost unnoticed, and this imagined tragedy may easily become a stark reality we all shall know."[66]

Most of the book is a careful exposition of the available scientific knowledge about the effects of DDT and other synthetic substances on the natural world. It shows how these chemicals kill far more than the species at which they are aimed. It demonstrates that the poisons remain in the environment for many years, contaminating the soil, rivers, lakes, coastal waters, and underground aquifers. It illustrates how the poisons pass through the food chain and become more concentrated the higher on the chain they get. It makes clear that these poisons carried in the chain eventually reach the men, women, and children who eat contaminated food or breathe contaminated air or drink contaminated water. It warns not only that humans are in danger of being poisoned by these substances but also that humanity is in grave danger of genetic damage from repeated exposure. "For the first time in the history of the world, every human being is now subjected to contact with dangerous chemicals from the moment of conception until death."[67] These substances, moreover, were changing the very fabric of nature. "The most alarming of all man's assaults upon the environment is his contamination of air, earth, rivers and sea with dangerous and even lethal materials. This pollution is for the most part irrecoverable; the chain of evil it initiates not only in the world that must support life but in living tissues is for the most part irreversible. In this now universal contamination of the environment, chemicals are the sinister and little recognized partners of radiation in changing the very nature of the world—the very nature of its life."[68]

Although the book is calm and reasoned in tone, many of its chapter titles make it clear that Carson consciously wrote a polemic intended to stir people to political action: "Elixirs of Death," "Needless Havoc," "And No Birds Sing," "Rivers of Death," "Indiscriminately from the Skies," "Beyond the Dreams of the Borgias," "The Human Price."

But *Silent Spring* ends on a hopeful, not a despairing note. There is an alternative to destroying nature with synthetic poisons—"The Other Road" Carson called it, a reference to Robert Frost's poem "The Road Not Taken." That road is a gradual turning away from pesticides and other life-killing synthetic substances. Alternatives such as biological controls on insects are available. She urges that people be informed of the danger so they may decide for themselves whether the risks are worth it. She calls for increased government action to monitor and regulate it. She urges that humans give up their arrogant efforts to control nature.

Carson did not do much of the research that showed the dangers of DDT or other synthetic substances. She was not even the first to cry the alarm—Bookchin, the naturalist Edwin Way Teale, and a number of others had already sounded public warnings.

What Carson did in *Silent Spring*, however, was to present the scientific evidence in clear, poetic, and moving prose that demonstrated how the destruction of nature and the threat to human health from pollution were completely intertwined. She showed how all life, including human life, was affected by misguided technology. The book synthesized many of the concerns of the earlier conservationists and preservationists with the warnings of newer environmentalists who worried about pollution and public health. It made frighteningly clear that they were all skeins of a large web of environmental evil settling over the nation and the world. What killed trees and flowers, birds and animals, she demonstrated, could also sicken and kill human beings. She combined a transcendentalist's passion for nature and wildlife with the cool analytical mind of a trained scientist and the contained anger of a political activist. She touched an exposed wound.

By the late 1960s public awareness of the misuse of the land and its resources, of the toll that industrial pollution and dangerous new synthetic substances were taking on the air, the water, and human beings, reached a critical threshold. The fervor, activism, and ethical sensibilities of Bob Marshall, Aldo Leopold, David Brower, and other pioneer conservationists had driven home to many Americans the message that their land and resources were being badly abused. Lewis Mumford, Barry Commoner, René Dubos, and Murray Bookchin demonstrated how uncontrolled science and technology and unresponsive social organization were responsible for the degradation of the natural environment and represented a growing threat to humans themselves. Fairfield Osborn, Garrett Hardin, Paul Ehrlich, and the Club of Rome were among those who alerted the public to the danger that too many people were making excessive demands on air, water, food, and other resources needed to support life. Ralph Nader underscored the role of the corporation in polluting the environment and depleting resources, and William O. Douglas and David Sive were prominent among those who demonstrated that the law could be a weapon against environmental injustice.

Thanks to these and many other vigilant guardians of our ecological household, environmentalism in the United States had become a powder keg ready to explode. With *Silent Spring*, Rachel Carson lit the fuse.

SAVING

OURSELVES

I am myself and what is around me,
and if I do not save it, it shall not save me.
　　　　—*José Ortega y Gasset*

On April 22, 1970, a crisp, sunny day over much of the country, some 20 million Americans, many of them young, massed in the streets, on campuses, on riverbanks, in parks, and in front of government and corporate buildings to demonstrate their distress and anxiety over the state of the environment. It was called Earth Day. A revolution, of sorts, had begun.

Earth Day was not a spontaneous uprising. The sense of mounting ecological crisis had begun to penetrate the national consciousness well before. We have already noted the growing concern and activity of the environmental groups and the government in the 1960s. A series of well-publicized ecological insults in the years following publication of *Silent Spring*—including a huge spill from an oil rig off the coast of Santa Barbara, California, the Cuyahoga River in Cleveland bursting into flames because of the heavy concentration of inflammable industrial chemicals in its waters, the choking of Lake Erie by phosphates, the dumping of toxic PCBs into the Hudson and Housatonic rivers, the dense smog blanketing many of our major cities, the contamination of food fish by mercury, the fouling of beaches by sewage, and dozens of other notorious episodes—directed the country's attention to the worsening condition of the natural landscape.

The conservation movement was a response to nineteenth-century abuses of the land and its resources. The twentieth century would turn out to be far more dangerous to the natural environment and to the humans and other creatures that live within it. A few names and phrases evoke the environmental havoc wrought during this century: Killer smog. The Dust Bowl. The Cuyahoga River. Bhopal. Toxic waste. Three Mile Island. Chernobyl. PCBs. Love Canal. Times Beach. The *Exxon Valdez*. Lead paint. DDT. Minimata disease. Radioactive waste. Whales and dolphins. Gridlock. Rain forests. Inner city. Acid rain. Asbestos. Garbage mountains. Endangered species. Mass extinction. Strip mines. The ozone layer. The greenhouse effect. The possibility of a "nuclear winter." Threats to the environment sped far ahead of their solutions, overmatching the strength of the fledgling conservation movement.

Individual citizens were already expressing alarm and anger over the insults done to the natural world by human mistakes, excesses and abuses of technology, and the economy.

Smog and other pollution were suffocating a growing number of cities and producing pressures for action on political leaders. Well before 1970, Senator Edmund Muskie, a Maine Democrat, was preparing legislation intended to ensure that Americans could enjoy clean air. In 1990, another Maine Democrat, Senate Majority Leader George Mitchell, would describe Muskie, who played the key role in shepherding the nation's basic clean air and water laws through Congress, as the greatest environmental legislator in congressional history. The air pollution law was drafted in the late 1960s by Leon Billings and Thomas C. Jorling, staff members of the Senate Environment and Public Works Committee.

Even President Nixon, no tree hugger, found it expedient to declare in his February 1970 State of the Union message that the 1970s "absolutely must be the years when America pays its debt to the past by reclaiming the purity of its air, its waters and our living environment. It is literally now or never."[1] His cabinet secretary, John

C. Whitaker, later recalled, "When President Nixon and his staff walked into the White House on January 20, 1969, we were totally unprepared for the tidal wave of public opinion in favor of cleaning up the environment that was about to engulf us."[2]

But April 22, 1970, is as good a date as any to point to as the day environmentalism in the United States began to emerge as a mass social movement. The American people, demonstrating the power of a democracy to address a social crisis, started taking matters into their own hands. The time had come to save ourselves.

Much later, Earth Day would be described by Denis Hayes, the national coordinator of the event, as "the largest organized demonstration in human history."[3] It may or may not have been the largest such event in history, but "organized" is hardly the word for the varied and often highly inventive happenings staged by demonstrators around the country to express their distress over ecological threats. The day was chiefly and surprisingly lighthearted. Participants picked up litter, planted trees, and adorned themselves with flowers. In San Francisco, a group calling itself the "Environmental Vigilantes" poured oil into a reflecting pool in front of the offices of the Standard Oil Company of California to protest the oil slicks discoloring offshore waters. In Tacoma, Washington, a hundred high school students rode horses down a superhighway to call attention to pollution from automobiles.[4] Junior high school students in White Plains, New York, painted a ramshackle railroad station and cleaned up the trash surrounding it.[5]

Many of the day's activities focused on the dangers of pollution to human health, the issue that would be at the core of the new broad-based environmentalism. On Fifth Avenue in New York City, demonstrators held up dead fishes to symbolize the contamination of the Hudson River and shouted to passersby, "You're next, people!" New York's Mayor John Lindsay gave a speech in which he stated that "beyond words like ecology, environment and pollution there is a simple question: do we want to live or die?"[6]

With Earth Day, the fears and frustrations felt by the American people after years of environmental neglect began to shape a new political energy. After Earth Day, nothing was the same. The demonstrations of that April day forced government and industry to open the gates of change, however slowly and grudgingly. The millions of Earth Day demonstrators touched off a great burst of activism that profoundly affected the nation's laws, its economy, its corporations, its farms, its politics, science, education, religion, and journalism, created new institutions, and, in time, changed the physical world itself by reducing pollution and preserving open space and other resources. Most important, the social forces unleashed after Earth Day changed, probably forever, the way Americans think about the environment. We now look at a safe and aesthetically pleasing environment not only as necessary to our happiness and well-being but as a right due us along with freedom and opportunity.

In the years following Earth Day, environmentalism, once regarded as the self-serving indulgence of a privileged elite, became "America's cause," to use Peter Borelli's phrase[7]—an expanding mass movement that could in the not too distant future become one of the dominant features of the nation's political life. Although environmentalism certainly was born long before April 22, 1970, it takes no great license to proclaim that day the dawn of the environmental era.

While a number of people had proposed setting aside a day of demonstration of concern for the environment, Earth Day was in large measure the creation of Gaylord Nelson, a Democratic U.S. senator who had previously been governor of Wisconsin. Nelson, the son of a country doctor, had read Aldo Leopold's *Sand County Almanac*, Fairfield Osborn's *Our Plundered Planet*, and Rachel Carson's *Silent Spring*. Built like a middle linebacker, Nelson is an eloquent, humorous, sometimes hard-drinking, passionately liberal Wisconsin progressive who had actively pursued an environmental agenda on Capitol Hill. But even in the late 1960s, he recalled, there were only four or five senators and four or five congressmen who could be described as environmentalists. "I hoped that the politicians, the Presidents, and governors would start talking about the issue, but they never did. The climate was there, though, because I could feel it every time I spoke . . . There were some other issues but mainly it was pesticides, herbicides, air pollution, water pollution. And everybody around the country saw something going to pot in their local areas, some lovely spot, some lovely stream, some lovely lake you couldn't swim in anymore."[8]

After meeting in September 1969 in Santa Barbara with Paul Ehrlich, who had sounded repeated alarms about the effects of overpopulation on the environment, Nelson flew to Berkeley, California, to give a speech, and while en route read an article in *Ramparts* magazine about teach-ins to protest the war in Vietnam. "I thought, my God, why not a national teach-in on the environment?" Returning to Washington, he enlisted the support of Republican congressman Pete McCloskey of California to make the effort bipartisan, found space in the offices of Common Cause, and began hiring a staff, headed by Denis Hayes, then a Harvard Law School student, to begin organizing Earth Day. The money came from Nelson's speaking fees, a few personal and corporate contributions, and a small amount given in response to an advertising appeal. April 22 was chosen, Senator Nelson explained, because it was when most colleges around the country were neither on holiday nor in the middle of examinations. "Within the week the John Birch Society denounced this event, saying this was a thinly veiled attempt to honor Lenin's birthday." Nelson responded by noting that "the original conservationist, St. Francis of Assisi, was born on April 22; Queen Isabella was born on April 22; and my Aunt Tillie was born on April 22."[9]

Denis Hayes believes that the energy that exploded on Earth Day sprang from the social activism on the nation's campuses and the restless discontent of the young.

> There was this broad, sort of all-encompassing sense that things were falling apart. We got a charge of new life in the Kennedy era as we were all getting out of high school and then there was this whole string of assassinations, finding ourselves up to our gills in a land war in Asia, seeing the racial situation in this country becoming increasingly polarized and watching—I don't know—just the general

deterioration of the quality of life . . . somehow, this concern with the environment and the quality, as opposed to the mere quantity, of what was being produced by society seemed to capture that.[10]

Many of the young activists who leaped into the crusade to save the environment shortly before or immediately after Earth Day and who now provide much of the leadership of the national environmental groups did so out of a broad sense of social justice rather than a specific interest in pollution and resource issues. Richard Ayres, a founder of the Natural Resources Defense Council and one of the many Yale University Law School graduates to become a professional environmentalist, explained that in the 1960s "there was a whole series of issues which people my age saw as part of one seamless web of need for social change—ending the war, a better criminal justice system, dealing with poverty and protecting the environment, which was a newly emerging or reemerging issue at the time."[11] Ayres, a boyish-looking and deceptively mild-mannered crusader, and David Hawkins, another lawyer who joined the Natural Resources Defense Council in the early months of its existence, spent virtually all of the 1970s and 1980s at the center of the political and legal struggle to strengthen the Clean Air Act and to make it work effectively.

The links between the Earth Day activists and the other causes of the 1960s, including the antiwar, civil rights, Native American rights, and feminist movements, were direct. Pollution and the exploitation of public resources to create private wealth were regarded as expressions of social inequity. James Gustave (Gus) Speth, another founder of the Natural Resources Defense Council and later chairman of the Council on Environmental Quality and then president of a think tank called the World Resources Institute, recalled that the idea of an organization devoted to litigating for a safer, cleaner environment came to him one day in the late 1960s while reading an article in *The New York Times* about the NAACP Legal Defense Fund. A few pages later there was a story about the environment and, said

Speth, "it just occurred to me that there really should be an NAACP Legal Defense Fund for the environment."[12]

To Speth, "unregulated discharge pipes, fish kills, urban air pollution, all kinds of industrial pollution—those were the issues that originally turned my head. It was not establishing wilderness areas in Montana." Yet like many militant new environmentalists, he was also appalled by the aesthetic degradation of the landscape. He had grown up in rural South Carolina before going to Yale, and "coming out of this beautiful pristine area and hitting the Northeast megalopolis up there in New Haven and looking at all the pollution in Bridgeport . . . I remember it shocked me."[13] Speth, a thoughtful, pleasant, round-faced man who retains his Carolina drawl, has been especially effective in defining, explaining, and documenting the major national and international environmental issues. As chairman of the Council on Environmental Quality, he was the key architect of President Carter's environmental program, which briefly reasserted federal leadership in anti-pollution and resource protection during the late 1970s.

The environmental impulse that came to a boil on Earth Day, however, has many roots other than the social unrest and campus revolts of the 1960s. Samuel Hays has pointed out that new values arose among the increasingly affluent Americans of the post–World War II period, many with greater leisure and higher levels of education than the prewar norm, who demanded different consumer "amenities" than industry was providing. These included improved standards of health and physical fitness, better living conditions generally, and wider opportunities for recreation and leisure.[14] While this was only one tendril of the flowering environmental movement, it was crucial because it helps explain why a great many Americans who were wary of joining other social causes of the period and tended to remain on the sidelines enthusiastically supported this one. Sociologist Denton E. Morrison commented that the environmental crusade "came as something of a relief to a movement-pummeled white, middle-class America and its representatives in the power structure. The environmental movement especially seemed to have potential for diverting the energies of a substantial portion of young people away from more bothersome movements and into [groups] that seemed to stand for something close to Country, God, Motherhood, and Apple Pie, and that, at worst, were still clearly the safest movement in town."[15]

Many Americans responded to the rallying cry of Earth Day not because of any aesthetic or mystical affinity for nature, to fight for social justice, or to search for new consumer amenities or a more pleasant lifestyle, but out of fear—fear of cancer or other disease caused by toxic substances, fear for the future of their children, and fear that the value of their property would be diminished by pollution or inappropriate development. Americans who worried about PCBs in mother's milk, about polybrominated biphenyls in Michigan cattle, about poisons leaking from rusty drums in their backyards, or about strontium 90 from atmospheric testing of nuclear weapons or radiation from Three Mile Island were not asking for new consumer items. They were expressing outrage and demanding change.

The older conservation groups—the Sierra Club, the National Audubon Society, the National Wildlife Federation, the Izaak Walton League, and others—played little or no role in Earth Day and, in fact, were surprised by the surge of national emotion. Still preoccupied by traditional land and wildlife preservation issues, most—although not all—of the old guard had remained blind and deaf to the growing national anger over pollution and other environmental threats to human health.

"We were taken aback by the speed or suddenness with which the new forces exploded," Michael McCloskey, then executive director and later chairman of the Sierra Club, recalled during an interview in 1989. The club had reemerged on the national scene in the 1960s, he recalled, by taking on and winning fights to preserve national parks and defend the beauty of the Grand Canyon. In the "Lady Bird Johnson years, the watchword became recreation and then natural beauty and environmental quality and all of that." Then, suddenly, there was a "whole new agenda" that seemed to have nothing to do with the old issues, an agenda that focused almost exclusively on pollution and waste, he said. "We were severely disoriented suddenly to find that all sorts of new personalities were emerging to lead something new, mainly people out of the youth rebellion of the 1960s who had all sorts of notions that just came out of nowhere . . . I remember being amazed at a meeting of a New Orleans group when someone said, 'Oh, we're not using paper napkins anymore. You can't do that.' I said, 'What's wrong with paper napkins?' 'Oh, that's the new ecology movement that says we can't do that.' "[16]

For their part, the young militants who joined the movement during the Earth Day period tended to look at the old conservation groups as irrelevant. Denis Hayes, who would also organize the national celebration of the twentieth anniversary of Earth Day in 1990, recalled that "by and large, there was, I think, a pretty deep amount of ignorance of all of that and even some tendency to sort of distance themselves from the rest they termed 'the birds and squirrels people.' "[17]

In remarkably few years, the fissure between the traditional conservation groups and the pollution- and public health-oriented activist national organizations was narrowed and largely—although not entirely—closed. Those concerned with public lands and wildlife realized that air and water pollution did not stop at the boundaries of the national parks and that Americans deprived of their health by industrial poisons could not enjoy the wonders of nature. The social militants, for their part, soon discovered that the assaults of technology and commerce on the environment were inevitably also attacks upon human beings; that oil spills that destroyed wildlife in Alaska and strip-mined mountains in Appalachia were part of the same abuse of the natural environment that threatened the health of people living in cities or workers in their factories. Just as George Perkins Marsh, John Muir, Aldo Leopold, René Dubos, Rachel Carson, and others had foretold, human beings were not isolated from the natural world and the injuries they inflicted upon it. The cause of reducing pollution and protecting public health was clearly inseparable from the cause of saving the land and preserving nature. The principles of ecology, both scientific and moral, welded the old and the new environmentalism into a movement of fiercely competing but relatively unified national organizations.

The passions that swept through the nation's campuses in April 1970 soon died. Within a few months, young, middle-class Americans in and emerging from the universities once again grew increasingly self-absorbed and sought individual rewards rather than social reform. Especially during the Reagan era, that search for individual fulfillment centered on the accumulation of wealth and material possessions. Many of the angry demonstrators of the late 1960s and early 1970s became the investment bankers and corporate lawyers of the 1980s. The peace movement ebbed with the end of the Vietnam War. The Nixon administration and then the Reagan administration turned their backs on the civil rights movement and so did much of the country. The feminist struggle became to a large extent tied up in the ugly confrontation over abortion rights.

But the environmental movement, despite predictions that it would collapse, particularly during the energy crises of the 1970s, did not fade away. A chain reaction had started on Earth Day and, while it was slowed from time to time, it could not be broken by the apathy of the erstwhile student activists, the long lines at gasoline filling stations, the short attention span of a public conditioned by television, or even by the hostility and active opposition of a President of the United States. The interest and anger displayed by millions of Americans had caused the politicians, the news media, the universities, and other power centers to pay heed. With each passing year the environmental impulse become more deeply enmeshed in the nation's institutions, its laws, and its daily life.

In the aftermath of Earth Day, new environmental institutions such as Greenpeace emerged that combined a strong social sensibility with concern for the natural world. Political agendas that embraced the environment, such as social ecology, gained new adherents. The environmental movement itself soon began to grow a radical wing.

Religion, science, education, communications—virtually all sectors of American society found themselves changed by its power.

The institutions most immediately and overwhelmingly affected by the surge of public interest generated by Earth Day, of course, were the environmental groups themselves. The old-line conservation clubs and societies, the *ancien régime* of the movement, though slow off the mark, were swept into the rushing current. The membership of most of these groups doubled and doubled again. So did the size of their staffs. At the same time, a variety of new organizations sprang up to fight the environmental battles on a broad front. The Sierra Club created a legal defense fund as an independent organization to pursue its goals through the courts. Environmental Action, formed in 1970 to coordinate Earth Day activities, stayed in business as an aggressive lobbying and public information group that focused on issues like solid waste and alerted voters to the "Dirty Dozen," the companies with the worst pollution activities. The Environmental Policy Institute, splintered off from Friends of the Earth in 1974, formulated and lobbied for policies for governmental action on environmental issues.

Growing public opposition to nuclear power, both for weapons production and testing and for the generation of electricity, was a strong thread in the new fabric of environmental activism. A number of ad hoc but broadly representative groups were organized to oppose nuclear generating plants such as those planned for Seabrook in New Hampshire and Diablo Canyon in California. Like many grass-roots environmental organizations, the anti-nuclear movement was born more of fear for personal safety than of ideological opposition to nuclear power.

One major international environmental group—Greenpeace—was organized in the early 1970s around efforts to block the testing of nuclear devices in the Pacific Ocean. Although founded by Canadians from Vancouver, among them David McTaggert, Robert Hunter, and Patrick Morre, the Greenpeace movement quickly spread to the United States and other countries. Encounters with whales by

Greenpeace members who sailed small boats to interfere with nuclear tests at sea led the organization to expand its mission to include protection of marine life and other parts of the natural world. The Greenpeace modus operandi of putting the bodies of its staff at risk to defend whales or stop nuclear tests is based, according to the group's former U.S. executive director, Peter Bahouth, on "the Quaker philosophy of bearing witness and trying to stand in harm's way."[18] The group also incorporated the tactics of nonviolent resistance pioneered in this country by Dr. Martin Luther King, Jr., and his allies in the civil rights movement. When some members of Greenpeace, led by the Canadian Paul Watson, adopted an aggressive eye-for-an-eye approach—for example, blowing up whaling ships—they were forced to leave the organization and in 1977 formed a new group called the Sea Shepherd Conservation Society. Sea Shepherd, named after Watson's boat, is part of a tiny but active radical wing of the movement that considers sabotage to be a legitimate weapon against large-scale activities that harm the environment.

Leaders of a number of the national groups pooled resources in 1970 to create the League of Conservation Voters, which became the major political arm of the movement. Led for many years by Marion Edey, and later by Alden Meyer and then Jim Maddy, the league kept track of the voting records and policy decisions of members of Congress and the executive branch and endorsed and organized electoral support for environmentally minded politicians while attempting to maintain a bipartisan approach.

The petroleum shortages created by the international oil cartel in 1973 and 1979 raised anew the specter of dwindling reserves of vital but finite resources and gave birth to several new environmental groups that focused on energy issues. Perhaps most influential in shaping the environmental response to the energy crisis, however, was Amory B. Lovins, who, together with Hunter L. Lovins, formulated a policy that called on the nation to turn away from the "hard energy path" of reliance on fossil fuels or nuclear power and travel the "soft path" by meeting our needs through conservation and more efficient use of energy and the development of renewable, non-polluting new sources, particularly solar power.

The "green" organizations gradually built highly professional staffs of lawyers, lobbyists, scientists, economists, organizers, fund raisers, publicists, and political operatives to influence government decisions. Previously, the contests in the nation's capital over legislation and administrative decisions had been fought chiefly among representatives of business, labor, and agriculture, with industry usually dominating. Suddenly, the environmental groups challenged industry's efforts to dictate legislation, shape the rules put out by the regulatory agencies, and contest governmental decisions through the courts. In a modest way, the environmentalists also started to vie with business lobbies to manipulate the political process itself. The environmentalists remained heavily outgunned in money and manpower by the corporations, but industry no longer had the field to itself in Washington. The green activists were able to attract the sympathetic attention of the mass media and through that powerful ally won wide support among the American public.

While the national environmental groups work within the established political and economic systems, a small but growing radical fringe rejects the compromises accepted by mainstream environmentalists, saying their methods are doomed to failure. Worse still, the radicals complain, the national groups seek only to meet human needs instead of protecting the right of nature to exist.

These radicals, notably members of Earth First!, choose instead to defend the natural world by direct action, civil disobedience, and the kind of ecosabotage romanticized by the novelist Edward Abbey as "monkeywrenching." Earth Firsters, some of them remnants of the back-to-the-land movement of the 1960s, have thrown themselves in front of logging trucks, pulled up survey stakes for an oil exploration project, chained themselves to the upper branches of centuries-old trees marked for the chain saw by timber companies, and driven iron spikes into trees to make it dangerous for loggers to cut into the wood. In May 1989, Dave Foreman, a co-founder of Earth First!, and three of the group's members were arrested by the Federal Bureau of Investigation on charges that they were planning to topple a tower carrying power lines to the Central Arizona Project, a massive federal irrigation program.[19] The group's advocacy of draconian measures to reduce world population, including letting famine-stricken peoples such as those of East Africa starve to death, is only one of its controversial positions.

Earth First! loosely adheres to the principles of a radical philosophy called "deep ecology." Formulated in large part by the Norwegian philosopher Arne Naess, deep ecology regards all life as having intrinsic rights equal to that of human beings. It rejects mainstream environmentalism as "shallow ecology," which engages in piecemeal efforts to protect only those elements of nature that are seen as of service to humans. In 1988, Naess and an American disciple, George Sessions, drafted a "platform for deep ecology" which begins with the principle that all life on earth has value and that the value of nonhuman life is independent of its usefulness to human beings. "Humans have no right to reduce this richness and diversity except to satisfy vital needs," the platform asserts. Further, human population and manipulation of the nonhuman world are now excessive and are not consistent with the flourishing of both nature and humans. Policies must therefore be changed to achieve a substantial reduction in world population, Naess and Sessions insisted, and they emphasized that the quality of life is more important than an ever higher level of material consumption.[20]

Also on the radical edge of the environmental movement are some of the militant animal rights groups, including the Animal Liberation Front, some of which resort to sabotage and other forms of physical coercion to save animals from being used in painful medical experiments and to protest the killing of animals for their fur.

Another philosophical strand of today's environmentalism is represented by the social ecologists whose goal is the restructuring of society along lines that will serve the ecological health of the planet. Reflected in the concepts of E. F. Schumacher, presented in his book *Small Is Beautiful*, and the ideas of Murray Bookchin and, to some degree, Barry Commoner, social ecology, unlike deep ecology, does not reject humanism or even technology. It does, however, seek to reorient economics, institutions, and political relationships to create a lifestyle that is harmonious for both nature and humans. Social ecologists believe—to oversimplify somewhat—that decentralized economies with more local self-reliance and benign technologies, combined with direct, participatory democracy, will lead us out of the ecological cul-de-sac created by industrial society. One manifestation of this philosophy is "bioregionalism," which seeks to create a new economy based on small, self-sufficient geographic units.

Social ecology, smacking as it does of utopianism, is a minor tributary of the environmental movement in this country. But if one were to ask mainstream environmentalists to pause in their hectic daily efforts to influence legislation, ban toxic chemicals, save a particular piece of land, or elect sympathetic politicians, and think of the kind of world they are working for, many of them would probably respond with goals similar to those proposed by the social ecologists. And, on a larger canvas, the principles of social ecology are really the foundation of the whole notion of sustainable development that is now so fashionable in national and international circles.

The new environmentalism has made significant inroads into religious thought. In 1967 a historian from the University of California in Los Angeles, Lynn White, Jr., published a short essay in *Science* called "The Historical Roots of Our Ecological Crisis."[21] Its message was blunt. Christianity or, more broadly, the Judeo-Christian tradition, "bears a huge burden of guilt" for the destruction of nature by the science and technology of Western civilization. Christianity, especially in its Western form, "is the most anthropocentric religion the world has seen." Unlike the religions of the pagan world and of Asia, which regard nature as sacred and humanity as part of nature, Judeo-Christian beliefs "not only established a dualism of man and nature but insisted that it is God's will that man exploit nature for its proper ends." The book of Genesis, White noted, makes it clear that God created the heavens and the earth and all of its creatures for man's dominion and benefit. Man "is not part of nature; he is made in God's image." This dichotomy between humans and nature encouraged the development and growth of a science and technology dedicated to exerting human power over nature, which in turn led to the destruction of nature.

Although we imagine we are living in a secular age, the Judeo-Christian tradition continues to dominate the way we think and act. The present disruption of the global environment, White said, is a product of the scientific dynamism that arose out of the Christianity of the medieval world. "Hence we shall continue to have a worsening ecological crisis until we reject the Christian axiom that nature has no reason for existence save to serve man."

White was not the only scholar to find the roots of the environmental crisis in the Judeo-Christian religions; nor was he the first. The great French priest, theologian, and paleontologist Pierre Teilhard de Chardin had long since criticized Christian doctrine for concluding that nature has been static since the creation and insisted that nature was a growing, self-creating force. Humans, Teilhard contended, did not save themselves by freeing themselves from nature, as Christianity taught, but by working with and becoming one with nature.[22]

White's argument was sharply challenged by several scholars and theologians. One of the critics was René Dubos, who noted that many non-Christian cultures, including those of Egypt, Mesopotamia, and Persia, had turned fertile countrysides into barren deserts by their misuse of the land and that "ecological disasters are not peculiar to the Judeo-Christian tradition and to scientific technology."[23] Lewis Mumford, in the rhetorical role of an Old Testament prophet, had spoken of the urgent need for the modern world to undergo a "religious conversion" from a lower to a higher plane of values in response to the ecological crisis.[24]

White's essay, however, published as environmentalism was emerging as a major social force, touched off a ringing debate about the responsibilities of religion in confronting the environmental crisis. It also produced a great deal of soul-searching within the churches. Both the debate and the soul-searching are still in progress. That is not to say, however, that the nation's churches and synagogues have fully embraced "ecotheology." While environmentalism is on church agendas, it is fairly well down on the list of social causes. Carl Casebolt of the National Council of Churches explained that new doctrines make their way very slowly downward in the hierarchical structure of the churches. Christians are reluctant to adopt White's ideas of the need for a new theology to embrace nature because "people have spent two thousand years thinking of the earth as a way station."[25]

Yet there is ample evidence that environmentalism is causing an upheaval in Judeo-Christian thought. The churches have searched assiduously for a creation doctrine that supports the concept of a Christian love of nature. Wendell Berry, poet, farmer, and Christian ecologist, found that "the ecological teaching of the Bible is simply inescapable: God made the world because he wanted it made. He thinks the world is good, and he loves it." Berry also insisted that Scripture called for a usufruct approach to nature as part of man's obligation to be a good steward of the world God gave him.[26]

Although there are many exceptions within its clergy, the Roman Catholic Church was a bastion of resistance to the ecotheology movement. But on December 5, 1989, Pope John Paul II issued a startling twelve-page document entitled "Peace with God the Creator, Peace with All of Creation," which is likely to reverberate through the church for many years. "World peace," the Pope wrote, "is threatened not only by regional conflicts and by injustices between peoples and nations but also by the lack of necessary respect for nature, by the disordered exploitation of her resources, and by the progressive deterioration of the quality of life. The ecological crisis has assumed such proportions as to be everyone's responsibility." The world's ecological problems, the document stated, show that "greed and selfishness, individual and collective, have gone against the order of creation."[27] Cardinal Roger Etchegaray, president of the Pontifical Commission for Justice and Peace, said that the document underscored that, to the Pope, "ecology is a moral imperative, not simply a fashion or a political movement."[28]

So religion, too, is caught up in the environmental revolution.

Roderick Nash found that "by the 1980's, 'ecotheology' had become not only a new word but a compelling world view."[29]

Salvation, it would seem, now means saving ourselves not only for the next world but in this one as well; saving not just our own immortal souls for eternity but our own posterity and all of God's creation.

THE

ENVIRONMENTAL

REVOLUTION

Hurry up please its time.
—T. S. Eliot

The federal government, which frequently moves at a glacial pace in dealing with social problems, responded in the 1960s and 1970s with surprising speed to the rising concern over the deterioration of the environment. In the 1970s, Congress churned out a series of environmental laws that, taken together, must be regarded as one of the great legislative achievements of the nation's history.

On January 1, 1970, President Nixon signed the National Environmental Policy Act, which requires the federal government to analyze and report on the environmental implications of its activities. A Council on Environmental Quality was created later that year to oversee compliance with the law by federal agencies. The council also was assigned the job of preparing an annual report on the state of the environment and, at least in theory, of advising the President on it. Under Russell Train, its first chairman, and two of his successors, Russell Peterson, former governor of Delaware, and Gus Speth, the council played a significant role in prodding the government to take an active role in protecting the nation's resources and fighting pollution.

Another agency created by act of Congress in the seminal year 1970 was the Occupational Safety and Health Administration, or OSHA as it is commonly called. The new agency was given authority to ensure that the workplace was safe and healthy and that employers did not subject workers to toxic chemicals or other dangerous substances such as asbestos and cotton dust or to unsafe machinery and equipment. The new agency gave workers and their unions a potentially powerful new tool for protecting themselves from careless or unscrupulous employers. The same law that created OSHA established the National Institute of Occupational Safety and Health to do research into the causes of workplace accidents and illness and to design criteria for lowering risks. While the Labor Department sometimes administered the law in ways that seemed more inclined to placate employers than to protect workers, that was not the fault of the statute.

The Environmental Protection Agency, the most powerful and controversial environmental institution in the federal government, was a product of congressional inaction. In December 1970, President Nixon, responding to the rising political winds, submitted a reorganization plan to Congress, lumping a number of federal public health and regulatory bureaus and programs into a new patchwork organization called the EPA. Neither house of Congress voted against the reorganization, which would have killed the new agency. The EPA, which was to be the federal government's watchdog, police officer, and chief weapon against all forms of pollution, was thus created without benefit of any statute enacted by Congress. It quickly became the lightning rod for the nation's hopes for cleaning up pollution and its fears about intrusive federal regulation.

William D. Ruckelshaus, appointed by President Nixon as the agency's first administrator, later recalled, "From a management point of view, the task was daunting: how to form a cohesive integrated, functioning entity out of fifteen different agencies and parts of agencies throughout the federal government."[1] Ruckelshaus said during an interview in 1989 that the normal condition of the EPA was to be ground "between two irresistible forces. Here was one group, the environmental movement, pushing very hard to get [pollution] emissions down no matter where they were—air, water, no matter what—almost regardless of the seriousness of the emissions. There was another group on the other side [industry] pushing just as hard in the other direction and trying to stop all of that stuff, again almost regardless of the seriousness of the problem."[2]

The EPA had no choice but to hit the ground running. To carry out the Clean Air Act of 1970, it was required to come up with rules for reducing air pollution 120 days after it opened its doors. Congress passed one law after another that added to the agency's mandate. Ruckelshaus soon banned the use of DDT by administrative order, something that Congress had been unable to do by legislation. The agency established regional offices and research and testing facilities in a number of states. Its presence was soon felt—and usually resented—by a wide swath of industry, municipal governments, and even other federal agencies. The role of the EPA is not only to force polluters to obey the laws but also to explain the laws, to provide information and technical assistance to help polluters comply with the laws, to identify the sources of danger within the environment, and to inform, educate, and assist the public on how to protect themselves and the environment.

Although political pressure by industry—all too frequently supported by the White House and members of Congress—and the EPA's often excessively bureaucratic approach to its task have tended to blunt the agency's sword, it is today still the single most effective guardian of the nation's air, water, and soil.

A cascade of environmental legislation flowed from Capitol Hill during the Nixon, Ford, and Carter administrations. The Federal Water Pollution Control Act was adopted in 1972. Also enacted in 1972 were the Federal Insecticide, Rodenticide, and Fungicide Act (the nation's basic pesticide control law), the Noise Control Act, the Coastal Zone Management Act, and the Marine Mammals Protection Act. The Endangered Species Act was passed in 1973 and the Safe

Drinking Water Act in 1974. Pausing for a deep breath in 1975, Congress produced in 1976 the Toxic Substances Control Act and the Resource Conservation and Recovery Act (both dealing with the control of dangerous materials), the Federal Land Management Act, and the National Forest Management Act the following year. In 1977 the Clean Air and Water laws were expanded and strengthened.

In 1980, after an epic legislative battle between environmentalists, who wanted to preserve as much as possible of our last wild and primitive state in a pristine condition, and those who wanted to exploit the land and resources for economic purposes, Congress enacted the Alaska National Interest Lands Act, setting aside over 100 million acres in perpetuity for the enjoyment of the American people. Millions of acres were also designated by Congress in the lower forty-eight states during the 1970s and 1980s as protected wilderness areas, wildlife refuges, and parks. In a lame-duck session in 1980, Congress passed the Comprehensive Environmental Response, Compensation, and Liability Act, or Superfund as it is commonly known, more or less successfully establishing a well-financed program for cleaning up the thousands of dangerous abandoned toxic waste sites around the country. Many other environmental laws of somewhat lesser significance also emerged from Congress in those years.

While no major new environmental statutes were enacted during the Reagan presidency, many of the existing laws were renewed and strengthened, often over the objections of the White House and, on occasion, despite a presidential veto.

A number of these statutes were amendments to existing legislation. But they gave such sweeping new powers to the government to protect the environment that they were in effect new pieces of landmark legislation.

Most of the new statutes placed the burden of proof on the polluter to show that his activities did not harm the environment. The laws set uniform national standards defining acceptable levels of pollution, thus making it more difficult to blackmail state and local enforcement authorities. The laws also sought to address the problems of interstate pollution, although, as the long battle over acid rain demonstrated, they were often unable to do so. They extended the police power of government, placing the environment as well as people and property under a mantle of protection.

Armed with the new laws and inspired in large part by the Supreme Court under Chief Justice Earl Warren, which demonstrated that the judicial system could be a powerful instrument for social change, many activists turned to the courts as their primary tool for environmental reform. With few effective statutes on the books prior to 1970, individuals and groups had to resort to common law to seek compensation for environmental injury. Law professor Martin H. Belsky of the University of Florida noted, however, that "to succeed in such an action, the plaintiff had to overcome an almost insurmountable burden of proof"[3] under tort law. Although some states had adopted environmental statutes, they were generally ineffective because states were reluctant to constrain industry that generated jobs and income within their borders. Companies sometimes practiced "environmental blackmail" against states that tried to enforce more protective anti-pollution laws by threatening to lay off workers or to move their operations to a more permissive jurisdiction. Moreover, state laws could not address the problems of pollution that crossed state lines. The flood of legislation after Earth Day changed all that, or, at least, was intended to do so.

The legislation of the 1970s combined with a willing judiciary gave environmentalists and their causes standing in the courts, creating a major new field of law. During an interview in 1989, John Adams, a former Assistant U.S. Attorney who has been director of the Natural Resources Defense Council since it was founded, noted, "In 1970 there were no environmental laws. There were zoning laws, public health laws, but no real environmental laws. Now we have forty or fifty federal statutes. Today we have laws across the United States—every county, every town, every city. And even though we've had ups and downs in environmental awareness between 1970 and now, the fabric gets built up each day—more people, more environmental analysts, more enforcers, more this, more that."[4]

J. William Futrell, longtime president of the Environmental Law

Institute, commented, "The courts are now open to environmentalism as a value. They were not open in 1970. For those of us who want to work to protect the environment . . . there are ways that were blocked in 1970. There is now a level playing field in which citizens can work to protect the environment."[5]

Environmental law has been for some time the fastest-growing sector of the American bar. Futrell estimated in 1989 that there were some 20,000 environmental lawyers, more even than practice labor law. Of course, only a fraction of those lawyers work for environmental organizations. Most work in big law firms, for corporations, and for governments at all levels. Futrell noted that in 1970 environmental statutes filled fewer than 30 pages of the *Environmental Law Reporter*. By 1989 they filled more than 800 pages. By that year, Futrell estimated, federal courts had handed down at least 3,000 decisions on environmental cases.[6]

Yet many environmentalists and other commentators, including Futrell, have expressed disappointment over the results. The laws, Futrell contended, have made only spotty changes in the social and economic values that lead to pollution, and the results they have produced in restoring the environment fall far short of the expectations aroused by Earth Day. Futrell places some of the blame on the rigidity of the statutes. Adopted during the Vietnam War and the years of the Watergate scandal, many of the laws reflect Congress's distrust of the executive branch and contain detailed, prescriptive language that leaves little flexibility for the EPA or other regulatory bodies to maneuver and improvise. Statutes such as the Clean Air and Water acts are "command and control" laws. Not only do they set standards determining what constitutes acceptable maximum levels of pollution in the air and water, they also prescribe how those levels shall be reached—catalytic converters on auto tailpipes, scrubbers on power plants, filters on water discharge pipes. Critics said that the rigidity of the laws led industry to fight regulation every step of the way and that the costs of complying with them deprived industry of capital to invest in new, cleaner plant and equipment.

Virtually no part of the public and private sectors has remained untouched by the environmental revolution. A broad institutional network has been built up to monitor the environment and act to protect it. At the same time, history is likely to record the landmark environmental statutes of the 1970s and 1980s and the new institutions they spawned as the most consequential legacy of the environmental era. In response, there have been profound changes in government at all levels, in our science, our medicine, our education, and our mass communications. Because of environmentalism, we are a society transformed, although in ways that are still not broadly understood.

New departments, agencies, and boards for protecting the environment have proliferated at the state, the municipal, and, in many areas, even at the village level since 1970. While the federal government continued to set minimum environmental standards and to provide funding and technical assistance, the chief responsibility for carrying out most of the environmental laws was given to the states. Thomas C. Jorling, commissioner of New York State's Department of Environmental Protection, commented in 1989 that in the past the professional quality of bureaucracies at the state level dealing with environmental matters was very low. "Today, the quality of the professional institutions and staffs in many states is every bit as good as the federal government's." Jorling added that many Americans have already become accustomed to petitioning state governments to respond quickly to environmental hazards such as waste dumps and oil spills; many, if not most, state governments have the capability to deal with such emergencies. State responsibility for protecting the environment, he said, "has become so deeply ingrained it is now routine."[7]

Science and technology have been deeply influenced by modern environmentalism. Devra Davis, former staff director of the environmental board of the National Academy of Sciences, noted that environmental regulation is essentially "a shotgun wedding of science and law."[8]

A fundamental, if intangible shift in the basic values underlying science appears to have taken place in recent decades. Since the seventeenth century, Western science has tended to separate human beings from nature. Francis Bacon, the father of modern science, contended that "man, if we look to final causes, may be regarded as the centre of the world insomuch that if man were taken away from the world the rest would seem to be all astray, without aim or purpose."[9] Omnipotent humans, arranging the forces of the universe into rigid laws, assigning names to other forms of life and making use of that life, peering into the stars and the heart of atoms, were creatures apart from and above nature, were the rulers of creation, able to employ science and technology to bend a mechanistic world to their will.

This edifice of scientific faith, already shaken by Darwin and Einstein among others, is now crumbling under the accumulating ecological evidence that humans are, like any organism or microorganism, inextricably part of nature.

This evolving view of science has influenced medical research and practice and created a new field of environmental health. For example, physicians Irving Selikoff, Philip Landrigan, and William Nicholson at the Mount Sinai Hospital environmental health center in New York City not only have done crucial research on the dangers of asbestos, air pollution, and other environmental insults but also have helped shape public policy, through congressional testimony and stories in the news media, aimed at reducing the risks. The Health Research Group, an organization founded by Ralph Nader in 1971 and led since by Dr. Sidney Wolfe, has waged unrelenting, often successful war against the misuse of chemicals in the environment, particularly in the workplace. Wolfe was among the growing minority of physicians who preached that it is better to prevent illness by removing its environmental causes than to cure it.

American education has also been strongly, and yet inadequately, influenced by environmentalism. Environmental studies are now taught throughout the country from elementary through graduate school, albeit on a hit-or-miss basis. In 1970 President Nixon signed the Environmental Education Act, intended by Congress to help correct what it had found to be the lack of understanding about the need for "environmental quality and ecological balance." Although its purpose was to help launch environmental studies programs around the country, the act was never adequately funded and eventually it was killed by Congress.

The story today, said William Clark of Harvard University's John F. Kennedy School of Government, is not the number of graduate schools with centers for environmental studies but efforts, like those undertaken at Tufts University under Anthony Cortese, dean of environmental studies, to introduce environmental curricula—and environmental literacy—into all departments and schools of the university.[10]

The mass media have probably been more effective than the slow-off-the-mark schools in educating the American public about the nation's ecological problems—although not necessarily about potential solutions. In the 1960s and early 1970s, only a handful of journalists—John B. Oakes, Gladwin Hill, and E. W. Kenworthy of *The New York Times*, Luther Carter of *Science*, Robert Cahn of the *Christian Science Monitor*, Ed Flatteau, a syndicated columnist since the early 1970s, Casey Bukro of the *Chicago Tribune*, and Tom Harris of the McClatchy newspaper chain, among the most prominent— wrote regularly about conservation and pollution issues. Gershon Fishbein founded the influential *Environmental Health Newsletter* in 1961. Michael Frome, a writer-activist, contributed hundreds of articles to the periodical press on parks and public lands issues.

Today, it is safe to say, there are few major news organizations without at least one full-time environment reporter, and many smaller newspapers and television stations give prominent coverage to such stories. While many reporters with no background in the complex issues are assigned environmental stories, a growing number of journalists are providing increasingly sophisticated and accurate coverage. In 1990 the Society of Environmental Journalists was formed to upgrade the quality of environmental reporting, and by 1992 it had about 700 members.

Documentary films about the natural world presented on such programs as the *Nature, Nova, National Geographic*, and *Audubon* series undoubtedly played a significant role in awakening Americans to the joys of and the threats to the natural world. Even Hollywood got into the environmental act. Actors and rock stars lent their names and made appearances to support battles against oil spills, ocean dumping, pesticides in foods, and the destruction of the rain forests. Television writers began putting ecological messages into their scripts. *Time* magazine noted in a 1989 article, "The Greening of Hollywood," that "Tinseltown has a boffo new cause: saving the planet."[11]

National and even local environmental groups grew increasingly adept at using the media as a tool to call attention to their issues and to prod government into responding. Several environmental leaders, including Rafe Pomerance, a former president of Friends of the Earth who later joined the World Resources Institute, played valuable roles as intermediaries between the scientific community and reporters, alerting the media to new scientific findings and explaining the complexities of the findings as well as their political implications.

Editors and producers, however, still tend to give stories about pollution or natural resources second rank in the competition for space in newspapers and magazines or time on the air. A residue of skepticism lingers among some media managers who have not become attuned to the key issues of the late twentieth century.

Environmental values understood by so broad a spectrum of society gave new political potency to environmental issues.

Gaylord Nelson pointed out that while there were perhaps a dozen members of Congress in the 1960s who could be called environmentalists, by 1990 there were at least 200 who would answer to that description.[12] Even more startling, however, is the fact that there is hardly a member of the Senate or House of Representatives who does not claim to be an environmentalist no matter how vigorous an enemy of environmental regulation he or she may be. Whatever their failings, our legislators vibrate like tuning forks to the signals sent by their constituents and, as the polls have made abundantly clear, the public overwhelmingly supports strong laws on the environment.

Because of this broad public support, the national environmental groups are now featured players on the policy-making stage in Washington, D.C. John Adams of the Natural Resources Defense Council recalled in 1989 that in his organization's early days "we would come to EPA meetings and they would ignore us and do everything they could to make us go away. They'd fight us and tell us we didn't have any right to be there. Everything we did in those early years was really resisted by government—I mean really resisted. Well, clearly that's not true anymore. When we go and see someone at EPA or a senator or congressman or governor or even a President, they listen. They may not necessarily like everything we say, but now we are a respectable part of society in terms of the message we have to deliver and the constituencies that we represent. I mean, that's like jumping from one world to the next; it's that big a gap."[13]

Of course, business and other opponents of environmental regulation or programs to protect public resources still throw considerable weight around in the nation's capital. They have been effective in influencing the White House and frequently prevail through the Office of Management and Budget. But it is a lot harder for them to win than it used to be.

The Earth Day revolution changed virtually every sector of the nation's economy.

Most immediately, the environmental laws gave birth to a major new industry—pollution control. It is now estimated that by 1987 total direct spending to comply with federal pollution control programs reached an annual level of $81.1 billion.[14] By 1992 the level had probably surpassed $125 billion. That is a substantial amount of money even in a $5 trillion economy. Those figures include only the direct costs of programs for dealing with air and water pollution and solid waste disposal. They do not include spending on mandated programs for reducing pesticide pollution, noise, or radiation, or on efforts to protect natural resources such as acquiring and operating national parks and other lands or reducing soil erosion.

The percentage of total industry investment in new plant and equipment allocated to pollution control peaked at 4.2 percent in 1975.[15] But such investments are likely to go up sharply in the coming years as the nation comes to grips with acid rain and smog under the requirements of the far-reaching Clean Air Act amendments of

1990, replaces chlorofluorocarbons in industrial production, and assumes the substantial expenditures that will be required to slow the warming of the earth from the greenhouse effect. Paul Portney, vice president of Resources for the Future, estimated that by the end of the 1980s, the pollution control industry was employing between half a million and a million people in the United States, or roughly 0.5 percent to 1 percent of the nation's work force.[16] Of course, that only includes the direct employment of men and women in pollution control and regulation. When the money spent by the industry in procuring materials and supplies and the wages of its workers are included, there is a multiplier effect that substantially increases the impact on the economy. "Today," said Roger H. Bezdek in 1989, "this industry represents an important driving force in the U.S. economy."[17]

The large sums spent on pollution control have had some dampening effects on the American economy, of course, although their magnitude is a matter of dispute. A study published late in 1989 by Dale W. Jorgenson and Peter J. Wilcoxen of the Harvard University Institute of Economic Research found that, because it siphoned off capital investment, environmental regulation produced a small, but significant reduction in the rate of economic growth. Between 1974 and 1985, the study found, the diversion of investment capital into pollution control programs and the cost of running those programs reduced the nation's potential gross national product by an average annual rate of nearly two-tenths of 1 percent. The environmental laws had a particularly sharp impact, according to the economists' models, on polluting industries forced to make the biggest investment in control technology, the automotive industry in particular but also the coal, steel, and chemical industries, the Harvard report noted.[18]

Economist Paul Portney contends that the environmental laws discouraged investment in industrial facilities because the pollution control requirements for new plants are much stricter than for existing power stations or factories. "New plants in some cases would be environmentally cleaner than the old plants that they would replace.

But we don't build them because it's cheaper just to keep the old ones clunking along with baling wire and tape."[19]

Because the benefits of regulation and spending are much harder to quantify than the costs, they tend to be neglected by the economists. These benefits include better health, less money spent on medicine and hospitals, a longer life span for Americans, fewer days spent away from their jobs by workers, cleaner air, more productive farms, forests, and fisheries, cleaner cities with less erosion of buildings and other structures, improved recreation, and enhanced aesthetic enjoyment of the natural world. It is much easier to figure out how much a piece of pollution control equipment costs and factor that into the GNP than it is to agree on the value of a human life or a clear, crisp day with perfect visibility from the World Trade Center in Manhattan or the rim of the Grand Canyon.

I have yet to see any credible national balance sheet on the aggregate monetary value of environmental benefits. As economists Kenneth Boulding, Hazel Henderson, and others have pointed out, there are anomalies in the measurement of economic values that would tend to make these measurements somewhat absurd from an environmental perspective. For example, the more people who sicken from air pollution and must be hospitalized, the higher the GNP, because spending on health care is considered part of economic growth. On the other hand, air or water fouled by pollution or land rendered unusable by chemical poisons or erosion is not counted as a debit on the national ledger, but the activity that caused these undesirable results is counted as a credit.

One of the fundamental questions raised by the environmental revolution has to do with the quality of our economic growth. Like the shark that cannot ever stop swimming because it would suffocate from lack of oxygen, the American economy operates as if consumption must continually expand, regardless of other values, such as preservation of the environment. John Maynard Keynes, whose theories dominated economic policy in this country for much of the century, advocated government intervention to stimulate mass consumption, which in turn would lead to investment and a rising national income. Continuous economic expansion in the United States has come to be regarded as synonymous with progress, with power, even with patriotism.

This endless expansion is fueled in turn by a constant increase in the consumption of goods and services, which means, among other things, that industry must constantly market new products. E. J. Mishan, the British economist, found that in his country and the United States, economic policy means "snatching at any technological innovation that proves marketable with scant respect for the consequences."[20] "Certainly the American economy presents us with the bizarre spectacle of growing resources pressing against limited wants."[21]

Americans, in my view, are manipulated by marketing, advertising, credit, and a variety of social pressures to maintain a high level of consumption, a good part of it dulling to the spirit and damaging to the environment. The United States, with about 5 or 6 percent of the world's population, consumes an estimated 40 percent or more of the world's resources. Since the distribution of wealth is uneven, a minority of Americans accounts for a majority of the consumption.[22]

The powerful opposition of large sectors of corporate America has been a major obstacle to the achievement of many environmental goals. But many companies did respond to the anti-pollution statutes with technological innovation and modernization, however reluctantly some of them may have done so. Every time Congress ordered the automotive companies to cut down on their tailpipe emissions or to improve fuel efficiency, they complained that such improvements were not technologically feasible or would make their cars too expensive for American consumers. Then grousing and delaying all the way, the industry would eventually meet the statutory requirements. Meanwhile, Japanese and European automakers raced ahead of Detroit in anti-pollution technology—and other engineering innovations—and in so doing made better cars and won much of the United States market, not to mention the international market, away from the no-can-do Detroit manufacturers.

Some companies discovered that their efficiency and profits went up as a result of technological changes to protect the environment. The Dow Chemical Company, for example, found that pollution control at its fourteen latex plants around the world, at a cost of \$2 million, cut operating costs almost \$2 million a year.[23] Dow also found that it could increase its earnings by reducing the amount of waste materials it produced. Dow went from being one of the bitterest opponents of environmental regulation in the early 1980s to a pacesetter in improving corporate environmental performance by the early 1990s. The pill of environmental regulation was not so difficult to swallow after all, some of the most recalcitrant opponents were learning. In fact, a growing number of companies were discovering that doing the right environmental thing could also help improve the balance sheet.

Finally, in the years after Earth Day, there was a dawning recognition in some quarters of government—excluding the Reagan administration and important members of the Bush White House—and industry that, far from impeding the economy, environmental protection is a necessity if economic growth is to be sustained over the long run.

As the years passed, business and industry were forced to recognize that environmental regulation was not a temporary inconvenience that would soon pass away but would be a permanent part of doing business in this country. The past twenty years and more have witnessed a dramatic change in the environmental actions and attitudes of many of the major corporations and, in many cases, major internal changes. Almost all these companies now have environmental departments, sometimes numbering in the hundreds of employees, headed by an executive of at least vice presidential rank. Almost all companies now feel it incumbent to portray themselves as good environmental citizens, and resistance to environmental regulation is much less overt. William Clark of Harvard University's Kennedy School has observed that many companies "have a corporate culture that is by now absolutely committed to playing the environment game right."[24] Russell Train believes that environmentalism has now "become institutionalized throughout the business community."[25]

How did some American corporate leaders suddenly become born-again environmentalists? One answer is that a new generation of executives, who grew up during the environmental era, is taking command of the nation's industry. James Range, vice president for government affairs of Waste Management, Inc., a major waste-handling company, said that people his age, who were in college during or just before Earth Day, "have an ingrained commitment to the environment just as we have an ingrained feeling about civil rights. And we are beginning to be vice presidents and senior vice presidents and even presidents of the corporations."[26]

Another answer was that even Ronald Reagan in the White House, with his perfervid distaste for government regulation, could not do away with or even significantly weaken the environmental rules despite his strenuous efforts to do so. There was no choice but to face reality. As Irving Shapiro, former chief executive of E. I. Du Pont de Nemours & Co., put it: "You'd have to be blind and deaf not to recognize the public gives a damn about the environment and a businessman who ignores it writes his own death warrant."[27] Moreover, many companies found that the costs of environmental regulation did not squeeze as hard as they originally feared. Shapiro was no environmentalist but a hard-nosed business leader. However, he was more farsighted than many of his fellow corporate executives whose perspective ranged no farther than the next quarter's earnings statement. Shapiro, whose support, as head of the world's biggest chemical company, for the Superfund law helped turn the tide in its favor in Congress, said that while the environmental laws imposed "enormous costs" on the chemical industry that were eventually passed on to its consumers, those costs have lost the industry virtually no business over the long run. "The fact is, Du Pont has not been disadvantaged by the environmental laws. It is a stronger company today than it was twenty-five years ago." But Shapiro, a lawyer who rose from the post of Du Pont's general counsel to head the giant corporation before retiring as its CEO more than a decade ago, cautioned that "where the environment is on the corporate agenda depends on the public. If the public loses interest corporate involvement will diminish."[28]

In a series of speeches in 1989, one of Shapiro's successors as CEO of Du Pont, E. S. Woolard, committed his company to a new standard of "corporate environmentalism," which he defined as "an attitude and a performance commitment that place corporate environmental stewardship fully in line with public desires and expectations." Environmentalism, he said, "is now a mode of operation for every sector of society—industry included. We in industry have to develop a stronger awareness of ourselves as environmentalists."[29]

There are, however, built-in limits to this transformation. While the law treats corporations as persons, they bear no resemblance to human beings. They have no soul, no conscience, no ethics, no long-term vision of where society or the economy should be headed, no purpose other than the generation of profits through the production of goods and services. This does not mean that corporate executives are soulless and evil. No doubt they are just as good or bad, wise or stupid, generous or mean as the rest of us. But the structure and tradition of American business and industry and the fierce competitive pressures of the market impose ironbound imperatives on those who would climb the corporate ladder. Annual profits must be maximized. Costs must be kept to a minimum. Interference with the corporate decision-making process, by law, by regulation, and by the public, must be resisted. Long-term planning is unrewarding to the manager seeking promotion or intent on retaining his top-floor executive suite; he or she must show results on the year-end balance sheet.

But change is taking place, however slowly. Environmental management is now well established in the curriculum of many business schools. Economic incentives are gradually making environmental standards and performance a legitimate line item on year-end balance sheets. Establishing environmental performance standards for business executives may sound like training tigers to be vegetarians, but new economic incentives, management training, and the widening environmental ethic may eventually do the trick.

Corporate executives discovered that it is not just workers or people living near mills or waste dumps who are threatened by pollution. Acid rain, global warming, and the depletion of the earth's protective ozone layer do not respect wealth or privilege, do not stay out of the better neighborhoods.

Unions, particularly in the building trades, frequently opposed pollution controls for fear of losing jobs. Conflicts between workers and environmentalists have been frequent. A dramatic example is the bitter dispute between the environmentalists who are trying to block the timber companies from cutting the last few million acres of old-growth forest in the Northwest and the loggers who fear that they will lose their jobs and that their communities will be disrupted. Estimates of the number of jobs that would be lost in the Northwest as a result of restrictions on cutting in the national forests ranged upward from 20,000. A major obstacle that had to be overcome before Congress could enact legislation in 1990 to address the acid rain problem was the fear that reducing pollutants would cost the jobs of many miners who worked in high-sulfur coal mines.

Many unions, however, have concluded that the interests of their members are best served by strong laws and rules to protect the environment, particularly the workplace. Workers whose life and health were jeopardized by chemical poisons, asbestos, cotton dust, radiation, or any of thousands of other occupational hazards they faced had a strong grievance against their employers. The Oil, Chemical, and Atomic Workers staged a long strike against Shell Oil to obtain better protection of their health and safety on the job. Cesar Chavez's United Farm Workers Union organized a national boycott of California table grapes to protest the use of pesticides that threatened the health of field workers. Many industrial unions, such as the United Steelworkers and the United Auto Workers, as well as the Industrial Union Department of the American Federation of Labor and Congress of Industrial Organizations, formed alliances—such as the National Clean Air Coalition—with environmental and public health groups to press for policies that would protect their members.

Union members, like the rest of us, are often ambivalent about economic trade-offs to protect the environment. But again, like most Americans, more often than not they agree that protecting the environment is so important that they are willing to risk some economic sacrifice.

In the more than twenty years that have passed since Earth Day 1970, American society has been quietly transformed by environmental values. An impressive body of environmental law has been enacted, new institutions have been created to carry out those laws, the courts have been opened to environmental causes, and environmental law has become the fastest-growing arm of the legal profession. Environmental laws and regulations have made a significant imprint on the national economy and altered the attitudes of powerful corporations and unions. Our science, medicine, education, mass communications, and even religion have changed in response to this environmental phenomenon.

Arising out of the transcendental and utilitarian streams of the old conservationism, the search for a better quality of life by affluent Americans in the post-World War II period, the demands for social justice that exploded in the 1960s and 1970s, the fear and anger of citizens whose health and families and property are threatened by pollution or rapacious development, and out of a slowly changing understanding of the relationship between humans and the natural world, the new environmentalism is helping create a new society.

But what about the American people? A social revolution cannot be built only by reforming laws and institutions—it must have the firm support of the public. Many well-informed people still question the depth of Americans' commitment to environmentalism. They cite the failure of environmentalism to influence electoral politics, particularly at the presidential level, as a telling indication of how superficially it has been adopted by voters.

My own view as a journalist who has observed environmental politics in the country for many years is that a large part of the American people, probably a majority, have become imbued with environmental values and are ready to respond to a call to arms to save the environment—and themselves. The anger and anxiety many

Americans feel about these issues and the sophistication they have acquired in understanding them have, I think, been grossly underestimated by all but a handful of politicians. I would guess that in a relatively few years, the environment will be one of the top two or three issues that will decide a presidential election.

In the meantime, the movement still had to tend to its traditional tasks. And it would soon become clear that saving the environment of the United States would also require working to save the global environment.

SAVING

LAND

Everything changes,
and nothing is more vulnerable than the beautiful.
                                        —*Edward Abbey*

In 1968 we bought some property for a summer home on a mountainside in Berkshire County, Massachusetts. We acquired the land cheaply because, by local economic standards, there is little to recommend it. Except for some low-lying boggy areas, it was covered almost entirely by skimpy, second-growth trees and thick tangles of mountain laurel, wild azalea known as swamp pinks, and woody blueberry bushes. A spade thrust into the ground strikes solid gneiss shelf after penetrating an inch or two of gravelly topsoil. The land could never have been farmed. At best, it may have supported a small dairy herd before it was abandoned, probably in the early part of the century.

What made the land unattractive to the country people was what made it appealing to us—its remoteness. Five miles from the nearest village and a mile and a half from a paved road, the property is reached by a narrow, rutted lane with high banks and a surface that turns into a sticky morass during spring mud season. When we bought the land there were perhaps a half dozen old houses and cabins within a two-mile radius. Except for deer-hunting season, when orangeshirted men with rifles invaded our woods without invitation, we were free of human intrusion.

Weary as we were of city crowds, noise, and traffic, of restricted vistas filled with concrete, steel, and glass, and of damp, gritty air, the fresh, quiet forest was just what we were looking for. Using axes and saws, my wife and I and our two young children hacked out a small clearing in the woods for our homesite. To the great amusement of our contractors, local men who knew that one should build as close to the highway as possible, we had them clear an 800-foot driveway into the heart of our property, making the site even more difficult to reach in wet weather. We dug out one of our bogs to create a small swimming pond—not knowing in the late 1960s that it was best to leave wetlands alone. We brought in a couple of truckloads of topsoil for our kitchen garden. And every spring and summer for more than two decades we have played at being homesteaders, clearing a little land each year, cutting our own trees for fireplace and cookstove wood, and growing our vegetables and salad greens. Foolish, perhaps, but it gives us more pleasure than anything else we do with our lives. When we are up there, living seems more direct and vital. We feel somehow more attached to history—more American. We have re-created the middle landscape idealized by Jefferson and his generation—our own patch of pastoral terrain in the midst of a wilderness. Our garden may only be a thirty-by-fifty-foot plot with topsoil from somebody else's old potato patch. The wilderness may stretch only a few acres around our small clearing and the supermarket may be only a twenty-minute drive away, but we can stand on our doorstep and see only trees and boulders beyond the kitchen garden and the stone wall and think of ourselves as intrepid pioneers.

Over the years, a handful of other families moved into our area. Like us, they came for the trees and the silence and clean air and have burrowed quietly and inconspicuously into the forest. But recently our area has started to change. The developers have discovered Berkshire County. All around us, beyond our land, the forest is being cleared, roads cut across the thin soil, and sites laid out for tract homes. A speculator from Long Island bought the property immediately adjoining ours and has filed a plan with the township for the construction of twenty-eight homes. Another development is planned just down the road. Our narrow country lane inevitably will have to be widened and paved. The woods that have grown back and now accommodate growing populations of bobcat, black bear, and wild turkey will be cut away to accommodate a ring of modular homes. The quiet and solitude we cherish will be broken. The middle landscape will turn into suburbia.

What is happening to our little patch of the countryside is all too symptomatic. The American land—and the life on it—are under enormous and intensifying pressure. In the second half of our century, a rapidly growing number of increasingly mobile families are filling up the empty spaces described by the pioneers and their successors over the previous 150 or so years. Across much of the continent, space between the cities is being occupied—developed for homes and vacation retreats, commercial enterprises, industry, highways, airports, reservoirs, and waste dumps. Places that were only visited in the past by a land-rich people—deep woods, steep hillsides, floodplains, shifting dunes on barrier islands, even the deserts—are increasingly being settled permanently and transformed to satisfy the growing hunger for space. By the mid-1970s, an estimated 1.25 million acres a year, a third of it once cultivated cropland, were being converted to intensive use.[1] The America of history and imagination, the America of the Indian, woodsman, and cowboy, of the yeoman farmer and small-town storekeeper, is vanishing before our eyes, swallowed by a hyperactive, motorized, urban civilization.

Perhaps the most serious casualty of this late-twentieth-century land rush is the nation's wetlands. These bogs and bottomlands, swamps, marshes, tundra, tidal flats, and prairie potholes are enormously valuable, irreplaceable resources. They are a vital habitat and spawning place for fish and wildlife. They support a vast diversity of plant and animal life. They filter pollution from flowing water, recharge underground water supplies, act as natural flood control barriers, soaking up overflows from rivers like a sponge. The potholes—shallow ponds that fleck the center of the continent from the Canadian plains to the Gulf of Mexico—provide indispensable nesting and feeding areas for the great North American bird migrations, particularly for waterfowl. As these potholes are drained and filled by farmers to increase their production, duck and geese populations are dropping rapidly. Over 400,000 acres of the nation's wetlands are now lost each year to dredging, filling, and development. Fewer than 100 million acres remain of the nearly 250 million acres of wetland that existed in the contiguous forty-eight states before the first Europeans settled here.[2]

The fate of Florida's Everglades, the nation's most famous wetland, is a poignant example of how we have been mistreating these rich resources. Called "the river of grass," the Everglades, a large part of which is now a national park, is formed by a broad, shallow, slowly moving flow of water that runs southward 250 miles from Lake Kissimmee to the southern tip of the state. It is an eerily beautiful, astonishingly fecund liquid prairie of mangrove trees and orchids, grass, and vines that is inhabited by a diverse wildlife— alligators, manatees, panthers, eagles, vultures, flamingos, and hundreds of other species. But more than a century of dredging, filling, and draining, of building canals, ditches, dikes, roads, farms, and oil wells, has drastically reduced the flow of water across the Everglades. The channeling of the Kissimmee River by the Army Corps of Engineers, an organization that until recently seemed to have the destruction of the nation's wetlands as its principal mission, turned that meandering, hundred-mile stream into a deep, straight fifty-mile canal. Hydrologists said that the taming of the river has had a disastrous effect on the natural balances of the great wetland. Runoff of farm chemicals and animal wastes has turned big Lake Okeechobee at the northern edge of the 'Glades into a eutrophied, dying body of water.

In 1986, Governor Bob Graham of Florida said when announcing a program to reverse the degradation, "In the process of draining the Everglades, the developers reduced a natural work of art into a thing pedestrian and mundane."[3] Despite such assaults, the Everglades is still the Sistine Chapel of wetlands. But other valuable works of wetland art throughout the country continue to be defaced and destroyed in defiance of the laws enacted to protect them.

Just how much farmland is being lost is a matter of dispute. Starting in the 1920s, millions of acres of rural land were drowned by big dams, particularly in the Tennessee, Missouri, and Columbia river basins. Between 1950 and 1980 about 40 million acres of farmland were converted to urban and suburban use, for roads, factories, and commercial centers, according to the U.S. Department of Agriculture.[4] In recent years, the amount of cultivated land in this country appears to have stabilized at somewhat over 400 million acres. And, of course, in the hands of American farmers, the land's productivity is very high and continues to feed hundreds of millions at home and around the world.

But the story is more complicated. Much of the converted land tended to be near cities, where historically most of the prime farmland was located. Many of the richest farms have been simply swallowed up by uncontrolled urban sprawl. New land brought under cultivation to meet the demands of a growing export market in the 1960s and 1970s was often marginal soil subject to erosion. An average of eight tons of soil per acre is carried off cultivated cropland each year by wind and water.[5] Farmlands and the freshwater aquifers beneath them are becoming increasingly toxified by the application of chemical pesticides. Irrigated lands in the West are experiencing growing salinization. While there is still unused farmland available, the Agriculture Department has determined that "by the year 2000, most if not all of the nation's 540-million-acre cropland base is likely to be in cultivation. When seen from this perspective, continuing *non*agricultural demands upon the agricultural land base become a matter for national concern."[6]

Forested land in the United States, both private and public, also remained relatively stable in the latter part of the twentieth century, as the regrowth of timber land cut earlier in the century about equaled the number of trees felled for wood and pulp and to clear land for industry and agriculture. But the second- and third-growth forests, of course, are not nearly as biologically rich as the virgin forests.

About 650 million acres of the country are classified as forest, about a quarter of which are in the national forests. But again, the overall figures are deceptive. In many places, the forests are being rapidly sold off by the timber companies that own them, as the value of the land for residential and commercial development exceeds the value of the timber resources. Logging companies and other big corporate landholders in northern New England and New York State's Adirondacks announced plans in the late 1980s to sell off as much as a million acres of their forests. Stephen D. Blackmer, policy director for the Society for the Protection of New Hampshire Forests, one of the nation's oldest private land protection groups, noted in 1988 that "the large forest ownerships of northern New England are an integral part of New England's economic, recreational, ecological, and cultural heritage. The threats to this heritage have never been greater."[7]

In the South, hardwood bottomlands are being drained for agriculture, mixed forests that permitted a diverse wildlife population are being replaced by softwood monocultures for pulp and paper mills, and growth rates of trees have slowed measurably for the past thirty years, a decline that is probably caused, in part at least, by air pollution. The great "old growth" forests of the Northwest, the final remnants of virgin forests that once covered much of the continent, are rapidly being leveled. Their shaggy, centuries-old Douglas firs and spruce trees are falling to the chain saw to feed the timber-hungry markets of Japan and the rest of the Pacific rim. In Alaska the Tongass National Forest, the only temperate rain forest in North America, is being decimated for the same reason.

Backpacking through the Maine woods a century and a half ago, Henry Thoreau was reminded "how exceedingly new this country is."[8] Today the America of Thoreau no longer exists. Even in carefully preserved wilderness areas, one is reminded by the empty Coke can on the trail or the jet aircraft high above that a high-tech, high-consumption urbanized civilization dominates the land. As the empty spaces fill up, however, more and more Americans increasingly cherish what is left of the unspoiled countryside and look for ways to save the land.

The United States has a better record than most countries in protecting the public domain as open space to be used by its citizens. President John F. Kennedy said in 1963, "The history of America . . . has been the story of Americans seizing, using, squandering, and, belatedly, protecting . . . their rich heritage."[9] Of the nearly 2.3 billion acres of land within the boundaries of the fifty states, the federal government holds today 730 million acres, nearly a third of the total. Some 155 million acres is owned by the states, 51 million acres by Indian tribes, and the rest is in private hands.[10] The public domain stretches from the mangrove swamps at the tip of Florida to the flat tundra of Alaska's North Slope, from the rocky coves of the Maine coast to a smoking volcano on Hawaii. Most federal land, however, is in the western states and Alaska. While the Defense Department and other federal agencies have substantial acreage under their management, most of the federal land is in the national forests managed by the Agriculture Department and in the national parks, the National Wildlife Refuge System, and the public range, all controlled by agencies of the Interior Department.

Bernard Shanks calls these lands "the spiritual heart of America."[11] They are what is left of the wild continent that awed and excited the first Europeans.

The protection of public land and its wildlife was the original impulse of environmentalism in the United States. The first conservationists and their organizations—Muir and Pinchot and Teddy Roosevelt, the Audubon Societies, the Sierra Club, the Wilderness Society—sought to conserve the land and its resources for the benefit of all and protect it from the rapacity of the few. To a certain extent they have succeeded. In this century the public domain has been largely preserved and has even been expanded. But saving these lands has been and continues to be a constant and close-run struggle. The pressure of economic interests to get at the public lands and resources for private profit is unrelenting and is quick to exploit any opening. The public lands are also under siege by an urban civilization that is exporting many of its problems—overcrowding, overuse, pollution, throwaway consumer products, crime, drug abuse, and the decay of the public infrastructure—to every corner of the land, including its parks, its forests, its refuges, and its open range.

The federal lands are the subject of many books and scholarly articles and I will only attempt here to give a general overview of the issues affecting them.

The national parks are arguably one of the great gifts that America has given to the world.

Today the National Park System includes over 68 million acres. Although over 48 million of them are in Alaska, there are national parks, monuments, and battlefields in every state except Delaware. Units of the park system range in size from the 9-million-acre Wrangell–St. Elias Park in Alaska, an area twice the size of Hawaii, to the memorial to the Polish-born Revolutionary War hero Thaddeus Kosciuszko that covers 0.02 of an acre in Philadelphia. They include wild areas like Glacier National Park in Montana and Big Bend Park in Texas but also parks in the middle of metropolises, such as Gateway National Park in New York City and San Francisco's Golden Gate National Park. Within the park system are seashores, islands, wild rivers, and national treasures such as the Statue of Liberty and the monuments along the Mall in Washington, D.C.

The big national parks in the West and in Alaska—Yellowstone, Grand Teton, Yosemite, the Grand Canyon, Zion, Bryce, Glacier, Olympic, Denali, and other crown jewels of the park system—are places of beauty, mystery, and enchantment. To a surprising degree they remain fresh and unspoiled. But they, like almost all the other parks, are threatened by a broad spectrum of internal and external troubles. A report by the National Park Service in 1980 listed seventy-three categories of serious problems facing the parks, including air and water pollution, toxic wastes, overcrowding by visitors, urban encroachment on park borders, and the development of oil, coal, uranium, and geothermal energy around the parks. Most of these problems have grown steadily worse since. While the eastern parks such as Acadia and the Great Smokies are the most overcrowded, almost all of the more popular parks, including the crown jewels, are in serious danger of being loved to death by the millions of visitors who pour into them each year.

The Park Service is increasingly torn by its dual mission of managing the parks as "a pleasuring ground for the people" and of preserving the parks and their natural features "unimpaired for future generations." Development is hurting many parks, such as parts of the Everglades National Park, which are dying as the flow of water vital to sustain its unique ecosystem is diverted for the swelling population of coastal Florida. Acid rain and smog are harming the water and trees of Acadia in Maine, Shenandoah in Virginia, and Minnesota's Voyageur Park. Civil War battlefields such as Antietam in Maryland, Gettysburg in Pennsylvania, and Manassas in Virginia are being nibbled away piecemeal by housing developments, shopping malls, and commercial strips. Some of our national seashores are being eroded by wind and water and by dune buggies that tear up the beaches. Industrial, commercial, agricultural, and residential development up to the borders of the parks is narrowing the habitat of the wildlife that lives within them but whose range cannot be confined to their boundaries. Bare-bones Park Service budgets have inevitably led to crumbling roads, bridges, trails, and other unsafe, unsightly visitor facilities within the parks.

By 1985, John B. Oakes of *The New York Times* would write, "The national parks are as sacred to most Americans as the flag, motherhood and apple pie, but unlike those other symbols of the national psyche, the National Park System is in imminent danger."[12]

Because Americans cherish their parks, they are not an easy political target. There is a sizable army of volunteers around the country ready to defend their integrity. One of the famous battles of conservation history was a successful effort in the 1950s led by David Brower and his Sierra Club, and joined by the Wilderness Society and other groups, to block construction of the Echo Park Dam in the Dinosaur National Monument on the Utah-Colorado border. (A national monument is a national park with slightly looser protection.) As Douglas Scott of the Sierra Club noted, the Echo Park issue was a matter of bedrock principle. "If we let them build a dam in one unit of the National Park System they can build one anywhere." It was Hetch Hetchy redux, but this time with the preservationists winning the fight. As Shanks observed, however, the Echo Park victory was "bittersweet" for the conservationists because at the same time they failed to block construction of the Glen Canyon Dam on the Colorado, which has ever since changed the character of that great river and the Grand Canyon through which it flows.[13]

In recent years, conservationists have carried their struggle to preserve the parks beyond park boundaries. In the face of development around them, many, if not most, of the parks are in danger of becoming isolated preserves surrounded by an urban, industrialized landscape—so many zoos and botanical gardens instead of the "vignettes of primitive America" that a 1963 report on the parks said they should remain. To prevent this, there is a growing belief that public and private policy should protect the parks and the areas around them as integrated ecological systems. The Greater Yellowstone Coalition, an alliance of environmental groups, is seeking to include the national forests around the park and other adjacent areas within the Yellowstone preservation system as a means of assuring adequate range for the park's threatened grizzly bear population and other wildlife. For some years now, there have been pending proposals to create inviolable buffer zones around other threatened parks.

Among Americans who cherish the national parks, there is a growing consensus that plans must be laid soon to save choice lands for the park system and to establish a strategy and provide the wherewithal to protect the parks for future generations.

Set in Florida's sparkling Indian River, Pelican Island is an unprepossessing three acres of sand, grass, cactus, and low mangrove trees. But squatting on almost every bush are brown pelicans looking like slightly streamlined pterodactyls, wood storks with puffed-out chests and haughty beaks, and slender great blue herons. The nests of the three species are occupied by naked, squawking chicks or fledglings almost ready to try their wings. Off-limits to casual visitors, the island remains as it was in 1903, when President Theodore Roosevelt designated it an inviolate bird sanctuary; it was the first such sanctuary in the National Wildlife Refuge System. The system was created piecemeal through presidential orders, acts of Congress, under the requirements of laws such as the Endangered Species and Migratory Bird acts, and through donations from private groups such as the Nature Conservancy. Today, there are 420 refuges covering 89 million acres, or about 10 million acres more than the entire National Park System.[14]

But though bigger than the park system, the refuges have a smaller budget, a less politically influential bureaucracy to protect them, and weaker support from a public yet to be educated to grasp the full significance and value of the system. The U.S. Fish and Wildlife Service, which manages the refuges, is unsupported by an organic federal statute to give it legitimacy. As a result, the refuges are even more threatened than the parks and less is being done to protect them. A 1983 survey by the service found that virtually every one of them is in trouble. Anecdotal information suggests that conditions have been worsening steadily since then. The most immediate problem for the refuges and their wildlife is water: either there is not enough or it is so contaminated that it threatens the birds, mammals, reptiles, and aquatic and plant life. The most notorious case of such contamination involved the Kesterson Refuge in California's Central Valley, where runoff of agricultural irrigation water was so badly poisoned by selenium and other chemicals that the Wildlife Service had to take measures of last resort as drastic as firing guns to keep migrating birds from setting down on the dangerous land and water.

The long-term health of the refuges is threatened by encroaching urbanization, poaching, imported exotic species crowding out native flora and fauna, air pollution, oil drilling, grazing, and heavy public use. Legal hunting is another threat to some of the refuges—contrary to wide belief, most of the refuges are not sanctuaries for wildlife. Federal wildlife programs are supported by sales of Duck Stamps bought by hunters.

The refuges remain vulnerable. They are increasingly isolated islands of natural shelter for birds and animals in a sea of human development. Without stronger statutory protection and more active political support, the refuge system may not survive.

To walk through a section of virgin old-growth forest in Oregon is to experience the land as it must have been when Indians were alone on the continent. Venerable Douglas firs, shaggy-barked and draped with moss, tower hundreds of feet above a forest floor dusted with the thin layer of snow that has managed to penetrate the high, tangled tree canopy. Dark, deep, lush, and fragrant, this old forest is North America untamed and unspoiled.

The last fragments of these ancient woods, which once covered the entire Northwest, are the object of an intense, sometimes violent dispute between the logging industry and its political allies and the conservation community and others who are fighting desperately to save them. The old growth, almost all of which is in national forests evocatively named Siskiyou, Unpqua, Siuslaw, Umatilla, Snoqualmie, and Wenatchee, supports dozens of communities that depend almost entirely on sawmills and logging camps for their economic well-being. The timber industry and its workers angrily defend their right to cut down the forests, saying that the environmentalists who are trying to stop them are tree-hugging radicals who care nothing about the well-being of the region. They were furious when the environmentalists successfully sued in court to block logging in large forest areas that are the habitat of the endangered northern spotted owl, contending that concern for the owl is only a ruse to halt economic use of the woods. The conservationists countered that the owl was an indicator species whose demise showed that the entire chain of life supported by the forest, including human well-being, was in danger. Efforts by area politicians to forge a compromise have foundered time and again.

But the struggle over the old-growth forests of the Northwest is only the latest episode of a fierce, century-long contest for control of the nation's publicly owned woodlands. As James Overbay, a deputy chief of the Forest Service, said in 1989: "This is really a debate over two philosophies: should the national forests be used or preserved?"[15]

The old philosophical debate between Gifford Pinchot and John Muir continues.

Today the National Forest System includes 155 forests and 19 national grasslands—191 million acres in all. There are big national forests in many of the eastern states, purchased in some cases by the federal government from private landholders rather than carved out of the public domain. As water quality was degraded in many areas, the forests became increasingly important as protectors of watersheds.

The Forest Service, the arm of the Agriculture Department that manages the national forests, while trying to balance the variety of demands placed on the lands in its charge, remains basically true to Pinchot's utilitarian philosophy. Their chief goal was to manage the forests to yield a large and stable supply of timber to the nation. Some 3 million board feet were cut annually before World War II. After the war, the service supervised a steadily increasing annual timber cut from the forests, expanding the number to over 11 billion board feet a year during the Reagan administration. To accommodate the increasing timber harvest, the service built hundreds of thousands of miles of road in the national forests. In many of the forests, trees are sold off to the timber industry at a price well below what it cost the Forest Service to survey the land, build logging roads, and manage the sale. These "below-cost sales" lose the U.S. Treasury hundreds of millions of dollars a year.

At the urging of conservationists, Congress passed a number of laws to protect public lands and resources, some of them specifically concerned with national forests. But as Samuel Hays has noted, the "bottom line" for the Forest Service has always been and remains the production of lumber.[16] Despite their Smokey the Bear image as protectors of trees, Forest Service rangers are trained to manage timber harvests and that is what many prefer to do. In recent years, however, a growing number of biologists and wildlife and recreation specialists in the service have other priorities and there has been a mini-revolt among some rangers against excessive road building and tree cutting. Nevertheless, a fifty-year plan for the forests, prepared under the National Forest Management Act and completed in 1986, called for a doubling of the timber harvest and the construction of over 100,000 more miles of road in the national forests over five decades.

Meanwhile, however, Congress continued to place large areas of forest in the national wilderness system; by the early 1990s nearly 35 million acres within the national forests had been officially designated as wilderness areas. The environmentalists sought to persuade the nation that the forests were of greatest value not as commodities but as places of refuge for humans and other life.

Nearly a century after Muir and Pinchot first clashed, their philosophies remain locked in battle over the use and future of the nation's forests. Pinchot's, now as then, is prevailing. But not easily and not entirely. The cult of wilderness inspired by Muir, Bob Marshall, David Brower, and others continues to flourish and its dedicated adherents have been successful in placing millions of acres of forest —and of public range and park land—off-limits to exploitation.

In 1964, President Lyndon B. Johnson signed the Wilderness Act and, in so doing, threw the authority of the United States government behind the radical idea that the land and its riches have value even when left undisturbed.

The statute defined wilderness thus: "A wilderness, in contrast with those areas where man and his own works dominate the landscape, is hereby recognized as an area where the earth and the community of life are untrammeled by man, where man himself is a visitor who does not remain." Stewart Udall, who was Secretary of the Interior when the law was adopted, noted that "wilderness, like the national park system, was an American idea. Many people at the time thought it was a crazy idea."[17] Crazy or not, the idea took firm root. Today there are more than 90 million acres inside the federal wilderness system, with more to come. George T. Frampton, Jr., president of the Wilderness Society, believes that there are another 90 or 100 million acres that should be protected as wilderness.

While the wilderness system is one of the great achievements of conservation, it also serves as a melancholy reminder of how completely we Americans have transformed our land. Far from being the dark and dangerous place the first Europeans believed they must conquer and "civilize," the wilderness, as James Oliver Robertson points out, is now "a resource in which naturalness is perpetuated."[18] Like the Native Americans, wilderness areas have been pushed onto reservations to preserve a semblance of their original state. In its very preservation, the wild land has been tamed.

If the national parks are fairly well protected from exploitation and national forests are a no-man's-land still contested by users and preservers, the public range managed by the Interior Department's Bureau of Land Management remains pretty much in the hands of ranchers and their allies in the mining and oil industries. And, probably, no category of federal land has been as abused and degraded.

With over 300 million acres in its domain, the Bureau of Land Management is the nation's biggest landholder. Almost all of that land is in the West and Alaska. In many of those states, the land agency controls a large percentage, sometimes over half of the land, administering, for example, 69 percent of Nevada and 41 percent of Utah. Bureau holdings account for nearly a quarter of the land in the West, more than the national parks and forests combined.[19] They were "leftover lands," the lands that remained after homesteaders, states, railroads, claimed their share and the federal government set aside land for parks, refuges, forests, Indian reservations, and military reservations. The bureau lands hold rich treasures of grass, trees, water, oil, coal, uranium, gold, silver, and other valuable metals. They also have beautiful mountains, magnificent valleys, austere deserts, forlorn badlands. They are home to elk and deer, cougars and coyotes, eagles and hawks, wild horses and burros, snakes and lizards.

Unfortunately, the public range of the American West provides a classic example of the tragedy of the commons, with individuals trying to wrest as much private profit as they can from public property without regard to the long-term fate of that property. The excessive numbers of cattle and sheep put on the range by many cattle and sheep ranchers badly overgrazed the land, causing the soil to erode and destroying streambeds and riparian habitat of wildlife.

For more than fifty years, starting with the New Deal, the federal government sought to control damage to the range through congressional action and regulations administered by the Bureau of Land Management. Not surprisingly, the stockmen, miners, and other range users, long accustomed to treating the public lands as a private fiefdom, reacted angrily to what they perceived as a threat to their rights and their livelihood. The result was the "Sagebrush Rebellion," the effort by entrenched western economic forces to wrest control of the land and its resources from the federal government. The rebels evoked states' rights, the free market, and rugged cowboy individualism to assert their right to use the land for grazing, to mine coal and other minerals, and to drill for oil. They demanded that the federal government turn over its holdings to them or to the states. They attacked, sometimes physically, and vilified federal land managers and sought to discredit conservationists as un-American left-wingers.

The environmentalists, in turn, branded the Sagebrush Rebellion as a naked land grab and the rebels themselves as profiteers out to enrich themselves at the public's expense. While in some cases that may have been true, the sources of the rebellion are more complex. In many respects it was the old West coming face to face with the emerging new West—the ranching and mining families that had been using the land for decades suddenly confronted with a growing influx of newcomers who wanted their share of the land and water, who were interested in recreation and conservation, in fishing and hunting and wildlife. While the rebels were defending privilege, it was privilege they had come to think of as their inherent right because the land had been used by their parents and grandparents.

Despite many rents in its fabric, the mantle of protection thrown over the public domain in the twentieth century remains largely intact. The challenge of the free-market libertarians and the corporate socialists who have exerted substantial political power in Washington, D.C., during the Reagan and Bush administrations was largely turned aside. The small band of passionate conservationists who began a movement to save the land nearly a hundred years ago has grown into an army of watchdogs who react vigorously to attempts to erode the federal estate. While there are still practitioners of the rape, ruin, and run school of resource development, no longer can they operate clandestinely on the public domain, in cozy cooperation with national and local politicians.

But progress in expanding the protected federal estate, as we shall see, came to a near standstill during the 1980s and early 1990s and existing lands and resources remain vulnerable. It will take broad-based public support, extending far beyond the ranks of traditional conservationists, to provide the political firepower necessary to preserve the public land in the next century as population grows and competition for increasingly scarce resources intensifies.

If a thin but serviceable cloak of law and environmental activism serves to protect the public domain, private lands and resources have little to shield them from development, growth, greed, and indifference. The nation's privately owned wetlands, farms, forests, coastal areas, and other open spaces are under enormous and growing pressure. Those who contend that only private owners with an economic stake in their property take proper care of the land have only to look at the desolation of the industrial parks along our superhighways, the inner-city holdings of slumlords, the used-car graveyards, the reeking dead zones around smelters, cropland now filled with treeless tracts of flimsy town-house projects, the unzoned suburban commercial areas, the slag heaps around abandoned steel mills, and countless other examples of how property owners abuse their own land. Efforts begun in the 1960s by Lady Bird Johnson to remove the blight of billboards from the nation's roadsides have failed as outdoor advertising agencies and their clients swarm through loopholes in the law. Greenery, privacy, fresh air, wild animals, clean streams, quiet places, wide spaces in which to run or throw a ball or simply stretch out and look up to a blue sky, are becoming increasingly remote, rare, and expensive. Except for some imaginative reclamation of waterfront areas in a number of our older cities, little has been done to create open space in our crowded urban areas.

The surface-mining law, if it were properly enforced, could protect or salvage some private mining land. The wetlands preservation provisions of the Clean Water Act could slow their loss, particularly if the "no net loss of wetlands" policy proclaimed by President Bush at the beginning of his administration is ever put into practice. Amendments to farm price support legislation theoretically encourage farmers to stop filling wetlands or planting obviously marginal land. Anti-litter and highway beautification statutes have made some headway in removing eyesores from the landscape, although a short drive almost anywhere in the country demonstrates the inadequacy of those efforts. Zoning laws are usually ineffectual barriers to development and abuse of the land. In most areas, long-range land-use planning is still considered politically anathema. Preserving land as open space is rarely considered an option for the use of private property—although, thanks to the efforts of land trust organizations, less rarely than in the past.

Time is running out for saving what is left of the American landscape. In 1986, Robert L. Bendick, Jr., then director of Rhode Island's Department of Environmental Management, warned with a sense of urgency if not a precise timetable that "we have five years to preserve what is important about our state."[20] Other state and local land managers and conservationists are feeling a similar urgency throughout much of the East and a substantial part of the West Coast as well. There may be more time in the West, but in places like Jackson Hole, Lake Tahoe, and other places popular for their beauty, recreational opportunities, or other development potential, open space is disappearing fast. America is becoming like Western Europe, built over and tamed, with the empty places filled in.

As the environmental impulse gains strength and the land ethic of conservationism takes deeper root, more and more private organizations and citizens are working to defend open space. The battle is fought on many fronts—from the well-endowed efforts of organizations such as the Nature Conservancy to buy large tracts of ecologically valuable land outright to the solitary act of courage of a man like Mark Dubois, who chained himself to a rock in a hidden cove along California's Stanislaus River to block those who wanted to build a dam on that wild and free-flowing stream. He succeeded, at least temporarily.

Rachel Carson
© 1961 ERICH HARTMANN
USED BY PERMISSION OF RACHEL CARSON COUNCIL, INC.

Barry Commoner   Paul R. Ehrlich   Thomas E. Lovejoy
                                         SMITHSONIAN INSTITUTION

Edward O. Wilson
MUSEUM OF COMPARATIVE
ZOOLOGY, HARVARD
UNIVERSITY

David Brower
EARTH ISLAND INSTITUTE

René Dubos
DON PERDUE

Gaylord Nelson
JANET FRIES

George T. Frampton, Jr.
THE WILDERNESS SOCIETY

Joan Martin-Brown

James Gustave "Gus" Speth

Michael McCloskey

Several states, including New York, New Jersey, and Massachusetts, have floated bond issues to raise money for acquiring and protecting land. But a lack of will on the part of politicians in many parts of the country, often men and women who owe their allegiance and their livelihood to those who develop and exploit the land, as well as a growing scarcity of public funds, means that the job of saving open space rests to a large degree with private citizens.

There are thousands of dedicated people across the country going about the job of saving the land with ever increasing zeal and ingenuity. The Rails-to-Trails movement is getting private companies, states, and railroads to convert abandoned rights-of-way into "linear" parks. Land trusts throughout the country are making use of a variety of techniques, particularly conservation easements, to preserve open space and wildlife habitat—often without buying the land. In Wyoming's Snake River valley, for example, the Jackson Hole Land trust bought scenic easements or persuaded ranchers to donate them to bar any development that would obstruct the view of the dramatic Grand Teton Mountains. In communities across the country, citizens have dug in for an acre-by-acre fight to save a natural landscape.

True land-use planning, however, is in its infancy at the local level, is rare on a regional scale, and remains politically anathema on the national level. Efforts to restore land ravaged by exploitation are few and far between.

The land continues to disappear.

SAVING

LIFE

Is the last dolphin dying?
Is there no friend left?
Are we here alone?
        —*May Sarton*

In his book *The Endangered Kingdom*, Roger L. DiSilvestro wrote, "It is said that from a distance the passenger pigeons' cooing sounded like the ringing of bells. We will never know it, never hear it for ourselves, because the twentieth century has inherited from the nineteenth a ravaged land."[1]

The destruction of wildlife has been especially dramatic in the United States because so much of it has been lost in a relatively short time. Wildlife in this country, unlike Europe, has always been regarded as a public rather than a private resource. It was a democratic view of how wild animals could be used. But it denied the protection that the lords and squires of the Old World insisted on for the game and fish on their estates. Fair game for everyone, so to speak, wildlife was more vulnerable in the New World.

In the centuries since the Pilgrims first came ashore at Plymouth, there were, according to biologists' conservative estimates, as many as 5 billion passenger pigeons. Contemporary accounts noted that it sometimes took ten to twelve hours for a single flock of those beautiful and useful birds to pass overhead. This great multitude of wild birds had been wiped out in 1899 by destruction of their forest habitat, by guns, by nets, by poisoned bait, and by fire. Often they were killed simply for the sport of killing. In 1914 the last of these creatures died in captivity.

The 50 million bison that roamed the Great Plains have been reduced to a few scattered herds, although they are now starting to make something of a comeback as domesticated animals. Before the arrival of the Europeans, the buffalo roamed so thickly across the landscape that one Indian described them as "a robe" that covered the prairie.[2] Ranchers wanted the prairies cleared for the longhorns, the farmers for their wheat and corn. Professional hunters, who could earn $2.50 a hide and 25 cents per buffalo tongue, could each kill 5,000 or more a season with their Sharps repeating rifles. By 1870, railroads were there to take the hides to market from remote parts of the West and year after year they were stacked for miles along the track. By 1890, it was estimated that no more than 1,000 of the great shaggy creatures remained.[3] Similarly, wolves, grizzly bears, mountain lions, coyotes, prairie dogs, and dozens of other creatures would be extirpated from much of their former range as dangers or nuisances that interfered with farming and hunting. The great auk is now extinct. So are the heath hen, the sea mink, the North Carolina parakeet, the Atlantic gray whale. The whooping crane is an endangered species; the California condor and the black-footed ferret are nearly extinct, with desperate efforts being made to save them. Relatively few colonies remain of the millions of prairie dogs whose towns covered much of the center of the continent. The flocks of wild turkeys that scuttled through the woods and across the prairie have dwindled to a few shy populations. The wolf, whose primal howl was once heard from central Mexico to the Arctic, was ruthlessly hunted and harried out of this country. The grizzly bear, the king of North American beasts, survives in a few out-of-the-way pockets of wilderness. Swarming shoals of salmon, shad, sea bass, and other fish have all but disappeared from most of our dammed and polluted rivers and estuaries. Great herds of deer, antelope, caribou, moose, were reduced to a small fraction of their former size, although in recent years they have made a comeback.

Slowing this wanton slaughter of wildlife was, of course, one of the earliest environmental impulses in the United States. As early as 1818, Massachusetts passed a law to prevent the killing of "useful birds" such as partridges, robins, and larks.[4] The Audubon Society, starting in the last decade of the nineteenth century, sought to slow the destruction of birds for their feathers. William Temple Hornaday, director of the Bronx Zoo from 1896 to 1926, carried on a one-man crusade to save North American wildlife. The Lacey Act of 1900, introduced by Congressman John F. Lacey and strongly backed by the Audubon Society, outlawed transporting across state lines any wildlife killed in violation of state laws. Theodore Roosevelt started the National Wildlife Refuge System in 1903. The Weeks-McLean Migratory Bird Act of 1913 extended federal protection to waterfowl and other migratory species. Other federal statutes, notably the Pittman-Robertson Act of 1937 and the Dingell-Johnson Act of 1950, established funds from excise taxes to support state and federal fish and wildlife management programs. The Izaak Walton League, the National Wildlife Federation, Defenders of Wildlife, were among many groups formed with the explicit mission of protecting and enhancing the nation's wildlife.

Along with new laws and institutions, the impulse to save non-human life was nourished by a spreading moral and ethical sense of human responsibility for nature to parallel our increasing domination of the natural world. By the beginning of the nineteenth century, doubt was beginning to spread that the conquest of nature was the proper goal of mankind.[5] People slowly became aware that in industrialized countries civilization had reached a point that demanded a new relationship between humans and the natural world. No longer did the wilderness, the forests, and the wild beasts have to be subdued and conquered. The balance had shifted so far that humans would have to protect and conserve other living things.

For millennia, Roderick Nash has written, Western ethics focused "almost exclusively on the conduct of people toward each other and toward various deities."[6] In Nash's view, however, we have gradually been widening the circle of those to whom we extend ethical behavior. At first individuals accorded rights only to themselves. Then the circle expanded to include family, tribe, nation, and, if only in theory, the entire community of *Homo sapiens*. In recent years, some environmentalists, ethicists, religious thinkers, and others in the United States and elsewhere have been demanding that this circle of ethical behavior be extended to its limits to embrace animals, trees, and even rivers and rocks, viruses, and the planet itself.

In his provocative scholarly essay *Should Trees Have Standing?* Christopher D. Stone argued in 1972 that natural objects were entitled to legal rights in our judicial system and contended that environmentalism had prepared the ground for this radical step. "We are not only developing the scientific capacity, but we are cultivating the personal capacities *within us* to recognize more and more the ways in which nature—like the Black, the Indian and the Alien—is like us (and we will also become more able realistically to define, confront, live and admire the ways in which we are all different)."[7]

Activists have shown that they are ready to fight, go to jail, and even die to protect animals, trees, and other aspects of nature. The Animal Liberation Front, which opposes cruelty to animals and seeks to free them from exploitation by humans, has demonstrated, sometimes violently, and broken into laboratories to free experimental animals.

Perhaps the most visible and effective expression of the widening conservation ethic is the global effort to save the whales. Although humans have regarded these vast, mysterious mammals with awe and even reverence, they have hunted whales since men first went to sea. Valued for their oil, meat, and baleen, whales have been destroyed in ever increasing numbers for hundreds of years. When Herman Melville wrote *Moby Dick* more than a century ago, he wondered "whether Leviathan can long endure so wide a chase and so remorseless a havoc; whether he must not at last be exterminated from the waters, and the last whale, like the last man, smoke his last pipe, and then himself evaporate in the final puff."⁸ Melville could not, of course, have imagined the havoc that future generations of whalers would wreak with fast motorized ships, explosive harpoons, sonar, and other efficient means of killing devised by technological ingenuity. Whaling in wooden sailing ships like Captain Ahab's *Pequod* would seem almost benign in contrast.

By the middle of the twentieth century, many of the great whales, including the blue whale, the right whale, the humpback whale, the bowhead whale, and the sperm whale, had been hunted to the verge of extinction. The blue whale, a gargantuan but gentle creature that can reach lengths of ninety feet and weigh over a hundred tons, once numbered in the hundreds of thousands. Today, only a few thousand remain.

In response to the steep decline in whale populations, maritime nations gathered in 1946 to form the International Whaling Commission. The commission was intended to do no more than set kill quotas in order to maintain commercially viable whale stocks. But determined conservationists such as Greenpeace, spreading concern for wildlife, and love of whales in particular gradually turned the commission into a vehicle for ending whaling. For a number of reasons—their legendary aura, their majesty, human romanticism, guilt, a true sense of justice or stewardship, and simply a good press—whales came to sum up for many the sad fate of the natural world at the hands of man. Increasing scientific knowledge about the intelligence of whales and other sea mammals such as dolphins, as well as about their family structure, their ability to communicate over long distances using repeated patterns of sound that to the human ear resembles singing, and their seeming ability to feel and express emotion, made the whales a symbol of humanity's kinship with— and estrangement from—the natural world. Human affection for the great sea animals manifested itself in the fall of 1988, when efforts to rescue three gray whales trapped beneath the ice of the Arctic Ocean on their migration to the Pacific captured the sympathy and rapt attention of millions of people around the world, many of whom may have rarely paused to express concern about the world's poor and suffering humans.

In 1983, the International Whaling Commission voted to impose a moratorium on hunting great whales, to take effect by the end of 1985. Congress adopted laws giving the President of the United States authority to impose sanctions on countries that violated the treaty. While Japan and several other nations continue to take hundreds of the sea mammals each year in the name—probably undeserved—of scientific whaling, the mass slaughter of the great whales was suspended. Leviathan has been saved for the time being. But the armistice in the war of the whales remains tenuous.

No doubt the concern of many Americans for whales and other creatures of the wild is sentimental and shallow, reflecting no more than a childhood exposure to Bambi, Dumbo, and other of Walt Disney's pastel animals. But the educational efforts of environmental groups such as the National Audubon Society, the World Wildlife Fund, the Humane Society of the United States, Defenders of Wildlife, the Animal Welfare League, and the Fund for Animals gave Americans an increasing understanding of the deadly pressures on wildlife. Widely viewed television programs such as Marlin Perkins's *Wild Kingdom, Nature*, and Jacques Cousteau's documentaries and popular books by naturalists and ethologists such as Gerald Durrell, Konrad Lorenz, Jane Goodall, and George Schaller were producing an increasingly sophisticated view and ethical appreciation of humanity's effect on wild animals and plants. As popular support for the protection of animals and plants grew, the conservation and animal welfare groups dramatically increased their political influence in this country and in much of the rest of the world.

A small but growing fringe of the environmental movement insists that ethical and legal rights be extended to all of nature. Most mainstream environmentalists, however, would agree that the alleviation of human wants and human suffering should take precedence over the liberation of animals, trees, and rocks. At the same time, most environmentalists would maintain that human welfare requires that nature be protected. A basic premise of environmentalism, as we have repeatedly seen, is that humans are interconnected with all of life and we throw away any of the pieces at peril to ourselves. As the great Harvard biologist Edward O. Wilson has pointed out: ". . . we are human in good part because of the particular way we affiliate with other organisms. They are the matrix in which the human mind originated and is permanently rooted, and they offer the challenge and freedom innately sought."[9]

Self-interest—the realization that the heedless, rampant destruction of wildlife has ominous implications for human beings—is an even greater incentive to protect wildlife. Does a world in which eagles can no longer survive pose serious dangers for men and women and children? Doesn't a stream too polluted to sustain salmon and shad threaten a source of drinking water and food for people? If pollution damages forests, reduces crop yields, and sterilizes lakes, doesn't that bode ill for the nation? Doesn't wildlife have value for science, agriculture, recreation? Should we not wonder whether the absence of the wolf, of the passenger pigeon, of wild orchids, chestnut trees, and peregrine falcons diminishes the richness and joy of our lives? Can we endure a world that has room only for humans and their works (shared, perhaps, with cockroaches and rats)? Are we not, as George Perkins Marsh, Henry David Thoreau, and countless others pointed out, inextricably enmeshed in the web of life?

For many, saving life is justifiable on purely utilitarian grounds. The Australian philosopher John Passmore recalled, "One of my colleagues, an ardent preservationist, condemns me as a 'human chauvinist.' What he means is that in my ethical arguments, I treat human interests as paramount. I do not apologize for that fact; an 'ethic dealing with man's relation to land and to the plants and animals growing on it' would not only be about the behavior of human beings, as is sufficiently obvious, but would have to be justified by reference to human interests."[10] Passmore also points out, however, that "in the biosphere . . . man has no tenure; his own folly may, at any time, lose him his precarious occupancy."[11] From a purely anthropocentric perspective, in other words, wild animals should be preserved because they might be useful to people or because their disappearance could signal a disintegration of ecological systems to an extent that could eventually threaten human well-being as well.

Whether, therefore, the destruction of wildlife is seen from a pragmatic, humanistic perspective or from an ethical, biocentric point of view, it is a tragedy that gives our own species much to answer for.

The landmark wildlife protection statutes of the 1970s gave formal legal shape to the evolving concept that nonhuman life is valuable for its own sake, not just for its economic worth. Indeed, they required that wildlife be spared even at the cost of economic sacrifice. They embodied, as Nash pointed out, "the legal idea that a list of non-human residents of the United States is guaranteed, in a special sense, life and liberty."[12] The Marine Mammal Act was intended to slow the slaughter of sea creatures for their fur and meat, and a convention was adopted to regulate and, in some cases, end trade in animals and animal products such as fur, skin, and ivory in order to discourage trapping or killing endangered animals in the wild.

But the Endangered Species Act was something more. Not only did it restrain human behavior by forbidding the destruction of certain plant and animal species, it placed a positive duty on the government to act to protect those species from extinction. This duty included preserving the habitat of threatened or endangered species and restoring plants and animals to areas from which they had been eliminated. Enacted to protect specific organisms at the edge of extinction, the law also expressed society's deeper concern that humanity was expropriating far too much of the world for its own use and that the rest of nature was being denied its share. Michael J. Bean, a lawyer and conservationist, asserted that the Endangered Species Act was "a turning point in our relationship with other living creatures with whom we share the earth."[13]

The endangered species law is a kind of ark constructed to save living creatures in danger of being lost. It is a small and leaky vessel with room on board—so far at least—for tragically few passengers.

By the early 1990s only about 1,200 species, half of them found solely in North America, had been listed by the U.S. Fish and Wildlife Service as endangered or threatened and so eligible for protection. Recovery plans for re-creating biologically viable populations had been prepared for only about 275 species. More than 4,000 species are being considered for listing, rather like animals lined up waiting for permission to board the ark. Several creatures, including the Guam rail, a flightless bird, have become extinct while waiting for protection under the law.[14] Reflecting public interest and attention, the law for a number of years concentrated on what M. Rupert Cutler, then president of Defenders of Wildlife, called "charismatic mega-fauna," appealing or storied mammals such as whales and grizzly bears, and gave relatively short shrift to what he characterized as "enigmatic micro-fauna and flora" such as insects, weeds, fish, and mollusks.

Still, a fair number of creatures that otherwise might surely have vanished have been pulled back from the brink thanks to the law. Whooping cranes, big, showy wading birds that had been hunted so intensively for their plumage that there were only 15 left by 1940, had been restored to a population of about 200 by the end of the 1980s, still a precariously low population but a step away from extinction. American alligators, hunted as a dangerous nuisance and for their meat and leather, had almost disappeared from the warm waters of the southeastern and Gulf states. After they were placed under the protection of the endangered species law, they recovered rapidly—so rapidly, in fact, that they are now a problem in some places, attacking children and pets and invading swimming pools. In some areas the alligator has been taken off the list of endangered species. The bald eagle, the peregrine falcon, and the brown pelican, nearly wiped out by DDT, which made their eggshells too fragile to hatch, made a comeback after the pesticide was banned. Painstaking efforts have restored the falcon and the eagle to some areas from which they had been obliterated. The red wolf, extinct in the wild and surviving only in one West Coast zoo, was restored to the wild when, after careful preparation, several breeding pairs were released in protected areas of the Carolinas. The wolves successfully reproduced and, as of this writing, it appears that the reintroduction effort will be successful. The remnants of several species virtually teetering over the edge toward annihilation, including the California condor and the black-footed ferret, continue to cling to existence only through the desperate efforts of a few biologists operating under the authority of the species law.

Granting plants and animals the legal right to exist inevitably produced conflicts with human demands on the land and its resources. While serious battles were surprisingly rare, when they did occur— examples are the snail darter and the Tellico Dam in the Tennessee Valley and the spotted owl and the Northwest timber industry— they tended to kindle with the intensity and passion of a religious war.

Despite the barricade of protective laws, and despite the sympathy and support of a growing number of Americans, wildlife continues to reel under the impact of a growing population and an expanding economy. The flood of civilization continues to rise, and there is little time left to load the ark.

Legal sport hunting in the United States has ebbed as a serious problem to wildlife, except, of course, in the eyes of those who believe that killing for pleasure is morally wrong. Regulated by permits, seasons, and bag limits, this kind of hunting rarely makes serious inroads into game populations. In fact, the taxes collected on hunting equipment help pay for research and management programs that protect and enhance game species.

At sea, however, excessive commercial fishing, the incidental killing of dolphins and porpoises by tuna boats, and the greedy depredations of drift-net fishing vessels continue to seriously deplete marine life.

Hunting, trapping, and gathering around the world are still taking a huge toll on plant and animal species. International trade in live and dead animals and plants and products made from them is huge, amounting to some $5 billion a year.[15]

Illegal killing—poaching—is another story. The federal and state governments have strong anti-poaching laws. Wildlife protection laws are enforced by some 7,800 state game and fish officers and 205 federal agents.[16] But despite the efforts of enforcement officials and stiff fines and jail sentences imposed on violators who are caught, poaching of protected animals and plants is a big business. In 1983, for example, Interior Secretary James G. Watt announced the arrest of fifty people who had slaughtered between 200 and 300 bald and golden eagles for commercial sale. Even in supposedly inviolate national parks such as Yellowstone, big game, including grizzlies, have been killed by poachers. Nor are plants immune. A number of species of cactus are now threatened with extinction because they are gathered illegally for sale to collectors.

But if poaching is harming wildlife in this country it has reached truly crisis proportions on other continents, particularly Africa, where elephants and rhinos and much of the rest of a once rich wildlife heritage is being destroyed with terrifying speed.

The rising value of wildlife and wildlife products among the very affluent in the industrialized and Middle Eastern oil countries, the desperate need of the poor and hungry in Africa and other third world countries where wildlife is found, the corruption in some first- and third-world governments, and flaws in the Convention on International Trade in Endangered Species have combined to encourage a flourishing illegal trade in wildlife.

Pollution—in all its forms—is a more dangerous threat. Sometimes poisons are placed intentionally to kill wildlife, as when ranchers leave poisoned bait to kill coyotes that prey on livestock. But the poison in a dead coyote or other animal can then spread through the food chain. In his book *Wild Harmony*, zoologist William O. Pruitt, Jr., described how a strychnine-laced caribou carcass intended for wolves in Alaska caused a widening circle of death. Adult wolves, scenting something wrong, avoided the bait. But two pups started eating the poisoned carcass. Suddenly, they both "gave convulsive grunts as their intercostal muscles hardened in strychnine tetany. They fell stiffly onto their sides. Blood spurted from their severed tongues as their contracting jaw muscles forced their teeth through the flesh . . . Long after the two wolves died, ravens circled down to the

exposed caribou meat. After feeding, they, too, died lingering deaths
. . . A fox found the raven carcass, devoured it, and died, convulsing,
on the snow. A wolverine loped over the lake surface, ate of the
poisoned caribou, and jerked through the snow into the forest. The
wolverine's amazing resistance to strychnine enabled him to travel
for two miles, struggling and snapping at the fire in his stomach,
before he, too, died."[17]

Pollution created by human activity continues to wipe out uncountable numbers of animals, birds, plants, and microorganisms
through acute or chronic contamination of their habitat.

When the *Exxon Valdez* ran aground in Alaska in 1989 and
cracked open on a reef in Alaska's Prince William Sound, it spread
a sheen of toxic crude oil like a dark shroud over hundreds of square
miles of that beautiful stretch of water. Of all the damage I observed
there, none saddened and angered me and millions of television view-
ers more than seeing seabirds, otters, seals, and other animals coated
with viscous oil and struggling—hopelessly in most cases—to stay
alive.

Pollution of a more mundane nature, but just as deadly to marine
wildlife, is caused by our ubiquitous plastic waste. Plastic from packaging, abandoned monofilament netting, and other waste dumped
into the sea strangles, chokes, drowns, poisons, starves, or maims as
many as a million seabirds, 100,000 seals and other sea mammals, as
well as countless numbers of other marine fauna each year. A South
American scientist reported pulling "enough plastic from a starving
leatherback turtle to make a ball several feet in diameter."[18]

Of still unknown, but potentially much more ominous consequence to the world's wildlife is pollution on a global scale that
threatens to change climate and the natural systems that support life.
The destruction of ozone molecules in the atmosphere by chlorine-
based industrial chemicals is permitting a steadily increasing level of
ultraviolet radiation from the sun to reach the earth's surface and
into its waters. A number of scientists fear that the radiation may
kill the small organisms such as phytoplankton at the base of the
food chain. Experiments conducted by Egyptian zoologist Sayed Z.

El-Sayed in Antarctica, where the loss of atmospheric ozone has been most severe, found that high levels of radiation caused a substantial dieback of phytoplankton in that part of the world, where they are the food source of small shrimp called krill. Krill, in turn, are the principal food of squid, fish, penguins, seals, whales, and other animal life in Antarctica. Dr. El-Sayed, speaking of Antarctica, says that if the ozone layer continues to be depleted by pollution, "we are going to be in some trouble. I can't predict how much trouble, but it does not bode well. If anything happens to the krill, the whole ecosystem will absolutely collapse. We can say goodbye to the whales, to the seals, to the penguins, et cetera."[19]

Perhaps the most dangerous pollution threat is posed by the carbon dioxide and other gases that are causing the greenhouse effect. Humans, through technology and social organization, may be able to adjust to what on a geological time scale is virtually instant warming. Such an alteration in temperature and climate in less than a century, however, could be fatal to many species of wildlife unable to adapt quickly enough to rapidly changing conditions. Some scientists, including Robert L. Peters II, a biologist with the World Wildlife Fund, warn that global warming could lead to "mass extinctions" in the next century.[20]

The fact that pollution continues to take a high toll of wildlife is depressing evidence of the inadequacy of our laws and conventions for cleaning the environment. Although a treaty for protecting the ozone layer was strengthened in 1990 to require that many of the problem chemicals be eliminated entirely, those chemicals are so tenacious that they will continue to build up in the atmosphere for the next fifty years. A stronger Clean Air Act, adopted by Congress in 1990, should help lessen the threat of acid rain, but the threat has not disappeared. And by the early 1990s little had been done to address global warming.

In our time, however, the greatest threat to nonhuman life is not pollution; it is the accelerating destruction of the natural world as human beings co-opt the resources of the planet for their own use. To feed ourselves, to survive, or, in the industrial world, to keep the engine of our economies running faster and faster, to make ourselves richer, to sustain our pleasures, our vices, our vanities, we are devouring an ever increasing share of the building blocks of life on earth and, in so doing, depriving other organisms of nourishment and space in which to exist. The great machine created to serve *Homo sapiens* is no longer simply intruding into the garden. It is devouring everything in it.

Although human beings are only one of millions of species on the planet, we have already appropriated for ourselves a grossly disproportionate share of the energy from the sun that is required to sustain life. Peter M. Vitousek of Stanford University and others have estimated that humans throughout the world, growing and consuming crops, raising cattle, cutting down trees, burning forests and grass or otherwise removing vegetation from the surface, now consume some 40 percent of the biomass produced by photosynthesis each year. All other life on earth must survive on the remaining 60 percent. Moreover, as Paul Ehrlich and others have warned, the human population is expected to at least double over the next century. So if our present consumption patterns are not changed, we will take even more of the food generated by solar energy for ourselves and leave little for other forms of life. Ehrlich has asserted that "there is no way that the co-option by one species of almost two-fifths of the earth's annual terrestrial food production could be considered reasonable, in the sense of maintaining the stability of life on this planet."[21]

Despite the Endangered Species Act and other laws and institutions created to protect wildlife, destruction continues in the United States. One particularly disheartening example is the steady decline in our populations of ducks, geese, swans, and other migratory waterfowl as a result of our progressive loss of wetlands. Although overhunting and agriculture sharply reduced the teeming populations of these birds, they remained in relative abundance until the last few decades. Then as coastal swamps and the shallow potholes of the heartland were filled in for homes, industry, and agriculture, the numbers started to plummet. By 1987, the breeding populations of the ten most common duck species had dropped to 30.3 million from

42.7 million in 1955, according to estimates by the Fish and Wildlife Service. And the 1955 populations were, of course, only a fraction of what they had been before the Europeans arrived in North America. Amendments were made to the farm law in 1986 to give farmers incentives to leave potholes and other waterfowl habitat alone. The United States and Canada joined in a last-ditch effort to save the continent's ducks and geese. But the prospects are not encouraging, particularly after the 1991 retreat of President Bush, in the face of heavy pressure from developers, farmers, and other large property holders, from his campaign pledge in 1988 that there would be no further net loss of the nation's wetlands.

If wildlife is in trouble because of habitat destruction in the United States, however, it is in extreme crisis elsewhere. This crisis is directly linked to the rapid disappearance of tropical forests in South and Central America, Africa, and Asia, which are now being cut, bulldozed, or burned at a rate of some 50 million acres a year —an area as big as the state of Washington is vanishing every twelve months. Although tropical forests cover only about 7 percent of the earth's surface, these fecund environments sustain about half its plant and animal species.

To date, about 1.4 million species of plants, animals, insects, fungi, viruses, and other life forms have been identified and classified. But biologists agree that this is only a small fraction of the number of species on earth. Estimates of the total range from a conservative 4.5 million to as many as 30 million. Dr. Edward O. Wilson of Harvard, who, along with the late Dr. Robert MacArthur of Princeton University, developed a widely accepted theory of projecting species loss, has estimated that at the current rate of habitat destruction, the earth is now losing between 4,000 and 6,000 species a year. "That is a rock bottom, minimum, ultraconservative estimate for the rain forest areas," Dr. Wilson noted. "But that is about 10,000 times the natural extinction rate. And the real number is undoubtedly much bigger."[22] Moreover, the rate of extinction is rapidly accelerating as more forest and other rich habitats such as coral reefs are destroyed. The biologist Peter Raven, director of the Missouri Botanical Garden in St. Louis, has estimated that 25 percent of the earth's species could be wiped out over the next three decades due to the loss of habitat and human preemption of the biomass that sustains life.

The world has undergone what Dr. Wilson describes as five great "extinction spasms" over the last 600 million years in which a large proportion of life forms were wiped out. The last such spasm came at the end of the Cretaceous period, 65 million years ago, when the dinosaurs disappeared from the face of the earth. "We're now in the middle of the sixth such spasm, there is no question about it," Dr. Wilson said. "But this one is human caused, and it can be human stopped!"

Dr. Wilson has called the destruction of species through human activity, and the loss of biological and genetic diversity such destruction brings with it, "the folly our descendants are least likely to forgive us"—worse even than energy depletion, economic collapse, limited nuclear war, or conquest by a totalitarian government.

Without even knowing they are there, we are eliminating not only potential sources of food, medicines, and other useful commodities but also the very building blocks of evolution. "We are," said Wilson, noting that there is more genetic information in a single organism than in an entire encyclopedia, "in the process of burning down our biological libraries—these are the libraries of Alexandria burning before us."

To Jay Hair, president of the National Wildlife Federation, the importance of saving species was changed from an abstraction to a dramatic reality by a personal tragedy narrowly averted. In 1984, Hair's nine-year-old daughter, Whitney, came down with a mysterious illness. She developed a lump in her groin and spots on her lung but, despite exploratory surgery, doctors could not diagnose her malady. Hair spent 109 nights in a row with her at the Duke University hospital as she grew sicker and sicker. One Monday morning, the doctors told Hair that though they still could not tell what was wrong his daughter was so ill she would probably die within four to five days.

"Four to five days. That is Monday to Friday. My daughter,

who is deaf, communicated to me that she knew she was very sick and she was saying, 'Am I going to die? What's it going to be like?' . . . But that Friday arrived and a rash had appeared on her chest. So, just in desperation, they biopsied the rash and sent it to the head pathologist at Duke . . . He said this is a very rare disease . . . called T-cell lymphoma, a type of blood cancer. It's never been reported in children. It's only a disease of adults and it's always terminal in adults."

But the hospital checked the data on the disease on its computer and found that two children at Sloan-Kettering in New York were being treated for the same illness with an experimental drug. The doctors told Hair that the drug would probably kill his daughter but there was no other choice.

"Well, to make a long story short, Whitney is a sophomore in high school this year, and this past fall she was declared completely, clinically cured, which means she is not in remission; she is cured of her cancer. The drug that saved her life was derived from a plant called the rosy periwinkle, which was found only in the forested area of Madagascar. Since the drug was discovered, ninety percent of Madagascar's forest has been destroyed and 100 percent of all the native habitat of the rosy periwinkle is gone forever. As a scientist I could talk to you for hours about the organization of complex communities and energy flow and all of that, but I could not tell you anything that made a bigger impression on me on why it is important to save tropical forests."[23]

Led by Drs. Wilson, Raven, and Thomas Lovejoy, an ornithologist who is assistant secretary of the Smithsonian Institution for external affairs, a growing number of scientists have been calling for a massive global effort to find, classify, and analyze for their genetic potential as many as possible of the earth's undiscovered organisms before they are wiped out forever. Dr. Wilson thinks that such an effort should be a major priority for our government and carried out on the scale of the Manhattan Project, the crash program to develop an atomic bomb in World War II. The United States ought to make the preservation of global biodiversity a major objective of its foreign policy and international aid programs, Wilson said, adding, "Our government needs to use all of its influence to bring about environmental revolutions in those countries that most need it." If only a fraction of the "staggering amounts" the United States has been spending on foreign military assistance were converted into environmental assistance, it could have enormous impact, he contended.

Dr. Lovejoy thinks some of the money spent on the U.S. space program could more appropriately be diverted to mapping the biosphere. A good start on such a program could be made, he said, for half the money spent to develop and launch the troubled Hubble space telescope.[24]

In the United States and many other countries, the loss of species is recognized and lamented and efforts have been started to save life. Natural areas are set aside as preserves. Seed banks are maintained to preserve plant species for use by future generations. Degraded wildlife habitat is occasionally restored. But the catastrophic loss of life—the "extinction spasm" that is now starting to shudder across the planet—cannot be addressed by any one nation. If we are to prevent millions of plant and animal species—a genetic legacy of incalculable worth—from being snuffed out like candles in a windstorm, strong, concerted, cooperative action must be taken on an international basis.

AVERTING

GLOBAL

DISASTER

The Earth is one but the world is not.
—Report of the World Commission on
Environment and Development

In the late 1980s, I wrote an article about the Massachusetts Audubon Society's work to preserve forest land in the tiny Central American country of Belize, thousands of miles away, in order to protect that country's winter habitat for the songbirds that nested in Massachusetts and elsewhere in North America in the spring and summer. As more and more of Central and South America was deforested for timber or to open lands for cattle ranches and farms, places to shelter a wide variety of migratory birds during the winter were becoming increasingly scarce. Each year, fewer warblers, thrushes, flycatchers, and other songbirds were returning to New England and much of the rest of North America because fewer were able to find food and shelter at the southern end of their range.

I had written many articles about the destruction of tropical forests and the consequent loss of biological diversity—even articles about the loss of wintering habitat for North American birds. But focusing on the fact that deforestation in Latin America was reducing the bird population in Massachusetts—*my* birds—made the issue suddenly very real and personal. The summer warblers of the Berkshires were my canary in the coal mine. Even more, that discovery placed on my doorstep gave clear evidence that environmental problems thousands of miles away had become my problem as well. The deteriorating state of the global environment, until then an abstraction, had become missing flashes of color in the trees around my house.

In their book *Only One Earth*, published in 1972, Barbara Ward and René Dubos observed that humans inhabit two worlds—the natural world of plants and animals, soil, air, and water, and the created world of institutions and artifacts.

> But today, as we enter the last decades of the twentieth century, there is a growing sense that something fundamental and possibly irrevocable is happening to man's relations with both his worlds. In the last two hundred years, and with staggering acceleration in the last twenty-five, the power, extent, and depth of man's interventions in the natural order seem to presage a revolutionary new epoch in human history, perhaps the most revolutionary the mind can conceive. Men seem, on a planetary scale, to be substituting the controlled for the uncontrolled, the fabricated for the unworked, the planned for the random. And they are doing so with a speed and depth of intervention unknown in any previous age of history.[1]

In the last decade of the century the pace and extent of ecological change caused by humanity are accelerating rapidly. The changes in the atmosphere now being made by pollutants from industrial activities, for example, have been described by an international panel of scientists as "the greatest uncontrolled experiment in history."

As Ward and Dubos wrote in 1972: "This is the hinge of history at which we stand, the door of the future opening onto a crisis more sudden, more global, more inescapable and more bewildering than any ever encountered by the human species and one which will take decisive shape in the life span of children already born."[2]

On April 22, 1990, more than 200 million people around the globe observed the twentieth anniversary of Earth Day. It was an amazing demonstration of international awareness that the world is at risk, that Mother Earth was being dangerously abused by her own children. People turned out on every continent to show their concern. The celebration was at once high-spirited and somber, with many participants troubled by the realization that the gravest threats to the global environment lie ahead.

In much of the developing world, population growth, poverty, and the destruction of the environment are intertwined. The 1987 report of the World Commission on Environment and Development, *Our Common Future*, found that population and economic issues could not be separated from environmental issues because poor people struggling to survive will destroy forests and agricultural land to scratch out a bare means of existence. When they can no longer do so they crowd into already congested and polluted cities.[3]

In North America, Europe, and Japan, however, it is not so much excessive demands on domestic resources—although that happens—but excessive consumption and polluting technologies that are mainly responsible for the decline of the global environment. The United States and the former Soviet Union alone, for example, produce 45 percent of the carbon dioxide that is creating the greenhouse effect. Over 90 percent of the chemicals that are destroying atmospheric ozone are produced and consumed in the industrialized countries. The demand of Americans for fast-food hamburgers has caused wide swaths of tropical forest to be cleared for cattle ranching. More forest is destroyed to supply logs for the elegant homes and furniture of affluent Japanese.

That is the situation today. But as Brazil's environment minister, José A. Lutzenberger, asked in 1990, what happens forty or fifty years from now when the world population reaches 10 billion and the average person in China, India, Indonesia, Nigeria, and elsewhere demands an automobile as Americans, Germans, and Japanese now do? Instead of the 350 million cars now choking roads and polluting air throughout the world, there could be close to 7 billion automobiles in use. "Suicidal," Lutzenberger said. "Unthinkable."[4]

To a growing number of thoughtful people in the United States and elsewhere, the threats to the global environment now represent the gravest long-term danger to the security of nations, particularly with the sudden end of the Cold War in the late 1980s and the collapse of the system of armed bipolarity that divided East and West for nearly half a century. The internal disorders, military clashes, and mass flight of refugees that can be traced, at least in part, to the inability of stressed ecological systems to support swollen populations in the Horn of Africa, the Sahel, Haiti, Central America, are probably a preview of environmental unrest in the coming decades. The Persian Gulf war of 1991 was partly a result of the failure of the United States and other industrial nations to end their dependence on oil, which contributes so much to global environmental problems. In an environmentally threatened world, strength of arms bolstered by a strong economy and firm alliances no longer suffices to assure the security of any nation, no matter how rich or powerful.

In a speech to the State Department's Foreign Service Institute in 1990, Peter H. Gleick of the Pacific Institute for Studies in Development, Environment, and Security contended that "by focusing solely on military threats to security, nations ignore other internal and external threats that may be even more threatening—threats such as conflicts over limited fresh water resources, access to increasingly scarce mineral resources and conflicts caused by massive population migrations and refugees." Speaking to the United Nations in 1988, Mikhail S. Gorbachev, then the Soviet leader, called for a new international emphasis on "ecological security." Writing in the journal *Foreign Affairs* in the spring of 1989, Jessica Tuchman Mathews, vice president of the World Resources Institute and a former member of the National Security Council staff, found that "environmental strains that transcend national borders are already beginning to break down the sacred boundaries of national sovereignty."[5]

The main body of the 1987 report of the World Commission

on Environment and Development begins by observing dolefully, "The Earth is one but the world is not."[6] The record of international cooperation to protect the environment is indeed a slender one, providing but a flimsy diplomatic and institutional foundation from which to confront the profound threats facing the planet. Until World War II, the few international environmental agreements that were negotiated were bilateral or involved a small number of countries dealing with a specific problem—a migratory bird treaty here, a water-use compact for a river basin there. Several efforts were made to organize broad cooperation to protect land, water, and wildlife, but they led nowhere.

Beginning with the creation of the United Nations in 1945, the postwar era has been marked by the expansion of multilateral cooperation for the maintenance of peace and economic security. But this spirit of collaboration did not extend to environmental matters —international diplomacy barely acknowledged that such issues existed. For many years the environment had no place on the agendas of the UN and its ancillary bodies, or of the World Bank and the regional development banks created by the Bretton Woods system, at summit meetings of the major powers, or anywhere else in the mainstream of international politics.

In the postwar years, the United States made significant strides in dealing with domestic environmental threats. But the U.S. Agency for International Development and, for that matter, U.S. foreign policy in general gave these issues very short shrift. In 1974, Congress imposed a Bureau of Oceans and Environmental and Scientific Affairs on an unreceptive State Department, which for many years proceeded to treat the bureau as an unwanted stepchild.

But the spreading menace of pollution, the accelerating destruction of natural resources, and the pressures of population and poverty on the earth's support systems could not indefinitely be swept under the rug. To confront the issue at last, the United Nations in 1972 convened a Conference on the Human Environment in Stockholm. The conference was not an unalloyed success. Some of the developing countries expressed the fear that environmental protection was yet another ploy by the rich industrial countries to keep them in a subservient economic position. But, with the United States in the vanguard, the conference did focus the attention of the international community on the environment. For the first time the problems of economic development were linked to environmental problems. Most important, the conference authorized the creation of the United Nations Environmental Program—UNEP.

Chronically and severely short of funds and staff, restrained by the labyrinthine United Nations bureaucracy, hamstrung by squabbling among regional factions of its member nations, UNEP has nonetheless helped to awaken the world to the imminent dangers to the environment and to prod sluggish governments into action. Under Dr. Maurice F. Strong, a Canadian industrialist who was its first director, and Dr. Mustafa K. Tolba, an Egyptian biologist who has been its director for nearly twenty years, UNEP has played an important role in monitoring environmental pollution around the world and in acting as a stimulus to international action to address ecological perils. But its mandate and its capabilities are severely restricted.

The initial efforts of international diplomacy to confront environmental problems were slow and stumbling. There was, however, some notable progress, such as the 1973 Convention on International Trade in Endangered Species, which sharply reduced commerce in animals and plants threatened with extinction. Other multilateral agreements included the London Dumping Convention, which established rules to protect the oceans from wastes. Governments in Europe signed the Convention on Long Range Transboundary Air Pollution in 1979. At the time of the Stockholm conference, only 11 nations had any governmental environmental agency. Ten years later 106 countries had governmental institutions devoted to the environment, 70 of them in developing countries. At the second United Nations Conference on the Human Environment, in Nairobi in May 1982, Noel Brown, the North American director of UNEP, said, "In ten years, environmentalism has become a global value."[7]

But the response of the international community remains inadequate to the gravity of the crisis.

One reason for this failure was that in the 1980s the United States to a great degree abdicated its role as leader of the international community's efforts to address global environmental problems. At the UN conference in Nairobi, it was apparent that a startling role reversal had taken place. Speakers from developing countries stressed that protecting the environment was necessary to enable them to expand their economies and improve the lives of their people. But representatives of several of the industrialized countries, most notably the United States, downplayed the need for international action. Anne M. Burford, administrator of the U.S. Environmental Protection Agency under Ronald Reagan and head of the U.S. delegation, admonished the conference to rely on the workings of the marketplace to solve their environmental problems.

Washington did maintain a presence, however. Ambassador Richard E. Benedick and EPA administrator Lee M. Thomas, who served later in the administration, in fact played a preeminent role in forging an international agreement for protecting the earth's atmospheric ozone from destruction by industrial chemicals. The ozone protocol was signed in Montreal in 1987. But the Reagan administration was divided even on this frightening issue. Interior Secretary Donald P. Hodel offered his considered opinion that instead of going through the expensive process of replacing the chemicals that caused the problem, the dangers could be avoided if people would simply wear hats, sunglasses, and suntan lotion to protect themselves from ultraviolet radiation. Mr. Hodel's ludicrous proposal was greeted with a wave of scorn, dismay, and amusement that may have helped build public support in the United States for strong international action.

Through most of the 1980s, the great void in international leadership on environmental problems left by Washington's abdication was filled, to a surprisingly large extent, by the efforts of private environmental and research groups in the United States and around the world. These groups monitored global environmental trends, kept the public and governments informed of developments, maintained an international communications network, developed policy alternatives, aroused public opinion, and prodded often reluctant governments into action. The environmental groups had demanded a place at the table of international policy making ever since the Stockholm conference in 1972. They were the sober, disapproving presence at the wasteful feast, refusing to let the global political establishment ignore the havoc being caused by the excesses of production and consumption.

Old-line conservation groups such as the World Wildlife Fund and the International Union for the Conservation of Nature had long been in the forefront of efforts to preserve wildlife and biological diversity on all continents. Newer groups, including the World Resources Institute, the Worldwatch Institute, the Center for Global Change, and Earthscan, assumed a vital role largely unfilled by official national and international institutions by monitoring the condition of the biosphere and its resources and reporting their findings on a regular basis. It was the World Resources Institute, for example, that reported in 1990 that the rate of global deforestation was 50 percent higher than previously realized. Scientists working for private groups, notably Dr. Michael Oppenheimer of the Environmental Defense Fund and Dr. Irving Mintzer of the Center for Global Change, kept a careful eye on emerging scientific information about global warming and the ozone layer and explained the significance of those findings. Rafe Pomerance of the World Resources Institute, David Doniger, Richard Ayres, and David Hawkins of the Natural Resources Defense Council, and Daniel Becker of the Sierra Club, among others, persisted in keeping the media, Congress, federal agencies, and the international community aware of the emerging threat to the atmosphere and the need to react to it.

International organizations such as Greenpeace and Friends of the Earth dramatized the global issues. Greenpeace experienced an enormous surge of support and growth around the world after 1985, when French agents blew up one of its ships, the *Rainbow Warrior*, killing Fernando Pereira, a photographer on board. The ship had been protesting France's nuclear testing in the Pacific. Bruce Rich and Scott Hajost of the Environmental Defense Fund, David Werth and Thomas Stoel of the NRDC, Barbara Bramble of the National

Wildlife Federation, and Frances Spivey-Weber of the National Audubon Society were among those who kept up pressure on the World Bank, AID, and other international development institutions to force them to stop merely paying lip service to the need to bring environmental considerations into their lending and grant programs and finally to do something about it. The Global Tomorrow Coalition, with Don Lesh as its director, provided a forum for bringing together the diverse groups and causes involved in international environmental issues. Many organizations continued to sound the tocsin about the threat of an uncontrolled global birthrate, particularly in the poorer countries. In the 1980s, private environmental groups increasingly served as an effective shadow government dealing with policies involving pollution and natural resources.

The environmentalists also were allied with a few courageous academic and government scientists, including Dr. Stephen Schneider of the National Council for Atmospheric Research and Dr. James E. Hansen of NASA, who sought to awaken the public and government to the reality of the greenhouse effect. Dr. F. Sherwood Rowland, one of the scientists who discovered the threat to the earth's ozone shield, actively pressed the American government to respond to the threat.

In Europe, over the past two decades, the environmental movement took a different historical tack. In addition to working outside government, many greens in West Germany and other European countries entered the arena of electoral politics and won seats in several parliaments, including the parliament of the European Community. While the number of elected greens remained low, their influence on policy and public opinion was greater than the votes they commanded within governments. Cities choked with pollution, the *Waldsterben*, or death of the forests, in Central Europe, the rapid erosion of ancient buildings and monuments, the massive spill of chemicals into the Rhine, and other insults were awakening Europeans to the overflowing cauldron of environmental ills bubbling in their midst. By the late 1980s, Western Europeans were looking up from their postwar preoccupation with growing rich and enjoying life to discover that their binge of getting and spending was taking a devastating and unacceptable toll on the physical world around them.

In Eastern Europe and the Soviet Union, environmental activists were the advance guard of the democratic revolution that changed the face of geopolitics in the late 1980s. Environmental abuses in that part of Europe were among the worst in the world. Anxiety and anger over the poisoned air and water turning much of the region into something resembling an ecological dead zone grew so intense that even the repressive Communist regimes were unable to put down protest against the abuse of the environment. The community and national groups that formed in opposition to nuclear power plants in the Baltic states, to hydroelectric projects in the Balkans, to the pollution of Lake Baikal and other ecological abuses in the former Soviet Union, were forerunners of insistent demands for freedom and democracy in Eastern Europe.

It is in the poor countries of the world, however, that the activist grass-roots environmental groups are particularly astonishing and significant. They are astonishing because, as Alan B. Durning of the Worldwatch Institute noted, poverty, whether in hungry peasant villages in Asia or in wretched urban slums in Africa, tends to make people passive and averse to taking risks. Nevertheless, Durning contends, a new generation of community organizations, formed largely for self-help, constitute a rising if "unnoticed tide" of activism in the developing countries. Villagers in Senegal worried about the spread of deserts into their cultivated fields, women along the Ganges watching their babies die of dehydration brought on by diarrhea, the native peoples of the Amazon seeing the forest, their ancient home and only source of subsistence, disappear in fires set by outside developers— these people know that they are victims of environmental assault. "To them," Durning wrote, "creeping degradation of ecosystems has meant declining health, failing livelihoods, and lengthening workdays. But they are not standing idle. In villages, neighborhoods, and shanty towns around the world, people are coming together to discuss and respond to the tightening ecological and economic conditions that confront them."[8]

Nobody knows precisely how many people are involved in these grass-roots organizations, but their numbers are estimated to be at least in the tens of millions and could conceivably be in the hundreds of millions. Collectively, however, these people represent a ground swell that even apathetic or corrupt politicians cannot ignore. The passion and resolution of Chico Mendes, willing to die to save the rubber trees of Brazil's Acre Province, and the Chipka villagers of India who protect trees from the chain saw with their bodies represent a powerful political and moral force that must be reckoned with. Together with their counterparts in the developed world, these community groups are helping to achieve environmental reform on a global scale.

By the summer of 1988, when Dr. James E. Hansen of NASA told a Senate committee that the greenhouse effect was probably already upon us, when heat and drought plagued North America, floods killed thousands in Bangladesh, and African nations warned that they would no longer tolerate being used as a dumping ground for toxic wastes from Europe and America, it was apparent that damage to the environment had become of global concern and environmentalism was well on its way to becoming a global movement. Then, of course, political leaders slowly developed an interest in environmental threats and began to respond to them.

While perhaps less dramatic than the end of the Cold War and the tearing down of the Berlin Wall in 1989, the sudden intense attention given to environmental concerns by world leaders may well prove over the long run to be an equally significant turning point in the history of nations. Until the late 1980s, ecological issues had been on the periphery of international politics. Almost overnight, it seemed, global warming, acid rain, the ozone shield, biological diversity, and other environmental issues had moved to the center of the diplomatic stage.

In a powerful speech to the United Nations in December 1988,

Mikhail S. Gorbachev mentioned the environment more than twenty times and compared its degradation to such threats as war, hunger, and disease. In 1989 Prime Minister Margaret Thatcher, who had long remained icily aloof from ecological concerns, made a speech to Britain's Royal Society in which she called the protection of the balance of nature "one of the great challenges of the late twentieth century." French President François Mitterrand, host of the 1989 annual meeting of heads of the world's leading industrial powers, dubbed the gathering in Paris the "green summit." The communiqué of that summit gave unprecedented prominence to pollution and the preservation of natural resources.

Even the year before the "green summit," Rafe Pomerance, a veteran environmental activist, said, "We are seeing a greening of geopolitics."[9]

The verdant political rhetoric was accompanied by intensified international scientific and diplomatic activity involving the environment. Following up its success with the Montreal protocol on the ozone layer, UNEP, in cooperation with the World Meteorological Organization, another UN body, created in November 1988 the Intergovernmental Panel on Climate Change to begin organizing the international response to global warming. The goal was a treaty to bring about international cooperation to reduce the magnitude of climate change and to slow its onset.

Almost weekly, it seemed, there was a major international gathering to discuss solutions to the global environmental dilemma. In March 1989, the heads of seventeen governments and representatives of seven other countries met in The Hague to discuss how the international community could address global warming and other broad environmental threats. The meeting produced a "Declaration of The Hague," which called for a new supranational authority that would make the decisions needed to deal with threats to the earth. Within a year, forty nations endorsed the declaration. Linda Starke noted in her book *Signs of Hope*, published in 1990, that while the declaration is not a binding document, "it is an important step in a new direction.

It means that forty governments have now indicated they would contemplate giving over some of their sovereignty. This is the heaviest piece of baggage the nations of the world need to shed."[10]

The environment-development dilemma was addressed in 1987 by the highly influential report of the UN-sponsored World Commission on Environment and Development, usually referred to as the Brundtland Commission after its chairwoman, Gro Harlem Brundtland, then between terms as Prime Minister of Norway. The solution offered by the report was "sustainable development." It means simply finding ways to assure steady, equitable economic growth that will enhance rather than damage and deplete the resources and support system on which human and all other life on earth depends.

Sustainable development was not an idea that emerged newly born from the womb of the commission. Sustainability of resources, after all, was the central intellectual premise underlying conservationism. Joan Martin-Brown, director of UNEP's Washington office, created the Bolton Institute for a Sustainable Future in 1971, a non-profit group dedicated, among other things, to training teachers and students to devise environmental and energy programs that could enhance sustained economic development. Ms. Martin-Brown, one of the most influential and effective of the environmental activists and thinkers during the 1970s and 1980s, also was among the first to emphasize that the poor in this country were the chief victims of pollution. As early as 1981, Lester R. Brown (no relation to Joan Martin-Brown) published his widely read book *Building a Sustainable Society*, in which he argued that the world was already placing intolerable pressures on its soil, water, air, forests, and other resources."[11]

With the Brundtland report, however, the notion of sustainable development made a decisive breakthrough into the global consciousness. The report was prepared by a commission made up of representatives from twenty-one countries, reflecting a broad spectrum of East-West and North-South economic, political, and cultural perspectives.

The message of the report was simple and not really new. The planet is in the grip of two "interlocking crises"—one environmental and one economic. Population growth, economic expansion, and technology were depleting resources and creating pollution in ways that profoundly affected the natural world. At the same time, this environmental degradation was increasingly an obstacle to economic growth, particularly in the developing countries, where poverty contributed to runaway population growth and destructive overuse of resources. "Ecology and economy are becoming ever more interwoven—locally, regionally, and globally—into a seamless net of cause and effect."[12]

In effect, the Brundtland report proposed what has come to be called a "global bargain." Under its terms, the rich countries of the world, which consume the bulk of the world's resources and, up to now, have been responsible for most of the pollution that has put the earth's support systems at risk, would preempt less of the world's wealth and reduce their contribution to the degradation of the biosphere. The richer nations would also make financial and technological transfers to the developing countries to enable them to raise the standard of living of their citizens. This would enable third-world countries to slow population growth, to expand their economies in ways that would preserve their land, water, wood, and other vital resources, and to industrialize in ways that do not add to the already frightening burdens on the earth's life support systems. "The global bargain," insisted Mustafa Tolba of UNEP, "is a clear-cut cooperative effort in which every human being in the world must be included, every country. North, South, East, West must be involved in the negotiation and bargaining on an equal footing and with a commitment that they will really honor what they agree on."[13]

Because the industrialized countries would be transferring wealth to the developing countries, the global bargain might seem, at first glance, to be one-sided. In the long run, however, it would be a bargain, indeed, for the United States, the countries of Europe, Japan, and other affluent nations. By the end of the century, the rich countries will account for only 20 percent of the world population. If the explosive growth of the third-world countries is not checked, the needs of their people for mere survival would overwhelm the biological, chemical, and physical systems on which all life, including the lives of the affluent, depend. To try to mitigate that disaster after the fact would be enormously expensive, assuming that it could be done at all. The global bargain, therefore, is what Jessica Tuchman Mathews calls a "division of labor" in which the rich would reduce their per capita consumption and pollution and the poor would lower their fertility rates and their destructive use of renewable resources. It would be an agreement to save the world.

That bargain has not yet been struck. Despite growing apprehension and quickening international diplomatic activity, the world's old ways of thinking about and acting on international issues have yet to be changed significantly.

Some leaders of developing countries still fear that an international environmental compact would be a new strategy by the industrialized world to keep them in economic subjugation and to erode their hard-won sovereignty.

While there is growing recognition within the industrialized North of the need to face up to its responsibilities for protecting the global environment, there is still reluctance, particularly in the United States, to commit the adequate economic resources and make the sacrifices necessary to seal the global bargain. Dr. Tolba of UNEP estimates that the current costs of international action to protect the environment would be about $30 billion a year.[14] Some estimates are much higher. The late Indian Prime Minister Rajiv Gandhi proposed that all nations, except the very poorest, contribute one-tenth of 1 percent of the gross national product each year to a global environmental fund. And, of course, much more than just monetary contributions will be needed. The terms of trade between nations would have to be adjusted to eliminate or reduce the current biases against countries whose economies depend largely on the export of raw materials. Privileged nations would have to voluntarily reduce their consumption of energy and other resources to allow developing countries to consume more. Current political relations will have to be adjusted to permit a more equitable sharing of global power. The lion will have to willingly reduce his share. The lamb must be given a place at the feast. It will not be easy.

Over the long run, environmental issues are increasingly likely to dominate the international political agenda. To meet the threats to their economies, the health of their citizens, and their national security posed by the decline of the global environment, the international community will have to cooperate and, in so doing, surrender some sovereignty. The consequences of global warming, the hole in the ozone layer, deforestation, and mass extinction of life could and should frighten the nations of the world as much as an invasion from Mars, and persuade them to join forces against a common enemy. By the early 1990s, a number of nations, including West Germany, France, Britain, and the Scandinavian countries, seemed ready to lead the world in a sustained, united response to these problems. The United States during the Reagan and Bush administrations, as we shall see, seemed prepared to be left behind.

Environmental isolation is bound, however, to be temporary. The global bargain is truly a global imperative. The problems facing the world are too compelling to be ignored for long. The political, social, and moral power of the growing environmental movement within this country will not long allow the American government to remain on the sidelines in the great task of saving the world. As Gro Harlem Brundtland stated, public opinion must be brought to bear to achieve political leadership strong enough to stand up to the economic forces that are profiting from and thus seeking to retain the status quo in international economic relationships.[15] Where appropriate, environmental organizations and other private institutions will work around the government in Washington to reach international goals through such means as consumer campaigns, boycotts, and debt-for-nature swaps. The 1992 United Nations Conference on Environment and Development in Rio de Janeiro—the "Earth Summit"— offered a rare opportunity for decisive action by the leaders of the international community.

As the second millennium of this era winds down, it is clear that environmentalism is growing among the peoples of the earth and is an increasingly decisive factor in affairs among nations. Whether environmentalism has or will have the strength to avert the grave dangers that now threaten us is a crucial question.

In *Only One Earth*, Ward and Dubos wrote that "the new ecological imperative can give a new vision of where man belongs in his final security and his final sense of dignity and identity."[16]

Let us hope they were right.

Chapter 10

THE

COUNTER-

REVOLUTION

I do not think they will be happy
until the White House looks like a bird's nest.
—Ronald Reagan

President Jimmy Carter appeared to have strong environmental instincts. He placed environmentalists in key federal jobs. He tried to do away with environmentally harmful pork barrel projects, such as unneeded dams and canals. He threw his support behind legislation such as the Alaska National Interest Lands Act and the toxic waste cleanup law that came to be known as the Superfund. His administration began to address international environmental problems such as overpopulation. In 1980, his Council on Environmental Quality, headed by Gus Speth, and the State Department, then led by Secretary of State Edmund Muskie, who had been known as "Mr. Clean" in the Senate because of his dogged insistence on strong environmental legislation, produced a landmark study of world ecological prospects called the Global 2000 report, which warned that "if present trends continue, the world in 2000 will be more crowded, more polluted, less stable ecologically and more vulnerable to disruption than the world we know today."

But Carter's environmental agenda was, to a significant degree, swept aside toward the end of the 1970s. Soaring inflation, unemployment, an energy crisis brought on by an Iranian oil embargo, the politics of budget balancing, and what was perceived to be a growing antipathy to government regulation reduced Congress's willingness to support environmental legislation. As a result, much of the Carter administration's agenda for environmental reform remained unrealized.

To some, it seemed that Carter's retreat on many issues, including stiffer air pollution regulations, signaled the beginning of the end for the era of environmental activism launched on Earth Day. In the late 1970s, attacks on the premises of environmentalism began appearing in print, usually written by conservatives who considered environmental problems to be transitory irritants that would easily be resolved by the marketplace.

One book that received considerable attention, *The Ultimate Resource*, was written by Julian Simon, a business professor who later became a senior fellow of the Heritage Foundation. It dismissed the warnings of the environmentalists as alarmist fantasy.[1] Simon contended that far from being a threat to the world, rapid population growth was a benefit, because human beings are the "ultimate resource" that would use their intelligence and skills to make the world a better place. In a similar vein, *The Resourceful Earth*, edited and in part written by Simon and the futurist Herman Kahn, directly attacked the Global 2000 report. Kahn and Simon and their contributors found that "the world in 2000 will be less crowded (though more populated), less polluted, more stable ecologically and less vulnerable to resource-supply disruption than the world we live in now."[2]

For a while there was a lively debate between the environmentalists, who warned of the dire fate awaiting humanity—the image of Chicken Little comes to mind—and the Panglossian anti-Malthusians such as Simon and Kahn, who insisted that environmental problems were mostly negligible and required no heroic solutions. Unfortunately, as we have seen, empirical evidence showing that the alarmists were right continued to mount.

Opposition to environmentalism, of course, is as old as the movement itself. Those who used public resources to create wealth for themselves—the timber and cattle barons, the mine operators, the oil companies, big agriculture—and industries that regarded air and water as free commodities, as a commons into which they could pour their polluting effluents, predictably and consistently reacted to efforts to control their activities with the tolerance of a nest of angry rattlesnakes. They often were able to enlist the sympathy of the political establishment, which they supported with their money.

But the election of Ronald Reagan and the triumph of right-wing politics effectively brought the federal government to a squealing stop as the chief engine of environmental progress in the United States. Through his appointments to the federal agencies and the judiciary, his budget decisions, and his program of "regulatory reform," Reagan transformed the executive branch from a champion to a foe of environmental protection.

The Reagan administration's philosophy of governance was an odd amalgam of libertarianism and corporate socialism. Reagan and his administration portrayed themselves as conservatives, but it was not the traditional conservatism of the Republican Party, which had a history of conserving lands and resources dating back to the presidency of Theodore Roosevelt.

The Reagan administration reflected a new kind of Republicanism. It turned its back on the party's eastern establishment and embraced the opportunism of Orange County and the Sun Belt and the run-and-gun cowboy capitalism that was to dominate the 1980s. In some ways, the Reagan administration appeared to be seeking a return to the robber baron, survival-of-the-fittest capitalism of the nineteenth century.

A blueprint for a moderate environmental program prepared for President-elect Reagan by a group of mainstream Republicans with environmental experience, including William Ruckelshaus, Russell Train, Nathaniel Reed, Dan Lufkin, and Henry Diamond, was scrapped and the aggressively pro-development recommendations of the right-wing Heritage Foundation were adopted. Even the Heritage

Foundation, however, could not stomach some of the Reagan administration's federally subsidized giveaways of water, coal, timber, and grazing rights and its expenditure of public funds to build dams used by agribusiness.[3] Reagan's government fostered a strange kind of conservatism that bred a world of junk bonds and leveraged buyouts, created the biggest deficit and national debt in the nation's history (to be exceeded by the deficits of the Bush administration), and produced in October 1987 the worst stock market crash since Black Friday of 1929. It was a neo-Keynesian conservatism that drenched the military-industrial establishment in public money and then pleaded fiscal poverty as an excuse for starving environmental and social programs. It was a conservatism that favored plunging ahead with radical technologies such as the breeder reactor and allowed untested and potentially destructive chemicals to remain on the market.

President Reagan read his overwhelming electoral victory as a mandate to get government "off the backs of the people." In the field of environmental regulation, and in many other ways, this translated into getting government off the backs of business and industry by easing or eliminating the anti-pollution rules and removing obstacles to commercial exploitation of the oil, coal, timber, water, grass, and other resources of the public lands. As political scientist Michael E. Kraft noted, when Reagan entered the White House in 1981, "the 'environmental decade' of the 1970's came to an abrupt halt . . . Like true believers in power, the White House seemed to disregard public criticism or consider it of no political consequence. The administration gave free rein to its conservative ideology in every area of environmental and resource policy . . ."[4]

California's environmental record while Reagan was governor was not bad—although he himself had little to do with it. He just was not interested in the issue, appeared not to understand it, and as President was unwilling to let environmental concerns stand in the way of his political agenda, which, in large measure, was aimed at shifting economic power out of the public sector and into private business and industry. He once said that most of the nation's air pollution came from trees. Reagan had nothing against environmental protection as long as it did not require the expenditure of federal funds or interfere with industry's right to pollute or to use the public domain for private profit. When the national environmental groups irritated him by criticizing his policies, he blurted out, "I do not think they will be happy until the White House looks like a bird's nest."[5] In Ronald Reagan's Manichaean outlook on the world, the environmentalists were his enemies because the national organizations had supported Jimmy Carter for the presidency.

Whatever his motives, however, Reagan's policies and especially his appointments constituted the most organized, sustained, and virulent opposition ever encountered by the environmental movement. In effect, he gave a free hand to the many political appointees in key positions throughout his administration who regarded environmental laws and values as an impediment to the free-market system. The tradition of bipartisanship in protecting the nation's environment was brought to an abrupt halt, at least in the executive branch—Congress for the most part continued to cling to the environmental values it had discovered in the 1970s. The democratization of public lands and resources that had begun with Theodore Roosevelt and the Progressive movement was thrown into reverse. The counterrevolution had found its leader.

The Reagan environmental counterrevolution was made manifest in the curious, almost cartoonlike incarnation of one James Gaius Watt. Tall, gaunt, and dressed in funereal black, with glittering eyes and a wolfish smile beneath a shiny bald pate, Watt descended on Washington like an Old Testament prophet bearing sword and scripture. Appointed by the newly elected President Reagan as Secretary of the Interior, Watt had led a right-wing legal foundation that represented businesses in fights against government regulation. He quickly became the leader and symbol of the new administration's efforts to halt and roll back federal activism in protecting the environment. In the name of patriotism, the free market, the Republican Party, and the Christian religion, he introduced policies aimed at

transferring control of public lands and resources to private entrepreneurs at a rate that had not been seen since the great giveaways
of the nineteenth century.

Like the administration he represented, Watt described himself
as a conservative but acted as a radical—radical since his actions
marked a sharp departure from the national policies of previous
decades. Environmentalists, he frequently asserted, had caused the
"pendulum" of public policy to swing too far toward conserving and
away from making efficient use of the nation's resources. He ques-
tioned their motives, suggesting at one point that their real goal was
to overthrow the political system of the United States. To assure
continued economic growth and protect national security, he repeatedly insisted, it was necessary to inventory all public holdings and
then transfer potentially productive holdings to the private sector so
they could be developed for the good of the nation. "I want to change
America," he declared. "I believe we are battling for a form of government under which future generations will live."[6]

Mr. Watt, a Christian fundamentalist acting as if he were leading
a religious crusade to save the nation, was serenely confident that he
was carrying out the bidding of the Almighty. Testifying before the
House Interior Committee about why he was speeding development
of public lands and resources, he replied that there was no point in
conserving resources for posterity because "I do not know how many
future generations we can count on before the Lord returns." To
members of another congressional panel he asserted that he was
changing land and resource policies so drastically because "failure to
know our potential, to inventory our resources, intentionally forbidding proper access to needed resources, limits this nation, dooms us
to shortages and damages our right as a people to dream heroic
dreams." Congressman Tom Lantos, a California Democrat and one
of the more sophisticated and literate members of Congress, noted
dryly, "One man's dream is another man's nightmare. Attila the Hun,
Genghis Khan, Napoleon Bonaparte, Karl Marx and the Ayatollah
Khomeini all had heroic dreams."[7]

Aggressive, bold to the point of recklessness, and clothed in impregnable self-righteousness, Watt did not seek to build a consensus for his policies but went about making changes with all the finesse of a wrecker's ball. Within weeks of taking office in 1981, he announced that he would open the entire billion acres of the Outer Continental Shelf to bidding, exploration, and drilling by oil companies. He offered millions of tons of publicly owned coal to mine operators at what an investigative commission later determined were giveaway prices. He did little to enforce the strip-mine law. He tried, unsuccessfully, to open wilderness areas to energy development and encouraged economic activity in the federal wildlife refuges. Consistent with his views that property is best used in private rather than public hands, he declined to spend money authorized by Congress to buy additional land for the National Park System. He tried to make the National Park Service subservient to political control and sought to give the private concessionaires who ran the hotels, restaurants, and gift shops increased authority in operating the parks and making park policy. He pitched in enthusiastically to make a success of President Reagan's "privatization" program—an effort to sell off as much as 30 million acres of public lands as well as other property in order to raise billions to lower the national debt. When real estate operators made it clear that they did not want so much property dumped on the market, and the privatization effort foundered, Mr. Watt said he had never been in favor of the program. He purged the Interior Department of civil servants he considered ideologically out of step and boasted that he was forcing the bureaucracy to "yield to my blows."[8]

But James Watt was no odd man out, no loose cannon on the deck of Ronald Reagan's ship of state. Watt's agenda was also Reagan's agenda. His policies were faithfully tailored to carry out the President's plans for shifting the balance of power away from the public interest to the private interest. But Watt's provocative style brought him wide notoriety and made him the focus of much of the unhappiness and anger generated by the Reagan administration's environmental policies. Within months, the National Wildlife Federation, the biggest and one of the most cautious of the national conservation groups, whose membership included a large proportion of Republicans, was calling for his resignation. The Sierra Club and Friends of the Earth circulated a nationwide petition for his removal, which attracted millions of signatures. With derogatory, off-the-cuff remarks he offended liberals, Indians, blacks, Jews, the handicapped, environmentalists, and pop music fans—the latter with a statement about the bad influence he said would be exercised at a Fourth of July concert on the Washington, D.C., Mall by the Beach Boys, a popular singing group. Although he had allies among the big western mining, ranching, and energy interests—the Sagebrush Rebels—and was supported by some western state governments, and although he was popular among the ultraconservatives of the Republican Party, it was soon clear that Watt was a political liability to the President. By October 1983, he was forced by the White House to resign amid a fire storm of criticism.

James Watt was only one of many Reagan appointees who had represented the interests of the very industries they were intended to regulate and were ideological or financial allies of those industries. The environmentalists repeatedly charged that the President's environmental appointees were "foxes guarding the henhouse."

As head of the EPA, Reagan installed Mrs. Anne M. Gorsuch —later Anne Burford after she married Robert Burford, a rancher and mining engineer who came to Washington at the same time to take over the Interior Department's Bureau of Land Management. Both had been members of a clique, self-styled "the crazies," within the Colorado state legislature, which consistently fought against federal environmental regulation. Both of them, along with Watt, were recommended by Joseph Coors, the Colorado brewer, a friend of Reagan's who had extensive mining and energy interests in the West that made use of federal resources. Coors was a founder of the Mountain States Legal Foundation, which Watt had headed before taking over the Interior Department.[9]

A bright, articulate, and attractive woman with a manner that projected no-nonsense efficiency, Mrs. Burford came to Washington with firm ideas about changing the environmental policies of the federal government but virtually no knowledge about how the federal government operated. "She had no management experience, no experience in Washington, D.C., and no in-depth knowledge of environmental policy,"[10] said J. Clarence (Terry) Davies, an officer of the Conservation Foundation who later became assistant administrator of the EPA for policy during the Bush administration. Upon assuming command of the EPA, Burford proclaimed that her function would be to help advance the Reagan administration's goal of "industrial revitalization." She said that she wanted to ease the regulatory "overburden" that the environmental laws had placed on industry and that she was not interested in how many cases the agency filed against violators of the law because that amounted to no more than "bean counting."[11]

Mistrustful of the career professionals on the agency's staff, Mrs. Burford surrounded herself with political appointees, many selected by the White House, who shared her ideological perspective and, in many cases, came straight out of the industries the agency was intended to regulate. They included Robert M. Perry, who came from the Exxon Corporation, as general counsel, and Frank A. Shepherd, a lawyer who represented General Motors, as associate administrator for enforcement. As special assistants she had Thornton Field and James Sanderson, both lawyers who had represented the Coors interests. Rita Lavelle, who had worked as a public affairs executive for Aerojet General Corporation, which the agency was supposed to be requiring to clean up its toxic wastes, was named assistant administrator in charge of the agency's toxic waste programs. Many of the experienced career officials in the agency quit in disgust or were forced to resign. Those who remained hunkered down and tried not to do anything that would arouse the ire of the political executioner. A hand-lettered sign hanging in the back of the office of a middle-level official summed up the prevailing mood. It said: "No Good Deed Goes Unpunished."[12]

Burford eventually came to appreciate the talent and dedication of the civil servants at the EPA, or so she claimed in *Are You Tough Enough?*, a memoir of her tenure at the agency. By the time she did, however, it was too late. Ideological arrogance, indifference to due process, favoritism to industry, and the political appointees' antagonism to regulation soon led the agency into deep trouble. Participants in a meeting in Burford's office reported that she had intimated to executives of an oil-refining company that they would not be prosecuted if they ignored the rules requiring a reduction of lead in gasoline. The agency planned to suspend a regulation forbidding hazardous liquid wastes in landfills, allowing the disposal of such wastes to continue, particularly in a landfill outside Denver which was heavily used by the Coors Company to dump hazardous wastes.[13]

In 1982, Congress began a series of investigations into the agency's operations, most of them concerning the Superfund law. It found evidence of cronyism with industry, illegal private meetings with representatives of regulated companies, and sweetheart deals in which chemical waste dumpers were allowed to settle with the agency at a small fraction of what it would cost to clean up the dangerous mess they had created. When Mrs. Burford, acting on instructions from the White House Office of Legal Counsel, refused to turn over documents sought by congressional investigators, she was cited for contempt of Congress.

To borrow a phrase from the Watergate years, Mrs. Burford was left by the White House to twist slowly, slowly in the wind. The Justice Department told her it would not represent her in the contempt proceedings, even though she had incurred the wrath of Congress by following the orders of the President. In March 1983, she resigned, at least temporarily broken in spirit. More than twenty other political appointees of the agency had to quit. Rita Lavelle was sentenced to six months in prison for lying to Congress, although of all the Reagan appointees at the agency she was probably the most naive. Burford and Lavelle both suspected that they bore the brunt of the scandal because they were women.

By the time Burford departed, morale at the EPA was shattered. Much of the professional talent had left. Its programs were in shambles. Its credibility with Congress, the media, and the public had evaporated. The agency had certainly been taken off the back of industry.

But the dismantling of the environmental agency also produced a strong reaction from Congress and from the American public, which continued to support environmental protection even while it accepted other Reagan administration initiatives to reduce the size and scope of government. The scandal at the EPA proved to be the most serious political threat faced by Reagan during his first term. He was forced to bring William D. Ruckelshaus, the first EPA administrator, back to the agency to restore order. Ruckelshaus, who had resigned as Deputy Attorney General rather than fire Watergate special prosecutor Archibald Cox during the 1974 "Saturday Night Massacre," enjoyed a reputation for integrity and independence. He managed to bring a measure of stability to the agency and to reduce public distrust. But serious, perhaps permanent damage had been done to the EPA and its reputation.

Two years after she was forced from office, Anne Burford, still smarting from the shabby treatment she had received at the hands of the White House, said that the Reagan administration "has no commitment to the environment and no environmental policy."[14]

It was not just the EPA. In the Reagan years, most of the federal offices responsible for the environment became foxes' dens for profit-making special interests. These political foxes did not have to sneak into the henhouses through a hole in the floor. They were handed the key to the front door and turned loose on the chickens.

At the Department of the Interior, Robert Burford, who as a rancher grazed cattle by permit on public lands for a low fee, became head of the Bureau of Land Management, which administers nearly 400 million acres of range, forest, and desert land in the West. Burford divested himself of his ranching interests when he took office, but at least some of those interests were taken over by members of his family. Burford made some improvements in the conduct of BLM affairs, including computerizing the massive land records that dated back to George Washington's time. But most of his actions strongly favored nd other exploitive industries over other users of the range.

ith partial success, to relieve BLM employees of respon-

managing the public lands and turn over management to ranchers who held grazing permits. The theory or, at least, the explanation was that the ranchers would find it in their own best interests to protect the land. But as Garrett Hardin pointed out in *The Tragedy of the Commons*, those who use public property for economic purposes try to maximize their own profits without regard to the future of the property. Burford encouraged profligate use of the range by keeping grazing fees below what ranchers would have to pay to pasture their cattle and sheep on private lands.

These arrangements pleased the Sagebrush Rebels, but they outraged small ranchers who did not have access to subsidized grazing, as well as local communities and conservationists who saw the range and streambeds degraded by overgrazing. Recreational users of the public domain and conservation groups also charged that the land agency was being managed against their interests.

Most of the other bureaus at Interior were headed by men like Burford who came out of the industries that had financial interests in having the use of federal lands and resources. Before Watt was forced to resign, he boasted that he had imposed such tight control over the bureaus by his appointments, his regulations, his operating manuals, and other bureaucratic tools that his policies would be embedded in the department for years to come.

Donald P. Hodel, who ran the department for most of the Reagan years after Watt left, while less controversial and confrontational than his predecessor, had pretty much the same agenda. Hodel, who as head of the Bonneville Power Administration had presided over a regional power plan relying heavily on nuclear energy that became a financial fiasco in the Pacific Northwest, had been Watt's under secretary and then later Secretary of Energy. The Sagebrush Rebellion eventually petered out because the "rebels" were handed what they wanted by a compliant Interior Department: virtually limitless access to federal lands and resources at bargain basement prices.

Reagan's Assistant Agriculture Secretary in charge of the national forests was John Crowell, who had been vice president and general counsel of the Louisiana Pacific Corporation, the biggest purchaser of timber from the public forests. Crowell, departing from the principle of sustained-yield harvest that had prevailed in the Forest Service since the days of Gifford Pinchot, called for a massive increase in the cut from the national forests and was thwarted only by a sluggish market for lumber. He tried to block transfers of national forest land to the national wilderness system and greatly increased the number of road miles within the forests. Crowell also set new records for subsidized sales of timber from the national forests. The Forest Service lost hundreds of millions of taxpayer dollars a year selling timber to profit-making companies, including Louisiana Pacific, for less than it cost to build the logging roads and make the necessary preparations for cutting down trees. In the Tongass National Forest in Alaska, North America's biggest temperate rain forest, millions of board feet of timber were cut under long-term contracts and sold to the Japanese at a fraction of their value as finished wood products. The same sort of practices were followed in the ancient forests of Washington, Oregon, and California.

At the Labor Department, Reagan installed Thorne Auchter, a building contractor, as head of the Occupational Safety and Health Administration (OSHA). Along with the EPA, OSHA was (and is) one of the government agencies most loathed by industry executives for its interference in their day-to-day operations. Auchter, who seemed to me to have little knowledge of or capacity for the intricacies of his demanding task, was quick to take OSHA not only off the backs of employers but off their property as well. He sharply reduced the number of agency inspectors authorized to look for violations of the health and safety rules and cut the number of inspections even more. Employers, he proclaimed, would be responsible for policing themselves. Regulations for protecting workers from dangerous chemicals on the job were loosely enforced, eased, or jettisoned.

But it was the President's power over the purse that proved most potent in bringing environmental reform to a near standstill.

The Office of Management and Budget, presided over in the early years of the Reagan administration by David Stockman, the "*Wunderkind* of budget-cutting conservatives and mastermind of environmental deregulation,"[15] enthusiastically set about bleeding the already demoralized and undernourished EPA and conservation programs at other agencies. Denying the environmental regulators money and workers was sufficient to render them weak and ineffective without changing the laws.

So enthusiastic was the budget office about slashing funds for the EPA that Anne Burford, hardly a big-spending New Dealer, protested to the President. In 1981, as the Reagan administration was drawing to the end of its first year, Stockman and company proposed to hack off more than a third of the environmental agency's funds. This was after Congress had just given the agency a major new antipollution program to administer when it passed the Superfund law. Burford complained that a cut of that size would leave the agency incapable of carrying out the programs mandated by statute and throw it into disarray.[16] By the end of Reagan's first term, the EPA budget, after discounting for inflation, was about where it had been a decade earlier despite a much heavier work load required by new laws.

Another early target of the Reagan administration was the Council on Environmental Quality, the White House body that advised the President on environmental matters and administered the National Environmental Policy Act. Over the years the council had incurred the hostility of a number of business groups by recommending policies they opposed. The President at first simply wanted to eliminate the council. But protests by members of Congress forced him to stay the executioner's ax. Instead he impoverished the council through the budget, forcing it to cut its staff from nearly 60 to 16. Frederick N. Khedouri, associate director of the OMB, defended the action on the ground that "a lot of what it does is duplicated by the Environmental Protection Agency." But Malcolm Baldwin, who had been on the council's staff during the Nixon administration and served as acting chairman during the early weeks of the Reagan presidency, argued for keeping it effective, saying, "I am a Republican and I voted for the President. I think we can justify a strong environmental program as good, conservative economics. You can't have a healthy economy unless there are long-range efforts to preserve the land, air, and water. But the market won't address those concerns."[17] His words fell on stone-deaf ears. The council was gutted and was almost totally ineffective throughout the eight years of the Reagan White House.

The budget cuts were accomplished in a more surgical fashion at the Interior Department. While the relative size of the reductions there was less than that at the EPA or the Council on Environmental Quality, the funds that were devoted to conservation programs, wildlife, recreation, and other ecologically oriented programs were gouged just as deeply. The money went instead to department programs to exploit the oil, coal, timber, grass, and other commodities on federal lands and on the Outer Continental Shelf. The department spent nearly a billion dollars to improve the buildings, roads, bridges, and other man-made structures in the national parks but spent next to nothing on acquiring or preserving wild land. The parks were not included in the administration's "privatization" efforts, but from time to time some of its free-market zealots floated the idea of selling off park lands. "If someone could make a profit running the parks, don't you think he would do a better job of running them than the Park Service?" a member of the White House domestic policy staff asked me in all seriousness during an off-the-record conversation in the early days of the Reagan administration.

One of the most damaging and inexplicable budget decisions of the Reagan presidency was its virtual elimination of spending on energy conservation and renewable energy sources. Reagan, Watt, Hodel, and other administration leaders spoke often of the need to provide "energy security" for the nation and reduce our dependence on oil from politically unstable regions of the world such as the Middle East. This was their chief justification for attempts to lease the Outer Continental Shelf, the North Slope of Alaska, federal wilderness areas, and unspoiled BLM lands to oil or coal companies. It was also an argument for the administration's unabashed promotion of nuclear power. But it ignored efforts to develop solar and wind power and other environmentally benign sources of energy. It vigorously opposed fuel-efficiency standards, which could have saved more oil than the amount anticipated from drilling offshore wells. Except for its efforts to encourage the development of natural gas sources, the Reagan administration's energy policies greatly increased the nation's dependence on foreign energy supplies and thereby compromised national security to a serious extent and added hugely to our negative balance of trade.

A foreign enemy could hardly have chosen a course of action that would make the United States more vulnerable to energy blackmail.

On February 17, 1981, President Reagan signed Executive Order 12291, which stated, in part, that "regulatory action shall not be undertaken unless the potential benefits to society from the regulation outweigh the potential costs to society." The order took a useful tool of economic inquiry—cost-benefit analysis—and made it an imperative of federal decision making. In the hands of the administration's political appointees, the order served as a meat cleaver with a keen edge to be wielded against regulations that cost industry money, particularly environmental regulations.

The concept seemed straightforward enough. Who could argue against weighing the costs and benefits of government regulation? Murray L. Weidenbaum, chairman of the White House's Council of Economic Advisers, gave an example of the General Motors Company being required to spend $100 million to install anti-pollution devices for reducing carbon monoxide from tailpipe exhausts. The rule prolonged twenty lives for one year at a cost of $25 million for each life, Weidenbaum said. If the money had been spent on special ambulances to rescue people with heart attacks, he said, the same money could conceivably save 500,000 lives a year.[18]

Using such dubious logic, the budget office subjected every regulation coming out of the EPA and other regulatory agencies to prolonged scrutiny, slowing the flow of environmental rulings to a trickle and in many cases killing programs that had been devised to reduce pollution and protect public health. An EPA decision to ban almost all uses of asbestos, for example, was imprisoned in the budget office for the better part of a decade.

Resources for protecting the public health and the environment are not limitless, of course. Priorities do need to be set for using those resources. Two internal studies conducted by the EPA suggested that it was spending too much money on environmental threats that presented a relatively low risk to public health—toxic waste dumps was one example—and not enough on more dangerous threats to health—such as poisonous industrial gases. The reason, the studies found, was that the agency was responding to the public's perception of risk rather than actual risk levels. Cost-benefit analysis, properly employed, certainly could be a more rational way of allocating resources.

One serious flaw of cost-benefit analysis, however, is that the costs are easy to calculate and easily inflated, but the benefits are inevitably difficult or impossible to quantify. Industry often exaggerated cost data to defeat environmental legislation or regulations. For example, the Business Roundtable, a major lobbying group, estimated the cost of a Senate clean air bill in 1990 as somewhere between $52 to $103 billion a year. Even the Bush administration, which strongly objected to the sweep of the Senate bill, put the maximum cost at $42 billion and that was found to be double the actual cost by the Congressional Research Service as well as by economists within the EPA. In fairness, it should be noted that environmental groups tend to inflate the benefits of environmental regulation.

But costs, at least, can be counted in measurable units—research, development, equipment, labor, substitute materials, and the like. When it comes to benefits of environmental protection, however, it often means placing a dollar figure on intangible values. How much is a human life worth? Human health? A view across the Grand Canyon unobscured by smog? Is a virgin forest worth no more than the market price of its timber? When asked at a news conference about the industry's estimates of the high costs of the Clean Air Act amendments of 1990, Senate Majority Leader George Mitchell, who was pressing for a strong bill, looked the questioner in the eye and asked, "How much is the life of your children worth?" "Trillions," murmured the questioner in reply.

Some economists claim to be able to place values on lives and sunsets. They take surveys of what people say they are willing to spend for amenities. They compare nonmarketable goods such as fresh air with commodities such as houses in different parts of Los Angeles with clean and dirty air. Undoubtedly there is some value to such efforts, but they hardly provide a precise measure of benefits. They are at best rough approximations of monetary values and at worst represent only the biases of those making the estimates. John Holdrin, an environmental and energy expert at the University of California at Berkeley, aptly described cost-benefit analysis as "the tyranny of illusory precision."[19]

More often than not, the alternatives offered by the Reagan cost-benefit analysts were specious and placed arbitrary limits on choices available to society. Take, for example, Weidenbaum's contention that society had to choose between additional auto tailpipe emissions limitations that could save twenty lives and ambulances that could save 500,000 lives from heart attacks. Even if his numbers were correct—and I am highly skeptical because they were probably based on industry data—why would we have to make that particular choice? Why not choose between reducing auto pollution and reducing expenditures on weapons systems such as the B-2 bomber? Or between spending on pollution and spending on subsidies for tobacco or low taxes on alcohol, which significantly increase the incidence of heart disease and cancer and cost society many billions in medical bills and lost productivity of workers?

Risk assessment was another analytical tool used by the Reagan administration to block or ease environmental regulation. Like cost-benefit analysis, to which it is related, risk assessment is potentially a neutral and useful way of evaluating environmental hazards. It examines the degree of harm that might be inflicted on human health or ecological systems by exposure to toxic substances or other pollutants and seeks to quantify their impacts. Risk assessors are increasingly armed with advanced monitoring technologies, which enable them to measure chemical contamination of the air or water down to trillionths of a gram.

Decisions taken in response to risk are called risk management. While there were no arbitrary risk limits established by government policy, the EPA prior to the Reagan administration usually sought to reduce risks from pollution that presented more than a one-in-a-million chance of causing cancer. But reducing risk also imposes economic costs on society. Former EPA administrator William Ruckelshaus liked to cite the example of a copper smelter in Tacoma, Washington, that emitted arsenic fumes. The fumes presented a cancer risk of nine in one hundred to the most exposed residents of Tacoma and caused an estimated four lung cancers a year in that city. Regulations proposed by the agency would have lowered the risk to two cancer cases a year. But the company that ran the smelter said the costs of complying with the rule would be so high that it probably would have to close the plant and lay off 800 workers. In this case, the complaint was not an attempt at "environmental blackmail." The economic pressures were apparently real. Ruckelshaus took the dilemma to the people of Tacoma, asking them to advise him on what he ought to do. "For me to sit here in Washington and tell the people of Tacoma what is an acceptable risk would be at best arrogant and at worst inexcusable."[20] Tacomans responded with suggestions on how to reduce the risk while keeping the smelter open.

In many cases, however, Reagan administration regulators were willing to permit high risks if substantial economic interests were at stake or if relatively few individuals were exposed to those risks. The EPA proposed rules that would let coke ovens emit benzene at levels that posed a cancer risk of more than one in a thousand because a stricter regulation would mean closing down many of the ovens. It permitted workers at uranium mines to be exposed to high risks of cancer because only a few workers were affected and so the number of cancer cases would be low.

The Reagan administration and its allies in industry and the scientific and medical communities approached risk assessment and risk management from several premises—chief among which was the truism that there is no such thing as a risk-free society. Ruck-elshaus put the case when he asserted that "in confronting any risk there is no way to escape the question 'Is controlling it worth it?' We must ask this question not only in terms of the relationship of the risk reduced and the cost to the economy but also as it applies to the resources of the agency."[21]

But there were other questions that government officials and other professors of the gospel of risk assessment consistently failed to ask. When Ruckelshaus asked if controlling the pollution from a manufacturing process or contamination of a consumer product was "worth it," he did not also ask if the process or product was worth any level of risk. Is it worth a single cancer death, for example, to use chemicals on foods to make them look prettier or shinier—to make a bottled cherry look unnaturally red? Should we have to expose ourselves and our children to higher levels of air pollution that damage our hearts and lungs so that someone can gratify his ego by driving around in an eight-cylinder automobile that spews high levels of toxic exhaust into the air? Is it right that a poor community should have chemicals from an eight-state region dumped into its drinking water because the community does not have the political power to block a hazardous waste treatment plant? Who profits from being relieved of the requirement of keeping toxic chemicals out of the air and who suffers? How often do the polluters lie about the risks of their prod-ucts? When risks to human health are assessed one chemical at a time, does that even remotely begin to estimate the risks to humans who are exposed to thousands of different potentially hazardous sub-stances every day? Are there no safe, economically viable alternatives to the risky products? Cannot jobs be created and preserved without threatening public health and the environment? Smoking and driving are voluntary choices. But suppose people do not want to be exposed to risks created by industry, even if they are low? If they are forced upon them against their will, isn't that placing a limit on their free-dom? Isn't that what Nader described as violence against their persons—a crime? These are complex questions that have to do not just with environmental law but with environmental equity as well.

Their answers are not to be found in a simplistic totting up of gains and losses in an inevitably politicized exercise in social accounting.

Nowhere was risk assessment more effective than in weakening the federal government's policies for protecting Americans from cancer-causing substances in the environment. Since Rachel Carson, eliminating industrial sources of cancer had been an increasingly important goal of the environmental movement. The environmental position was succinctly stated by Dr. Samuel S. Epstein, a professor of medicine at the University of Illinois's medical school in Chicago, who noted that billions of dollars had been spent on a fruitless search for cancer cures but that "little or nothing has been done to prevent exposure to carcinogenic chemicals in the environment—this despite ample evidence that chemical pollution of our air, water, and food is the major cause of cancer . . . But cancer remains a preventable disease. It is up to citizens to push for action."[22] In response to public anxiety, the EPA, the Occupational Safety and Health Administration, and other federal agencies had devoted substantial resources during the 1970s to investigating and regulating carcinogens created by human activity.

By the early 1980s, however, industry had mounted a full-scale attack on the federal cancer policy. It sought to reach the scientific community, the neoconservative intelligentsia, and the policy makers of the Reagan administration with the message that warnings about occupational and environmental causes of cancer had been grossly exaggerated.

The fullest expression of this skeptical view of environmental cancer was presented by Edith Efron in her book *The Apocalyptics*, subtitled *Cancer and the Big Lie*.[23] Those like Samuel Epstein who warned of a cancer pandemic from toxic chemicals and other forms of pollution, Efron said, were not reflecting scientific or environmental knowledge but were merely "the voice of the apocalypse in new secular attire." Fears about cancer and other environmental disasters that had spread widely since Rachel Carson's *Silent Spring* emerged out of a new ideology or "Carsonian religion," not from objective data. While some chemicals and other industrial products and processes had been found to cause cancer, they were relatively few in number and were far outweighed by the number of carcinogens in nature. Often, Efron argued, substances were classified as carcinogenic on the scantiest of evidence, usually based on false extrapolations from laboratory tests on animals. Her list of alarmist "apocalyptics" included Rachel Carson, Lewis Mumford, Barry Commoner, René Dubos, Paul Ehrlich, and a number of Nobel laureate scientists, the staff of the National Cancer Institute, and scientists in government research and regulatory agencies—a rather distinguished group.

Cynical disbelief in the anthropogenic causes of cancer dominated health regulatory policy during the Reagan years. The administration more or less abandoned the prevailing approach that viewed any substance that caused cancer in laboratory animals as a potential threat to humans at any level of exposure. Instead it assumed that there were different "thresholds" of exposure to chemicals that caused cancer, an approach that was gaining increased scientific credibility. It also relied less on the results of laboratory tests and sought evidence from records that showed patterns of sickness and death in human populations. In many cases the Reagan administration revised upward the acceptable risk of exposure to a carcinogen and eased regulations accordingly. Generally, a suspected cancer-causing substance was presumed innocent until proved guilty with a high degree of certainty.

The Reagan White House Office of Science and Technology Policy said that the new cancer policy reflected the latest advances in science and would add flexibility and credibility to regulatory activities. But many scientists viewed the change in policy as ideologically motivated. "Supply-side carcinogenesis" was how Dr. Myra L. Karstadt, then director of the Environmental Cancer Information Center at Mount Sinai Hospital in New York, described the policy. Dr. Marvin Schneiderman, former associate director for science policy at the National Cancer Institute, said that the Reagan administration was trying "to demonstrate something that they really believe—that there are far fewer things in the world that are hazardous and need to be controlled. But if you are health-oriented you want to find things that cause cancer and regulate them."[24]

of the Senate Environment and Public Works Committee, and John H. Chafee of Rhode Island, chairman of the Environmental Protection Subcommittee, in alliance with environmentally minded Democrats, Congress actually strengthened a number of the environmental laws, including the Clean Water Act, the Superfund, and the Resources Conservation and Recovery Act, during the darkest days of the Reagan era.

But the environmental momentum built up in the 1970s was slowed substantially in the 1980s. Lax enforcement of the environmental laws by federal regulators who winked at the polluters sent the message to industry that it was all right to go back to their old ways. In the name of the "new federalism," responsibility for carrying the environmental laws was shifted from Washington to the states even as they were starved of federal funds. Nothing was done to stop acid rain and little progress was made in shrinking the smog shrouding major cities. Washington looked on with benign approval as agribusiness contaminated our food and water with pesticides. For most of a decade, Washington refused to act on the grave threats to the global environment. Although Congress created millions of new acres of federal wilderness over the opposition of the administration, the growth of the National Park System slowed to a near halt and the condition of the parks deteriorated badly. The National Wildlife Refuges and federal grazing lands were in equally poor shape. Millions of acres of national forest continued to be clear-cut by the chain saws of government-subsidized timbering operations. Slipshod regulation of nuclear power plants, nuclear weapons production facilities, and nuclear wastes left a hazardous nightmare and a due bill of many billions of dollars for cleanup. The environmental and conservation agencies were starved for money and politicized and their staffs were cowed and demoralized, at least in the early years of the Reagan administration. The federal judiciary, which had played an active and key role in inculcating environmental values, was changed by an eight-year influx of Reagan appointees who, presumably, shared the President's antipathy to judicial activism.

There were a few oases in the desert of environmental policy during this period. In 1985, President Reagan, responding to wide-spread criticism of his administration's stewardship of the lands, ap-pointed a President's Commission on Americans Outdoors to study the open-space issues and make recommendations for future public and private action. The commission, headed by the Republican gov-ernor of Tennessee, Lamar Alexander, and composed largely of busi-ness executives, generally conservative members of Congress, and representatives of apolitical conservation groups, was expected to echo the administration's philosophy of letting the private sector worry about land and resources. Its report, completed in 1987, was reluctantly released by the administration, which found it to be an unwelcome surprise.

The commission, after holding hearings across the country, re-ported, "The Great Outdoors is still great. But we found that we are facing deterioration of the natural resource base, and of the recreation infrastructure. Accelerating development of our remaining open spaces, wetlands, shorelines, historic sites, and deferred maintenance and care of our existing resources, are robbing future generations of the heritage which is their birthright. We are selling the backyard to buy the groceries, and we must increase our investment today to protect what we have."[28]

The report did call for a private initiative and a "prairie fire" of community action to preserve open space. But it also called for sweeping government action, including a $1-billion-a-year trust fund dedicated exclusively to acquiring land and other outdoor resources. It recommended the creation of a system of "greenways"—or natural areas—linking cities and along river channels and more open green spaces inside cities. It recommended the creation of new public and quasi-public institutions that would plan and carry out long-range programs for preserving open space in the United States.

Although Reagan could not publicly disavow the report of his own handpicked commission, he did the next-best thing. A task force composed largely of right-wing, free-enterprise, privatization ideo-logues from within the administration was appointed to review the commission's work. It concluded, of course, that private and local initiatives—with the moral support of the federal government—were all that were needed to protect the land and its resources. Fortunately, the task force report was almost totally ignored except by like-minded ideologues. Few if any of the commission's recommendations have been put into practice.

A coincidence of fiscal conservatism and environmental goals led the administration to take the Interior Department's Bureau of Reclamation out of the dam-building business after nearly a century of hydro projects that helped open the West to settlement but wreaked havoc on natural ecological systems. The government played an active role in international efforts to end commercial whaling. The EPA, after initial reluctance, was prodded by the head of its policy office, Joseph Cannon, into speeding up efforts to remove lead from gasoline after medical evidence demonstrated conclusively that this toxic metal was present in high levels in the bloodstreams of most Americans and was causing serious learning impairment in many children.

By and large, however, "it was eight lost years—years of lost time that cannot be made up and where a lot of damage was done that may not be reparable," lamented George T. Frampton, Jr., the president of the Wilderness Society.[29] To John Adams of the Natural Resources Defense Council, the Reagan years were "absolutely thrown out the window with respect to environmental protection or any kinds of technological improvements in terms of energy conservation. All we did was hold our own and a lot of times we thought it was wonderful that we held our own." William Ruckelshaus conceded that the Reagan White House was not a friend of the environment. "They gave it the back of their hand; they told people it wasn't important . . . They clearly didn't care about it—and people can figure that out. They're not that stupid. And the American people said, 'We do care about it.' "

Because the American people do care, the Reagan environmental counterrevolution fell well short of its goals. It was unable to dismantle the environmental agencies, to gut the environmental laws, to "privatize" the public lands, to give away public resources as quickly as it wanted, or to subvert the environmental ethos that is putting down roots in American society. Membership in national and grass-roots environmental organizations, in fact, experienced unprecedented growth during the Reagan years. That is not as paradoxical as it sounds. Memberships lagged in the late 1970s, sociologist Riley Dunlap said, because people thought that environmental problems were being taken care of by the government. But as Denton Morrison pointed out, public concern and activism mounted "in *reaction* to the Reagan administration's anti-environmental policies and anti-environmental appointees."[30] Members of Congress discovered that it meant risking their seats to vote against environmental legislation. A Reagan veto of legislation to strengthen the Clean Water Act, for example, was overridden by Republicans as well as Democrats in both houses. To the consternation of industry, state governments across the country beefed up their environmental budgets and staffs to fill the vacuum created by the federal government.

Reagan was a popular President and was able to impose his will on most issues. On environmental policy he was often thwarted. The environmental values of the American people, it seemed, were too deeply implanted to be uprooted, even by a determined right-wing administration. The fears of Americans about the future were not allayed by Reagan's feel-good rhetoric. The Bhopal tragedy, Three Mile Island, the hole in the ozone layer, the mounting evidence of global warming, the failure to deal with urban smog, the rising tide of garbage, made the public realize that the threats were both real and urgent.

Eight years had been lost and there was much ground to make up. But around the country, a host of citizens, alarmed and angry over the continued degradation of the air, the water, and the land, were taking matters into their own hands.

THE

NEW

PEOPLE'S

ARMY

Man's capacity for justice makes democracy possible,
but man's inclination to injustice makes democracy necessary.
                                        —*Reinhold Niebuhr*

One August evening in the late 1980s, my wife and I drove to the town office of Becket, in the Berkshire Hills of eastern Massachusetts, to talk to the members of the local conservation commission. We wanted them to investigate whether a subdivision planned for property close to our vacation house would damage a nearby wetland. When we arrived, Main Street was dark and deserted except for a small cluster of teenagers lounging in front of the general store at the far end of the little village. Only the perfunctory song of a cicada broke the quiet of the mild night.

When we entered the ramshackle frame building, the three-member commission was seated at a table under a naked light bulb talking with a man who wanted permission to use chemicals to kill weeds that were choking the lake in front of his summer home.

Standing to one side of the table as they spoke was Jay Walker, who, with his wife, Mary, led the Becket Concerned Citizens, an organization of local residents angry about the explosive growth of second-home developments that in recent years has been transforming the forested, rural character of the township. Walker, a young building contractor and carpenter, took notes on the discussion and would later report on the proceedings in the group's newsletter. Seated on the other side of the table was Joe Engwer, another young local businessman, who represented the Hilltowns Alliance, a citizens group from Becket and adjoining Washington Township organized a couple of years before for a successful fight to block a proposed cloverleaf off the Massachusetts Turnpike that would have swallowed a large chunk of the countryside. Engwer raised a number of objections to the proposed use of chemicals in the lake, talking knowledgeably about the ecological dangers posed by the specific weed killers under discussion. The commission eventually refused to authorize the use of chemicals, urging that the weeds be raked from the water instead.

Our own business with the commission was quickly dispatched. We paused outside the building for a few words of mutual commiseration with Walker and Engwer about how the rapid, unplanned development, taking place with what they believed was the collusion of some of the town officials who profited thereby, was degrading the very qualities that had made Becket so desirable a place to live. Then we left. As we drove home, however, it struck us that we had just witnessed something remarkable. Twenty-five years before, there would have been no local conservation commission to protect wetlands under state charter. Even more astonishing, however, was the existence of two citizens groups dedicated to protecting the environment of this little community of some 1,200 souls. Here was grass-roots democracy, working to preserve the land, air, water, and quality of life. Here was the sinew of the environmental revolution.

Scenes such as the one that took place in the cluttered town office of Becket are acted out every day in many thousands of villages, towns, small cities, and inner-city ghettos. Communities across the country have organized to save themselves from environmental horrors in dozens of ways. There are no reliable data on how many such grass-roots organizations there are or how many Americans belong to them. But some estimates put the membership of environmental groups at over 25 million people, with the great majority belonging to local organizations.[1]

While the legislative and legal battles won by the big national groups provided many of the tools used by grass-roots organizations, the activities of the national groups have little immediate relevance to the local organizations fighting their acre-by-acre, dump-by-dump battles. Some of the national groups, including Greenpeace, are starting to build community affiliates across the country. A number of national networks, including the Citizens Clearing House for Hazardous Waste, the National Toxics Campaign, Clean Water Action, the Public Interest Research Groups, and the National Coalition Against the Misuse of Pesticides, provide organizational skills and technical assistance. But most of the grass-roots organizations sprang up spontaneously to confront local problems. As William Ruckelshaus noted in 1989, "since the early seventies the public concern has taken on a kind of momentum of its own and would be there regardless of the [national] environmental movement."[2] A Gallup poll taken as the 1980s were drawing to an end found that three-quarters of all Americans considered themselves to be environmentalists.[3]

Unlike the national groups, whose staffs are mostly white, well-educated, relatively affluent middle-class professionals, the membership at the grass roots cuts across class, racial, political, and educational lines. Workers who live in the shadow of smokestacks or within smelling distance of waste dumps are often the most active members of these groups. Also unlike the mainstream organizations, the local anti-pollution fighters are more often than not led by women. Where the national groups are prone to settle their differences with polluters through compromise, the grass-roots groups usually will settle for nothing less than complete victory because the health of their children as well as their own and the habitability of their homes are on the line. "It's a survival issue," said Lois Gibbs, who in 1978 organized the community of Love Canal in Niagara Falls, New York, to demand relief from the threat of dangerous chemicals in the soil and water beneath their homes and schools. "People are going to fight like hell because they don't have a choice."[4]

Gibbs was a twenty-seven-year-old housewife when she started her long struggle against the government and the chemical industry. She recalled her experience during an interview in 1989: "In 1974 I moved into Love Canal with my husband and my one-year-old child and bought the American dream. I had the picket fence. I had the swing set. I had the mortgage. I had two cars. I had HBO. I had a school three blocks away. It was literally the American dream in every aspect of what society perceives the American dream to be."

The dream faded quickly. Her son, Michael, developed asthma, epilepsy, a blood disease, and a urinary tract disorder which required two operations. Her daughter, Melissa, born after she moved into the community of small bungalows built over Love Canal, developed a rare blood disease. "I kept on talking to my pediatrician about 'What am I doing wrong?' I mean, I was the Suzy Domestic housewife who did everything. My whites were the whitest whites and the cleanest cleans, the foods were right and the kids got the sunshine and took their naps and I didn't overload them with junk. It just didn't make sense to me."

It was not until 1978, when a local newspaper reporter, Michael Brown, wrote an article about the dangerous chemicals buried beneath Love Canal and the diseases they could cause, that Gibbs "figured out what was going on." First she tried to persuade the local school authorities to close the elementary school on the edge of Love Canal and was rebuffed. Then she contacted local elected officials to try to persuade them to take action on the school. Nothing. Finally, she got in touch with local environmental groups but found that they knew little about pollution from chemical poisons or how to respond to the problem.

"So from there I decided to do the only thing I knew from being a homemaker full-time. People were always at my door with petitions, so I said, 'Well, I'm going to petition to close the school.' And when I walked around the neighborhood I discovered it wasn't just the schoolchildren; the entire community—men, women, and children alike—were all suffering health problems. I talked to folks and eventually we organized the grass-roots community group called the Love Canal Homeowners Association."

As the months went by, Gibbs recalled, she and her neighbors were given little help in extricating themselves from their poisoned surroundings. In fact, they were told repeatedly that their community was perfectly safe. Gibbs and the other members of the association became progressively more frustrated, angry, and militant. They educated themselves in science, in media relations, in politics. They took their case to the governor of New York and even to President Carter, trying to explain the danger they felt themselves to be in and asking for the financial assistance they needed to extricate themselves. At one point 500 members of the association surrounded two officials visiting from the EPA, holding them hostage in one of the houses for five hours in defiance of warnings of FBI agents. "I mean, these are law-abiding citizens, blue-collar workers who pay their taxes," Gibbs emphasized.

Such tactics, combined with bulldog persistence, finally attracted the nation's attention to the plight of the Love Canal residents and brought pressures on the government to act. Eventually, the federal government agreed to pay $17 million to evacuate Love Canal families that wanted to move. The Justice Department also went after the Hooker Chemical Company, which was responsible for burying the poisons in the area, bringing legal action that required the company to pay large fines and to take steps to prevent the contamination from spreading.

Like many of the citizens' groups that organized successfully over a specific environmental problem, the Love Canal Homeowners Association stayed in business even after it won its victory. The lessons it learned about mobilizing public opinion and forcing the political process to respond to citizens' needs were used to fight other environmental battles in the Niagara Falls area. A number of such groups, having discovered the power of a united community to correct inequity and bring about change, have widened their activities to pursue a range of social goals, including improved housing, more public services, and economic opportunity.

Gibbs herself moved to the Washington, D.C., area to found the Citizens Clearing House for Hazardous Wastes. Her marriage had been a casualty of the Love Canal war. "My husband worked in the chemical industry; he was a chemical operator. And, the poor man, he really wanted a homemaker, someone to stay home and have dinner on the table at five and all of these things, which I was willing to be at one time. And suddenly he was babysitting, because men don't take care of children, they babysit. Only women are parents. You know, he was fixing his own dinner; he was doing his own laundry. He was getting harassed like hell by his co-workers, who were saying, 'What is your wife doing? Is she trying to shut down the industry? Who is she sleeping with?' . . . I said, 'I just can't go back and do what I was doing.' And he said, 'That's what I want.' And so he has since remarried and has a new wife and a new baby and he's quite happy. And I have since remarried, and I have a new baby and I'm quite happy." Her older children are now in good health.

Gibbs formed the clearing house, she said, to help communities across the country with the lessons learned at Love Canal. "And the thing that we learned, and we learned it by the seat of our pants, was that these issues are not scientific issues. They're not legal issues. They're political issues. It was a hard lesson to learn but we did learn it . . . I didn't want anybody to have to reinvent the wheel." The lesson, Gibbs explained, was that the corporations, with the connivance of government, dump their pollution and poisons on people who don't fight back. If the people don't fight, industry easily manipulates government bureaucracies. Communities that don't want to be a dumping ground for pollution have to exert countervailing pressure on government.

By the late 1980s the clearing house was working with over 5,000 local organizations around the country, some with as few as fifty members, some with over a thousand. It provides its members with scientific expertise and other information and helps them organize. The grass-roots groups, Gibbs said, "are doing some terrific stuff. People are following the strategy. They're stopping landfills, stopping incinerators, and backing up the wastes. They're plugging up the toilet."

Plugging up the toilet. Not letting polluters flush their dirt out of sight in places where people live and work. There is another term for it: Not in My Backyard, NIMBY. No nuclear waste repository. No mass burn incinerator. No toxic waste treatment plant. No garbage barge. No aerial spraying of pesticides. Not in my backyard. It is happening with such regularity around the country that some speak of a "NIMBY movement."

Industry spokesmen and some government officials describe the NIMBY phenomenon as an expression of social selfishness. They say that waste and power plants and chemical factories have to go somewhere. Those who attempt to block the siting of such facilities, these critics claim, are hurting the economy and seeking to shift the burden to others in order to protect their property values or out of groundless fear for their health and safety.

When a community refuses to have a shelter for the homeless or a drug treatment center in its midst, it may reflect selfishness. But where it is aimed at rejecting environmental hazards, NIMBY is the authentic voice of people stating in no uncertain terms that they do not want the assault on their air, water, and soil to continue. To Lois Gibbs, the people who are saying, "We don't want this in our backyard," are also saying, "We don't want this in anybody's backyard."

NIMBY is a demand for reform, coming from ordinary people, telling the leaders of the country that the system is not working. It is heartsick mothers in Jacksonville, Arkansas; Woburn, Massachusetts; Friendly Hills, Colorado; and hundreds of other communities going from door to door in their neighborhoods tallying the number of children with cancer, neurological disease, or birth defects. It is Big Willie Tillman, a former Army sergeant who is helping lead the fight against a nuclear waste incinerator which was planned to be erected a few thousand feet down the road from his tiny bait and tackle shop outside St. Paul, North Carolina. NIMBY is a widening popular challenge to the faith that every scientific or technological innovation is by definition desirable, that the hand of the free market can do no wrong. It is a warning to industry to do its business without fouling the landscape and threatening the health of citizens, to adopt processes and make products that produce the least waste possible, to build factories that do not pollute. It is a message to politicians that if they connive with the polluters in putting their constituents in danger, they do so at the risk of their political future.

Public opinion polls consistently confirm that most Americans are willing to make some economic sacrifice if that is necessary to protect the environment. They are increasingly reluctant to harm the environment for economic gains. Of course, such an attitude could change in the face of real economic hardship. In the absence of a catastrophic downturn in the economy, however, public demands for environmental safeguards are likely to increase rather than diminish.

It is also clear that concern for the environment is becoming embedded in the social values of a wide spectrum of Americans.

One of the most telling pieces of evidence to show that environmentalism has penetrated deep into the national consciousness and is poised to serve as a springboard for broad social change is an article I clipped a few years ago from *Environmental Action* magazine. The author of the article, Sam Love, had himself snipped an item from his hometown weekly newspaper in Alabama, the *Pickens County Herald*. It read as follows:

> The Carrollton Garden Club met in the home of Ruby Windle . . . Those present enjoyed the fellowship time and

the delicious refreshments . . . Irene Owings introduced Hazel Mullenix, the guest speaker for the day. She is a devoted advocate for proper control of the chemical waste disposal site at Emelle, Alabama. Thanks to her persistence in seeking facts, she quoted frightening information concerning a situation that could involve this area. An immediate danger locally is the possibility of a spill from one of the many trucks hauling wastes through our town. All club members felt the need to become more knowledgeable and to become involved in spreading the concern.[5]

When the members of the Carrollton Garden Club of Pickens County, Alabama, become environmental activists mobilizing to do battle with Waste Management, Inc., the biggest waste management company in the country, it is fair to say that the revolution has not only started—there is a good chance it will prevail.

In the spring of 1986, I went to Robeson County, North Carolina, to talk to Willie Tillman, owner of a bait and tackle shop, and other local citizens who were unhappy about plans by industry, in cooperation with the state government, to build a big toxic waste treatment plant on one side of the county and an incinerator to dispose of low-level radioactive waste thirty-five miles away on the other side of the county. Unhappy is really not the right word—the people of Robeson County were burning with outrage and a sense of injustice.

The county is one of the poorest in the United States—its median income is about half the national average. A majority of its population consists of African-Americans and Lumbee Indians. Like many deprived groups, the poor whites, blacks, and Indians of the area competed with each other for the inadequate economic pie available to them—sometimes murderously. It was a badly divided community with a long history of racial strife.

Spokesmen for both the companies building the facilities and government officials said that waste disposal facilities had been planned for that county because of its favorable geographic location. They also said it would bring badly needed jobs to the depressed

ꞏnts of the county knew better. It had been selected,
ꞏ government and industry thought that such a poor,
..nity lacked the power to resist.

ꞏt is the same waste management equation that is being used all over the country," said the Reverend Mac Legerton, a clergyman who spearheaded local resistance to the two waste plants. "You take a poor, rural county, add a high minority population with historical racial, political, and economic divisions, and you have the most vulnerable community for the siting of massive waste treatment facilities."[6]

The people of Robeson County surprised proponents of the waste plants. They united to resist their construction. One evening while I was visiting the area, whites, blacks, and Indians joined in a rally, lighting candles, linking arms to sing hymns, and pledging, as one speaker put it, to protect "our homes, our water, our air, our children's future."[7] Tenant farmers, mill hands, shopkeepers, mothers on welfare, local clergy, worked together to take their case to the state legislature, to the media, to the Environmental Protection Agency.

Neither waste plant has been built.

The Robeson County episode crystallized for me two important truths about environmentalism. One was that environmental threats, almost more than any other stimulus, can bring a community together in common cause. People who compete for money, who are divided over race or religion, who are separated by schooling or manners, who are politically apathetic or even politically at odds with each other, will become aroused over the degradation of their community's environment and will put differences aside to deal with the threat. The promise of jobs and other economic benefits did not sway the impoverished people of Robeson County as they fought against the waste facilities.

Of course, when workers are in danger of losing their jobs and livelihood as a result of some plan to protect the environment, they will oppose that plan, particularly if the environmental problem does not directly threaten them or their families. A classic example was the passionate opposition of loggers in the Northwest to proposals to

save the spotted owl by prohibiting tree cutting on milli
of ancient forest. But if the government and environm
devised a plan to assure continued employment for the worκ.̣.
sparing the old forest, the opposition might not have been disarmed
but would almost certainly have been less angry.

An even more important lesson I took out of Robeson County
was the realization that pollution and degradation of the land are of
a piece with other forms of social injustice in the United States and,
I suspect, in most other countries as well. It is the poor, the powerless,
the politically neutered on whom an unfairly high share of the nation's
environmental evils are unloaded. A 1984 report by the Urban Environment Conference found, as Congressman John Conyers, Jr.,
stated in its preface, that "minorities are the targets of a disproportionate threat from toxins, both in the workplace, where they are
assigned the dirtiest and most hazardous jobs, and in their homes,
which tend to be situated in the most polluted communities."[8] In
1986 a report prepared by the government's General Accounting
Office for the congressional Black Caucus found that hazardous waste
disposal facilities tended to be placed in areas with high minority
populations and much poverty. The Black Caucus, not so incidentally,
has the best voting record, year in and year out, on environmental
issues of any interest group in Congress, according to tallies made by
the League of Conservation Voters. A study by the United Church
of Christ's Commission for Racial Justice issued in 1987 found that
"race has been the most discriminating factor of all those tested in
the location of commercial waste facilities in the United States." The
report found it "shocking to discover that African Americans, Hispanic Americans, Asian Americans, and Native Americans disproportionately lived in communities with a dangerous concentration of
hazardous waste sites. And, in 10 major metropolitan areas, more
than 90 percent of the African Americans lived in areas with uncontrolled waste sites. Even more outrageous, we have found that this
reality is no accident, no mere random occurrence . . . It is, in effect,
environmental racism."[9]

Toxic wastes are by no means the only environmental insults

heaped disproportionately on minorities, blue-collar workers, and the poor. Health-threatening air pollution is worst in the inner cities. Peeling lead-based paint and old lead-soldered plumbing are found mostly in the decaying apartment houses of urban slums. Low-income areas are often chosen for neighborhood-destroying freeway over-passes, which bring more foul air and noise pollution. Migrant farm workers—often Hispanic Americans or West Indians—along with other poor people in rural areas, are the chief victims of pesticides. The rural poor are also more likely than other Americans to have only contaminated water available. Blue-collar workers in lower-paying jobs are the ones who confront environmental hazards such as cancer-causing chemicals, cotton dust, and asbestos in the work-place. Women who work in plants that use chemicals that can harm fetuses have been asked to choose their jobs or sterilization.

Many of these victims of environmental violence are too preoc-cupied with survival, with finding enough food and keeping a roof over their heads and paying for clothing for their children, to fight back against the polluters. But a growing number of community organizations that serve the poor and minorities, originally organized to bring economic relief or to improve housing or fight crime in their neighborhoods, are putting environmental abuses on their agendas. In Brooklyn, New York, for example, the Williamsburg Around the Bridge Block Association obtained foundation funding for a campaign to prevent the renewal of a permit for a radioactive waste storage facility one block away from a neighborhood public school. The Minnesota Project in Preston, Minnesota, drafted a model ordinance for protecting the state's local water supplies from contamination.

Richard Grossman, former executive director of Greenpeace U.S.A., who has written on issues of social equity and the environ-ment, contends that the white middle-class professionals on the staffs of the national environmental organizations generally fail to under-stand the relationship between the powerlessness of the poor and the degradation of the environment. "They think, 'Well, if we can take care of this environmental problem and another one next week, then everything will be all right.' "

But poor people, workers confronted with a problem such as chemical poisoning, "have a context to put it into," Grossman said. "They already have a sense that it is not an aberration. They say, 'I have a terrible job. I have terrible medical care. I live in a terrible house in a terrible part of town. Oh, I'm being poisoned, too? It's terrible but I'm not surprised.' They look around and see that 'the poisoner is my boss. And he controls the town council because of the money he gives—you know, those crooked politicians that handle my garbage pickup and my water supply. And it's all of a piece. So, if I'm going to stop the poisoning and save my family, I've got to deal with this in the really broader context.' "[10]

A citizenry angered and frightened by the threats to their environment and to their health is no longer passive and willing to accept revealed wisdom handed down from on high by a government, corporate, and scientific elite. Militant community organizations demand detailed information about what is being dumped into their neighborhoods and the right to participate in the process of deciding how to deal with environmental threats. Government has been forced to respond with "sunshine laws" that opened the decision-making process to public scrutiny and provisions in the environmental laws that require that information be made available to citizens. These laws also require public hearings and other standards to assure that affected communities will have a voice in determining their own fate. As the great community organizer Saul Alinsky realized many years ago: "When we respect the dignity of the people, they cannot be denied the elementary right to participate fully in the solutions to their own problems . . . denial of the opportunity for participation is the denial of human dignity and democracy."[11]

When Congress expanded the toxic waste cleanup law—the Superfund—in 1986, it included a new provision requiring businesses that make or use toxic substances to inform the local community of what kind and how much of such chemicals were on the premises and how much was released into the environment each year. The amended law also required the establishment of local boards to decide how to deal with potential health and safety risks at local chemical plants and made federal money available to community-based organizations to help them hire the scientific and technical assistance they would need to be able to participate in the decision-making process.

Little noticed at the time of its adoption, this amendment to the waste law is the prototype of what may be one of the most significant instruments yet devised for protecting the environment. At least in theory, it enables the victims or potential victims of chemical pollution to remove the threat to their health and their surroundings by providing them with the tools they need to deal with the polluters: information, technical expertise, entry into the decision-making process. As Ralph Nader noted, the government's regulatory apparatus has the *authority* to stop or control pollution, but as the continued defiance of the law by many polluters and the ongoing degradation of the environment demonstrate, it does not necessarily have the *power* to do so. Real power to stop the polluters, he said, would come from an environmental agency, fully staffed by local residents, in every congressional district in the country and "a store-front environmental group, like an H & R Block, in every community. That would be a shift of power, focusing the concerns of people into cutting-edge advocacy—political, economic, legal—all kinds of advocacy, which can then trigger authority into doing its job."[12]

Systematic democratization of the process of environmental protection is not yet in sight, except in theory. But the rising tide of concern over the environment is bringing a growing number of Americans into the process with each passing day. "This is the greatest accomplishment of the environmental movement," wrote Janet Welsh Brown of the World Resources Institute, "this revolution in awareness and understanding, this sense of urgency, this knowledge that environmental protection is not the luxury of the rich but a matter of survival of the poor, this realization that we share one finite earth and that all of us are responsible for what happens to it."[13]

Far from being elitist, as some of its opponents charge, environmentalism is taking root at the local level across the country. The worker families of Love Canal, the forced evacuation from Times Beach because of contamination by dioxin, the poor whites, blacks, and Indians of Robeson County are patently not elitists. Clean air and water, a healthy home and place of employment, open space in which to enjoy leisure, cannot by any stretch of the imagination be considered luxuries. Most Americans now demand them as rights which belong to all. The members of the local activist groups comprise a broad coalition, cutting across racial and class lines, that has proved so elusive in electoral politics. More often than not, the leaders of these groups are women.

It may not be too far off the mark, in fact, to conclude that environmentalism is evolving into a new popular movement that is different from anything this country, or the rest of the world, has yet seen. The political scientist Robert Paehlke, for example, contends that environmentalism has the potential to be the first major new political ideology since the rise of liberalism, conservatism, and socialism in the nineteenth century. It is an ideology that is inherently neither left nor right but combines elements of both, Paehlke says. He adds that "it is the first ideology to be deeply rooted in the natural sciences."[14] He found, however, that it is still a "truncated ideology" that focuses on a very narrow range of issues.[15] The British scholar Anna Bramwell, looking at what she calls the "ecology movement" in both Europe and the United States, concludes that "it represents a new political consciousness and direction. It has been struggling to see the light of day since the third quarter of the nineteenth century . . . like a brushfire the ecological world-view has spread and taken hold." She describes the movement as "a new political category in its own right, with a history, right wings and left wings, with leaders, followers and a special epistemological niche all to itself."[16] While Bramwell's conclusion that the ecology movement is seeking "a return to primitivism"[17] seems to me to be dead wrong, at least in the United States, she correctly identifies the movement as a "box" into which an astonishingly broad range of political thought can fit.[18] Samuel Hays noted that environmentalism "cuts across traditional ideology" by defining corporate leaders as radicals who are responsible for "the massive transformation of modern society" by large-scale alteration of the environment.[19]

It would seem, then, that environmentalism is a kind of platypus among social movements—it is not easy to classify. The issues it raises have relatively little to do with classic disputes over the sharing of national wealth or the division of power between the individual and the state. If one looked only at the environmentalists' demands for government regulation of industry or public ownership of lands and resources, one could conclude it was a left-wing movement. Roderick Nash describes the idea of extending rights and ethical behavior beyond the circle of human beings and including animals and plants in the community of law as an extension of American liberalism.[20] But the opposition to state-funded infrastructure such as big dams or superhighways, the desire to cultivate a simpler lifestyle and preserve the landscape and the quality of life, are distinctly conservative goals. Environmentalism is progressive in that it believes that human society can be changed for the better to curb pollution, husband resources, and protect life. It is conservative because it strives to conserve the natural world.

Above all, however, environmentalism represents a new set of democratizing values that may be in the process of replacing many of the principles that have long dominated our economics and our politics. Certainly the old arguments about capitalism and socialism are no longer germane after the dramatic changes in Eastern Europe and the former Soviet Union. A new definition of national security is clearly necessary—no longer can it be defined solely in terms of weapons systems and armies and no longer can our political leaders justify draining away so large a part of our national treasure to swell the coffers of the military-industrial complex. Security now depends on how we can protect the biological systems that sustain life, how well we can protect our health from pollution, whether we can consume enough energy for our economic well-being without degrading the local and global environment and using up tomorrow's resources. Security now means preventing wholesale degradation of ecological systems in developing countries, degradation that can make refugees of entire populations and disturb the political stability of large regions of the globe.

Some political scientists and sociologists have speculated that environmentalism is beginning to challenge the fundamental structure of beliefs on which our society operates—beliefs, for example, that the human destiny is to conquer, that science and technology are infallible, or that the accumulation of wealth and the production and consumption of goods and services should be the focus of human aspiration. Sociologist Lester W. Milbrath contends that the environmentalists "have become something of a vanguard pointing the way to a better society and also pointing out the dire consequences of continuing on our old path."[21] Contrary to the claim of its enemies, environmentalism does not reject science, technology, industrial production, and economic growth. It does, however, demand careful attention to the consequences of our scientific, technological, economic, and industrial decisions. It calls for long-term planning to conserve resources and to minimize human impact on the natural world. It is intensely concerned with the *quality* of human life.

While environmentalism has obviously not replaced traditional values with respect to the relationship between humans and nature or notions of what constitutes progress—and it is probably premature even to speculate on whether that will ever happen—only a hermit sealed in a cave for the past twenty years or so would not have observed a significant shift in the way Americans now view these issues. Riley Dunlap observed, "The dominant paradigm as of 1970 wasn't just non-ecological . . . ecology was irrelevant to it. Progress was the biggie—faith in science and technology, materialism and abundance. Environmentalists have slowly but surely hauled those things into question."[22]

Public opinion polls in recent years have consistently indicated a broad popular shift toward environmental values. Most show a steadily rising public awareness and concern and suggest that most people want tougher laws to protect the environment and are willing to pay for more environmental protection even if it entails some personal economic sacrifice. While there are shadings, these polling results are consistent across geographical areas of the country, racial and class lines, levels of education, conservative and liberal values, and Republican and Democratic party affiliation.

As Dunlap has suggested, however, polls offer only "superficial" insights into people's values and what they really care about.[23] It is possible that, for much of the public, environmental values also remain superficial. The ambiguity that has characterized Americans' relationship to the natural world since the earliest colonial days is still evident. After all, many Americans began demanding bigger, gas-guzzling cars as soon as the price of gasoline declined. People still look for more convenient throwaway products and heavily packaged items. Many continue unthinkingly to litter the landscape with their cans and bottles and paper. We consume ever more energy to save labor—to the silly point of using electricity to open our cans, cut our meat, and brush our teeth. Despite our fear of synthetic chemicals, we continue to demand, in ever growing volumes, the products made out of them or with them. Many of us mourn the loss of the rural countryside but patronize the shopping malls that have paved over the old dairy farms and woodlots. Millions of Americans who call themselves environmentalists vote for politicians who give little more than lip service to the environment. Public concern for the environment can wane quickly in the face of potential threats to jobs, or even inconveniences such as lines at gasoline stations.

But as the song says, "the times they are a-changing." There is nothing superficial about the anger and fear of millions whose health and property are threatened by pollution. With the increasing awareness of threats to the global ecosystem from the greenhouse effect and the destruction of the ozone layer, this sense of environmental danger is no longer localized—suddenly everybody's backyard is at risk.

Along with Ralph Nader and many others, I believe that a virtually universal love of nature for aesthetic and spiritual reasons is also a major force in recruiting soldiers into the environmental army. "The strongest impulse after survival in the human psyche, I am convinced after years of observation," Nader stated, "is not power, lust, greed, jealousy. It is beauty. That's the strongest impulse . . . And environmentalism has that going for it."[24]

So far, however, while members of Congress and other politicians have to take pains to portray themselves as environmentalists, they need do little else to assuage voters. The environmental impulse has yet to be reflected in the behavior of voters in any significant way at the national or even state level.

A major foray into electoral politics seems inescapably to be the direction that will have to be taken by the next generation of environmentalists. Decisions on the fate of the natural world and its inhabitants, human and otherwise, are largely made in the offices of elected officials and their appointees in the bureaucracy. Lois Gibbs reported that when the local citizens' groups she works with take on elected officials in the political arena, they prevail every time. They did not necessarily win every election, she explained, but the political pressure they exerted in election years achieved their environmental goals in every instance.[25]

If the popular energy represented by the environmental movement at all levels of society can be channeled into electoral politics, it could well prove to be irresistible in the coming years. No other cause commands the interest and emotional commitment of so broad a spectrum of the American people. Based as it is on a set of issues that directly affect individual and local communities and with national and grass-roots rank-and-file activists demanding a larger role in the process of governing, environmentalism could be the most democratizing influence on national politics in recent history, perhaps exceeding the trade unionism of the 1930s and the civil rights and feminist movements of the 1960s.

Dunlap considers that the reelection of Ronald Reagan in 1984, despite his patently anti-environmental sentiments and policies, is evidence that the environment has not emerged as a significant political force. That may be. Having followed politics for many years as a newspaper reporter, however, I am convinced that the American people are ahead of their leaders on these issues. The nation's politics have changed already in response to the environmental impulse but not as far or as fast as the public's awareness and concern. Sometime soon, I believe, a canny national politician may be able to seize the issue, run with it full tilt, and be elected President of the United States.

Jay D. Hair
ROBERT RATHE

Kathryn Fuller
SAM KITTNER

Frederic D. Krupp
© T. CHARLES ERICKSON

David Hawkins
© DANIEL GELBWAKS

John Adams
© 1991 CASEY CRONIN

Richard Ayers
© DANIEL GELBWAKS

Peter A. A. Berle
JEFFREY STERN

Lois Gibbs
CITIZENS CLEARING
HOUSE FOR HAZARDOUS
WASTES

James G. Watt
THE NEW YORK TIMES

William D. Ruckelshaus
U.S. ENVIRONMENTAL AGENCY

Russell E. Train
WORLD WILDLIFE FUND AND THE
CONSERVATION FOUNDATION

Douglas Costle
U.S. ENVIRONMENTAL AGENCY

Anne M. Gorsuch
U.S. ENVIRONMENTAL AGENCY

Lee M. Thomas
U.S. ENVIRONMENTAL AGENCY

William K. Reilly
U.S. ENVIRONMENTAL AGENCY

THE

THIRD

WAVE

*The destiny of humans cannot be separated
from the destiny of earth.*
                    —*Thomas Berry*

With the departure of Ronald Reagan, the political balance seemed to tilt back toward the environmentalists. Reagan's Vice President for eight years, George Bush, in effect repudiated his former boss's environmental hostility by promising during his first campaign for the White House to be "the environmental President."

Delegates to the Republican National Convention in 1988 were polled on environmental issues and overwhelmingly said they would pay higher taxes for a cleaner environment, even though Mr. Bush, the candidate they were about to nominate, had solemnly pledged not to raise taxes. The conservative magazine *National Review* commented, "The summer of 1988 may well have marked a turning point in political consciousness where the problem of pollution is concerned. The issue has been building for years, but this summer it crested. The environment is no longer a cult issue." Thomas H. Kean, the Republican governor of New Jersey, commented that "Republican environmentalist still sounds to many like an oxymoron . . . But you would make a serious mistake if you were to believe that."[1] Environmentalism had become fashionable across the American political spectrum, from left to right (although not on the far right). Political candidates of virtually every stripe paid due respect to environmental issues in their campaign rhetoric.

After Bush was elected, he proposed legislation to strengthen the Clean Air Act, he volunteered to serve as host of an international meeting to begin drafting a treaty to respond to global warming, he appointed William K. Reilly, a professional environmentalist, as administrator of the EPA, and he agreed to elevate the agency to cabinet status. He endorsed a moratorium on offshore oil drilling along much of the nation's coastline. His budget included money for a major reforestation program and he endorsed a number of other initiatives to protect the environment.

The counterrevolution was over.

Or was it?

A year into his first term and flushed by high ratings in the polls following a successful and popular military invasion of Panama, Mr. Bush appeared to lose much of his zeal for environmental reform. His concern about the costs of environmental regulation rose sharply. The President's rhetoric remained benignly green, but his actions belied his speechwriters. While he made good on his campaign pledge to support a strengthened Clean Air Act, his staff downplayed the threat of acid rain and inflated the cost of cleaning the nation's air. His White House chief of staff, John H. Sununu, filling the shoes of James Watt, aggressively trashed potentially expensive environmental initiatives, such as a national commitment to reduce carbon dioxide emissions or to stop any future net loss of wetlands, as proposed rules made their way through the White House. When Sununu was forced to resign because of his unpopularity within and without the White House, Vice President Dan Quayle, as chairman of the White House Council on Competitiveness, became the anti-regulatory champion of the conservatives. EPA administrator Reilly found himself increasingly isolated in the administration. Bush's environmental policies, it began to appear, were tempering rather than abandoning Reaganism.

When Manuel Lujan, Jr., an affable, mild-mannered, conservative former Republican congressman from New Mexico, was appointed by Bush as Secretary of the Interior, the ideological zealotry that had dominated federal land and resource policies during the eight years of the Reagan presidency ebbed perceptibly. The Watt plan to put the entire 1.3-billion-acre Outer Continental Shelf up for auction to the oil industry was scrapped. Giveaway leases to the coal industry were ended, and a more honest effort was made to enforce the surface-mining law, passed during the Carter administration to mitigate the destruction caused by coal mining. Political appointees no longer sought to undercut the land protection laws.

But many of the basic Reagan policies remained intact. The Bush administration continued to oppose any major expansion of the public domain. The last great addition to the estate of protected federal lands took place during the waning days of the Carter presidency when Congress passed the Alaska National Interest Lands Act. The statute, enacted in November 1980, protected over 100 million acres in Alaska from development, more than doubling the size of the nation's park and wildlife refuge systems, and presented a gift of incalculable value to posterity.[2] While Bush did call for somewhat higher expenditures for buying land, he clearly did not intend any substantial expansion of the park, refuge, or wilderness systems. Budgets for resource protection and recreation on the public lands continued to be starved. Forest Service timber-cutting targets remained high and thousands of miles of roads were built into undeveloped national forest areas. Bush, a former Texas oilman, continued to call for the development of oil reserves on the coastal plain of the Arctic National Wildlife Refuge (an effort blocked by the Democrat-controlled Congress) and for additional if more restrained drilling activity on the Outer Continental Shelf. Grazing fees for stock on the federal range remained lower than prevailing market rates. When the Endangered Species Act threatened to block a dam project in his home state, Interior Secretary Lujan urged that the law be weakened.

In its reluctance to take the steps necessary to meet the pressing international environmental threats—the vanishing ozone layer, global warming, the population explosion in the third world—the Bush administration was increasingly out of step with the global community. President Bush—heeding the advice of Sununu; his director of the Office of Management and Budget, Richard Darman; and Michael Boskin, chairman of his Council of Economic Advisers—held back on any specific commitments to reduce greenhouse gases and grew increasingly reluctant to commit funds to help poor nations make the transition to nonpolluting technologies. These advisers warned that the costs of direct action to curb environmental threats would be enormous and could lead to high unemployment and have other serious economic repercussions. While the President talked about leadership and boasted of United States initiatives such as planting a billion trees a year and devoting a billion dollars to research on global warming, he guided United States policy away from any immediate formal agreement to set specific targets and timetables for reducing the use of fossil fuels and other sources of the greenhouse gases, although virtually every other major industrialized country had done so.

Of course, Mr. Bush and his advisers might have been right in believing that the process of shifting from the use of fossil fuels and the other economic changes needed to address the great global environmental issues could increase unemployment and slow economic growth. Such fundamental changes could hardly be achieved without some hardship and loss of economic momentum—although their magnitude and duration are a matter of intense debate. But in placing short-term American economic interests above long-term global environmental necessity, the Bush administration was succumbing to what Gro Harlem Brundtland, former Prime Minister of Norway and chairwoman of the World Commission on Environment and Development, called "the tyranny of the immediate."

Mr. Bush's near-term need was to keep economic activity high and unemployment down to assure a favorable political climate for his reelection. Similarly, business leaders always have the imperative of maximizing profits to satisfy shareholders. Poor people struggling to feed themselves and their children face the day-to-day requirements of survival. To satisfy these demands, long-range goals are ignored or scanted—even when the goal is the long-range habitability of the planet.

Starting in 1990, moreover, the Republican right wing lashed out again with surprising fury at environmentalists. Richard Darman, director of the Office of Management and Budget, contended in a speech at Harvard University that with the decline of the East-West conflict, environmentalism is the "green mask" under which "competing ideologies will continue their global struggle . . . Americans did not fight and win the wars of the twentieth century to make the world safe for green vegetables," Darman proclaimed.[3] Patrick J. Buchanan, long an intemperate, bullying voice of the far right, devoted an entire edition of his quarterly newsletter in 1990 to "An Anti-Environmentalist Manifesto" by Llewellyn H. Rockwell, which employed a virulent rhetoric reminiscent of the anti-Communist excesses of the McCarthy era. In environmentalism, the "manifesto" warned, "we face an ideology as pitiless and messianic as Marxism," which "harks back to a godless, manless Garden of Eden." It seemed clear that the extreme right in America, which had fed for decades on the fear and hatred of Communism, was seeking a new devil around which to build its recruiting and fund-raising efforts after the collapse of the Soviet empire. The environmental movement was being tried as a likely candidate—a green menace replacing the red.

But the fact that President Bush felt it necessary to put on a pro-environmental face, false or not, suggested that environmental politics had entered a new era. No longer could a President—or a political party that wished to win the support of a majority of Americans—be openly hostile to environmental concerns. It was clear that the American people cared too much. If the counterrevolution was not defeated, at least it had been contained. Lobbyists for the oil, coal, power, mining, timber, agribusiness, auto, chemical, banking, construction, and real estate interests retained enormous power, but with the departure of President Reagan they were put at least temporarily on the defensive. The passage of new clean air legislation in 1990 demonstrated that environmental politics were revivified and potent. The law, fought for with great persistence and skill by some of the most able members of the national organizations, was the most far-reaching new environmental legislation they had won in a decade.

For the environmentalists, the late 1980s and early 1990s were a time of stocktaking and adjustment. Many of the national groups had emerged from the Reagan counterrevolution bigger and stronger than ever. In the early 1980s, James Watt and Anne Burford had been superb, if unwitting recruiting agents for the environmentalists. Later in the decade, Riley Dunlap found, a growing number of people recognized "environmental problems as truly serious threats—especially to human welfare." Survey results in the late 1980s and early 1990s, he noted, "reflect an extraordinary level of acceptance of a social movement and indicate how fully environmentalism has become accepted within our society."[4]

Membership in the groups and the size of their budgets grew rapidly. By 1990, Greenpeace U.S.A., which started the decade with under 250,000 dues-paying members, had 2 million members. The National Wildlife Federation, with a membership of about 6 million, up more than 2 million over the decade, had an annual budget of over $85 million. Its president, Jay Hair, predicted in 1989 that the budget would reach $250 million a year by the end of the century. Most other environmental organizations also expanded. During the recession that started in 1990, the growth of most of the groups slowed or halted and many were forced to retrench. But their membership base remained solid.

The environmental movement, too, has been changed by the social forces it helped unleash. New leaders with new ways of operating took over many of the groups. To some, the tried and trusted tactics of green activism—direct confrontation, litigation, and lobbying—were viewed as no longer adequate. Industry, finally awake to the environmental challenge to its freedom of action, was adopting aggressive and sophisticated new techniques to fend off environmentalists' demands in Congress, statehouses, and the courts. International and global threats to the environment were emerging that could not be addressed through United States laws and institutions alone.

The new generation of leaders brought many changes in the way the groups organized and acted and even a change in goals. Sometimes referred to as the "Third Wave" of environmentalism— the first being the old conservation movement and the second the militant activists who rose on Earth Day 1970—the new group was in many ways more pragmatic and professional, more inclined to cooperate with existing political and economic forces to achieve its goals. The newcomers also recognized that more complex problems, such as global warming and well-organized opposition by powerful industry groups who no longer dismissed them as long-haired tree huggers, must be met with improved tools. The national organizations learned how to use and exchange mailing lists, conduct door-to-door canvassing efforts, and plan skillful advertising campaigns.

By the 1980s, many of the national environmental groups were adopting some of the same mass-marketing techniques used by industry. Virtually all of them employed full-time media relations officers and in some cases established public relations departments. The League of Conservation Voters, the Sierra Club political action committee, and other arms of the movement were endorsing candidates and spending millions on political campaigns. Rock singers and movie stars were enlisted for the environmental bandwagon. The National Wildlife Federation built its own office complex and conference center in downtown Washington, D.C. Almost all groups published slick, multi-color magazines and regularly sent newsletters to their members, the media, and opinion makers. Greenpeace U.S.A., according to Peter Bahouth, a former executive director, had more volunteers canvassing door to door than any organization in the country except the Girl Scouts. The publications of the World Resources Institute and the Worldwatch Institute were distributed widely and used as basic policy guides in countries around the globe. The National Audubon Society, the World Wildlife Fund, and the National Geographic Society produced environmental education films for national television. The Sierra Club's book publishing operations were expanded. The Natural Resources Defense Counsel forced Alar off the market with a media campaign that could be envied by a Fortune 500 corporation. "To answer the increasingly sophisticated response of those who would stop progress," said Frederic Krupp, executive director of the Environmental Defense Fund, "the environmental movement needs more scientists and engineers and economists."[5] Krupp, a vigorous, scholarly-looking young man who was a high school student on Earth Day 1970, became a leading practitioner of the Third Wave approach.

In 1991, the National Audubon Society, led by former New York State environment commissioner Peter A. A. Berle, dropped its traditional egret logo for a stylized blue flag in a well-publicized and controversial effort to remake its image. The venerable group, in stiff competition with other national environmental organizations for both members and money, wanted to convey the message that it is a broad-based institution with a sweeping agenda of national and international issues, not a quaint old club of birdwatchers in stout shoes. Protests from its members forced the society to readopt the egret. But the episode underscored the competitive pressures on the national environmental organizations.

One of the more interesting trends within the movement in the late 1980s and early 1990s was the advocacy by some of the groups of market incentives to achieve environmental goals. Under Fred Krupp, for example, the Environmental Defense Fund devised a system that would give "credits" to power plants that reduced the pollution that caused acid rain. Under the plan, those utilities that did more than was required by law to cut pollution could sell their credits to other power plants who might find paying additional cash less expensive than cutting down their own emissions. President Bush incorporated the plan in the acid rain legislation he sent to Congress in 1989 and it eventually became part of the law. The Environmental Defense Fund also helped craft "Project 88," a broad program based on market incentives that was proposed by Senators Tim Wirth of Colorado and the late John Heinz of Pennsylvania for tackling many of the world's critical environmental problems. This was a marked change of tactics within the environmental community. In the past the strategy was to get strong laws passed that commanded polluters to behave, and if they did not and the government refused to enforce the laws, then to sue the malefactors. Now some mainstream environmentalists openly embraced a market approach to addressing environmental ills.

Another Third Wave innovation tried by some of the environmentalists during and after the Reagan era was to negotiate with industry, often with the help of mediators, to work out pollution problems. Gail Bingham of the Conservation Foundation was among the trailblazers of this approach, helping bring about a tripartite environmentalist-industry-government agreement on the export of hazardous substances. The National Wildlife Federation formed a "corporate council," entering, Jay Hair said, an era of "corporate détente" in which industry and environmentalists could sit down and discuss "the tough environmental issues together."[6]

Some veteran environmentalists were a bit uncomfortable with replacing regulation with market economics and negotiating with polluters. Fighting pollution and preserving lands and resources, they pointed out, often conflict with purely economic concerns. John Adams said that the cause of environmentalism "is not well served by falling over and rolling over and talking about economics where it ought not to be talked about." Douglas Scott, who left the Sierra Club in 1991, said, "I am not a big believer in the Third Wave—this idea that we'll sit down with our friends in industry and they will come to terms. I think they will come to terms only if we create a climate in which they're under such pressure that they don't have any damned choice!"[7]

Nevertheless, a growing number of mainstream environmentalists conceded that the old approach of writing laws that set targets and timetables for reducing pollution and mandated precise measures for reaching those goals could only do part of the job, and might be approaching the limits of its effectiveness. New tools, including pollution taxes and economic incentives that make it financially worthwhile to industry to become good environmental citizens, were clearly needed. Moreover, the new conventional wisdom that economic development and environmental protection are mutually dependent placed on environmentalists the responsibility of supporting appropriate economic growth. If long-term economic prosperity could not be sustained without protecting the land, air, and water and making wise use of other resources, then it followed that those resources could not be preserved without a healthy economy and a population whose economic needs were satisfied.

A corollary to this determination is the growing recognition by environmentalists that environmental damage caused by technology often must be corrected by technology. Gus Speth, a confessed "former Luddite," called for "Twenty-first Century technologies that integrate environmental goals into the basic design of transportation, manufacturing, energy and other systems. An environmental revolution in technology is required . . ."[8] It is true that the environmentalists tend to emphasize smaller-scale, decentralized methods of production. But contrary to Anna Bramwell and others who view environmentalism as an impulse to return to the primitive, the mainstream of the movement seeks a more advanced technological society that turns to scientific innovation to replace outmoded technologies with benign, efficient means of production.

Barry Commoner, of course, has long placed the blame for the destruction of the environment on the use of the wrong technology, such as high-compression automobile engines and agricultural chemicals, and called for their replacement with nonpolluting technologies. In recent years, more and more mainstream environmentalists are issuing the same call. Few, however, share Commoner's conviction that the way to reach that goal is to socialize production. The former Soviet Union and other Eastern European countries, where production was highly centralized and socialized, are environmental basket cases. Commoner has explanations for this failure—the Soviet Union has not until recently permitted free expression to environmental advocates and its technology has been borrowed from the West.[9] But they are not very convincing. We have ample evidence that any political or economic system can design potentially destructive technology and then abuse it. The flexibility of the free market undoubtedly can more efficiently replace destructive with benign technology when society demands that transformation.

A number of veteran environmentalists were worried about the direction being taken by the movement. They feared that the professionalization of environmental groups was robbing them of the passion and moral zeal that had infused them with a sense of mission after Earth Day. They wondered if environmentalism was becoming just another career and its cadre was growing to resemble the corporate executives and government officials with whom they were supposed to be doing battle.

One of the more contentious expressions of this view was made by David Foreman, a former Washington representative of the Wilderness Society, who left to help found Earth First!, the radical environmental group that based its zealous activism on the principles of deep ecology. Eighty years after the death of John Muir, the environmental movement had turned its back on his moral vision, Foreman asserted. Today, "too many environmentalists have grown to resemble bureaucrats—pale from too much indoor light; weak from sitting too long behind desks; co-opted by too many politicians . . . By playing a 'professional' role in the economic rational game, we, too, acquiesce in the destruction of the Earth. Instead, we must redefine the battle. We must stop playing the games of political compromise the industrial power brokers have designed for us . . . The time has come to translate the non-violent methods of Gandhi and Martin Luther King to the environmental movement. We must place our bodies between the bulldozers and the rain-forest; stand as part of the wilderness in defense of herself; clog the gears of the polluting machine; and with courage, oppose the destruction of life."[10]

Other critics within the movement contend that, by collaborating with government and industry, the national groups are contributing only marginally to protecting the environment. Barry Commoner complained that the "old-line" environmental groups are "locked" into a strategy of working with government and industry to design standards for controlling pollution rather than demanding that pollution be eliminated. "But these efforts, however well-intentioned, have accomplished little because the controls that are supposed to implement the standards are ineffectual." It is the grass-roots environmentalists, Commoner insisted, who fight to block polluting operations in their communities, not the national organizations, that "are now at the cutting edge of the growing public movement to end the environmental crisis."[11]

Richard Grossman, the former head of Greenpeace, assailed the national groups for cooperating with the administration in 1990 to help pass what he said (wrongly, in my view) were meaningless amendments to the Clean Air Act. "Why after all these years are institutional environmental and conservation groups kissing Bush's ass and going for such a minuscule goal on clean air? How can that be? I don't understand it. It's so irrelevant, the debate that is taking place in Washington over clean air. It is so irrelevant to the problem and to the people who could provide the muscle to really bring change to the environment. To give the EPA a little more muscle doesn't mean shit to them because the EPA is so worthless it doesn't even exist in most people's minds."[12]

Douglas Scott wondered before he left the Sierra Club if the national environmental groups are too concerned about publicizing themselves to raise money and membership to be able to cooperate in major legislative campaigns. He said he doubted that the movement could today put together the kind of coalition that rammed the Alaska National Interest Lands Act through Congress in 1980, an effort that, after the legislative battle had been won, Congressman Morris K. Udall described as the best lobbying campaign he had ever seen.

But if the environmental movement had lost some of its youthful ardor, it also seemed to be slowly gaining a broader perspective of its role in society. Changes in the National Wildlife Federation are a case in point. Because of its conservatism as well as its size, the federation was long known as "the General Motors" of the conservation movement. With a membership composed heavily of hunters and rifle enthusiasts, the group was regarded for years—perhaps unfairly—as a kind of green extension of the National Rifle Association. Its members were interested primarily in narrow conservation issues such as the preservation of game species. "At our annual meetings in the 1970s you may have heard a debate on how you'd go about establishing waterfowl hunting regulations or something like that," said Jay Hair. But the group has undergone a transformation, he commented. "If you'd been at one of our meetings in the last couple of years you might have heard them debate about the environmental consequences of nuclear war. You'd have heard them debate and pass unanimously a resolution to launch an initiative to change the United States Constitution to add an environmental quality amendment to it."

Like other national environmental groups, the Wildlife Federation is starting to appreciate the link between social equity and the quality of the environment. "When I first came here eight years ago," Hair said in 1989, "somebody representing Coretta King asked me if I would participate on behalf of the federation in some kind of march here in Washington. I declined, saying that I believe very strongly in what Martin Luther King did, but I did not want the environment to become a subset of the larger social justice issues. But I don't think that way anymore, because I don't think that in many areas I can separate them. If you look at the people who are the recipients of many of the environmental abuses in this country, they are those who are politically underpowered and poor, whether they are urban people who are confronted with urban air problems or lead in paint or the rural poor. If you look at where hazardous waste sites are, they are in politically underpowered areas in North Carolina. If you look at who is losing land across America, they're poor people, not rich white folks. I very clearly see an association between environmental issues and social justice questions now that I would not have seen eight years ago."[13]

For the most part, however, the environmental community still has a long way to go in the last decade of the century to match its deeds to its perceptions and words, to link environmental degradation and social justice. Early in 1990, for example, a group of civil rights and minority community leaders, including Dr. Benjamin Chavis, Jr., director of the United Church of Christ's Commission for Racial Justice, and the Reverend Fred Shuttlesworth, co-chairman of the Southern Organizing Committee for Social and Economic Justice, wrote to eight of the leading national organizations accusing them of racism in their hiring practices. The letter also complained that the national environmental groups were isolated from the poor and minority communities that, it said, were the chief victims of pollution and other forms of environmental exploitation.[14]

The peremptory tone of the letter may have been unfair. The leaders of the environmental organizations were conscious of their dismal record on minority hiring practices and properly disturbed about it. Jay Hair insisted that nobody was as "aware of the whiteness of the green movement" as the environmentalists themselves.[15] In 1989, well before the letter from the civil rights groups, the organizations formed an Environmental Consortium for Minority Outreach. Some began trying to work on environmental problems in poor communities in the South and elsewhere. The National Audubon Society established an environmental education program aimed at poverty areas. The groups subsequently launched an organized effort to recruit minority staff and board members.

Still, at the time the letter was written, not one of the national groups had a black or Hispanic in its top leadership. None of them had recruited more than a tiny fraction of their professional staffs from minority groups. While they expressed increasing concern about the relationship between economic distress and environmental decline in the developing countries of Africa, Asia, and Latin America, the mainstream environmentalists did not have a significant place on their agendas for problems of poverty and discrimination in this country. Most of the groups probably devoted more of their time and money to dealing with environmental problems in the third world than to direct action in the inner cities or impoverished rural areas—although it should be stressed that their lobbying and litigation in the federal courts were carried out to the benefit of all Americans, poor as well as rich.

Change, however, was obviously in the wind. Some of the new groups that worked with grass-roots activists, including the National Toxics Campaign, the Citizens Clearing House for Hazardous Waste, the U.S. Public Interest Research Group, and others, did integrate issues of social equity into their daily operations. Large numbers of Americans, confronting toxic waste dumps, dying lakes, or choking smog, started to put two and two together, without the help of professional environmentalists. Recent years have witnessed an almost spontaneous upwelling of concern among Americans and people around the world, startling in its speed and intensity, about the threat our existing economic, political, and social systems are posing to the long-term habitability of our planet.

At this point, it would be appropriate to ask what has been accomplished by this social movement called environmentalism. We have seen that our institutions, our laws, and our economy have been altered, in some ways profoundly. Hundreds of billions of dollars have been spent by government, industry, taxpayers, and consumers to control pollution and to protect the land. Decisions affecting capital investments, the use of resources, and the broad range of public policy have been changed or modified by environmental laws or the emerging environmental ethic.

But what does it all add up to? Are we saving the environment? Are we saving ourselves? Has all the effort and expense been worth it?

It would certainly appear that daily life has changed in countless ways for millions as a result of the environmental revolution. In the morning I use shaving cream from which chemicals that harm the ozone layer have been banned. The electricity used by my toaster is more expensive because the power company raised its rates to pay for the scrubber it installed to lower sulfur emissions from its smokestacks. My minivan is equipped with a catalytic converter to remove polluting gases from the tailpipe exhaust, and I tank up with lead-free gasoline at a filling station that has installed suction devices on its pumps to eliminate dangerous vapors during refueling. As I drive along, I would not dream of throwing a paper cup out the window, as I might carelessly have done twenty or so years ago. I now compost the leaves I rake up in the fall because local laws prohibit burning them. When we remodeled our house in Maryland a few years ago, we installed a substantial amount of fiber-glass insulation in order to conserve energy. Although it is not yet mandatory in my community, I bundle up our old newspapers and regularly drop them off at a recycling station. The apple I have for lunch every day still contains pesticide residues, but fewer than it did a few years ago. If we want to drain our artificial pond in the Berkshires in order to pull out the weeds and remove the layer of silt that has covered its rocky bottom over the years, I will have to obtain a permit from the local conservation commission. A couple of decades ago the Potomac River near Washington, D.C., was a smelly, refuse-laden eyesore. Now I enjoy canoeing on the river and have even had the temerity to swim in it. The air in the city is by no means pure, but it has been cleaned enough so that it does not threaten my health—at least most days of the year. And while the air still is not crisp and clear, I no longer see thick particles of soot floating by when I look out my office window. If I see black smoke coming out of a factory or an office building smokestack or a truck tailpipe, I grow angry, wondering how the law can be flouted with impunity.

But what about the environment itself—the physical world we live in? Is it cleaner? Healthier? Safer? Are we using our resources wisely? Are we preserving the beauty of the land? Will we leave an undiminished legacy to our children and grandchildren?

Writing in 1990, twenty years after Earth Day, Barry Commoner found the answers to such questions to be "embarrassing." "Congress," he wrote, "has mandated environmental improvement; the E.P.A. has devised elaborate, detailed means of achieving this goal; most of the prescribed measures have been carried out, at least in part; and in nearly every case, the effort has failed to even approximate the goals. In both the columns of statistics and everyday experience, there is inescapable evidence that the massive national effort to restore the quality of the environment has failed."[16] Denis Hayes, the Earth Day organizer, lamented nineteen years later that "those of us who set out to change the world, who entered adulthood with dreams of global peace, racial justice, and a sustainable planet, are now on the threshold of failure. Those of us who were so outraged by the shape of the world we inherited are about to bequeath a much poorer planet to our children."[17]

That judgment is not universally shared. Lee M. Thomas, an earnest and capable public servant who was administrator of the EPA during the latter years of the Reagan administration, contended that "our accomplishments are impressive. There is no question that the air in most of our cities is far cleaner and healthier than it was in the 1960's. Thousands of miles of rivers and streams, and thousands of acres of lakes, have been restored and protected for fishing and swimming. In addition, we have taken extraordinary steps to improve the management of our hazardous wastes, toxic chemicals and pesticides."[18] His predecessor at the agency, William Ruckelshaus, asked us to consider "where we would be today supposing the federal colossus had continued to slumber and no response had followed the public demands of the late 1960s. Instead of the improvements we've witnessed, we'd have endured even greater degradation. We would find ourselves living in an increasingly inhospitable world. For a number of pollutants, the level of emissions would now be several times greater in many areas. In some cities, streetlights would come on in midafternoon because the air would be thick with particulate matter. People in Denver would be unable to see the mountains and people in Los Angeles would be unable to see one another. Rivers, many of which were bad enough in the late 1960s, would be fire hazards by now, so heavily laden would they be with oil and grease . . . The health effects would have been serious."[19]

Is the glass half full or half empty? What has environmentalism done for us and what has it not done?

Air Pollution: Advances have been made in reducing all six of the pollutants specifically identified for control in the Clean Air Act of 1970—sulfur dioxide, nitrogen oxides, carbon monoxide, ozone, lead, and solid particles. But except for lead in the air, which has gone down by 94 percent because its use in gasoline was banned, progress has not been very impressive. Many of our cities are still choked with smog, and visibility even in remote parts of the countryside is often limited by pollution from distant sources.

As for toxic air pollution—airborne chemicals that can cause cancer, birth defects, and other serious illness or even catastrophes such as the release of methyl isocyanate that killed over 2,500 people and injured hundreds of thousands in Bhopal, India, in 1984—the lack of progress is a national scandal. Between 1970, when the Clean Air Act was passed, and 1990, only eight of several hundred of these dangerous chemicals had been regulated.

After a decade of stalemate, Congress moved vigorously to correct the flaws of the Clean Air Act when it revised the law in 1990. The changes gave the EPA new tools for attacking acid rain, smog, and airborne toxics. But with a growing population and economy likely to create new sources of pollution, the act's goal of pure and healthy air still seems to lie beyond a distant horizon.

Water Pollution: The goals of fishable and swimmable surface waters established in the Clean Water Act of 1972 and of healthy drinking water set by the Safe Drinking Water Act of 1972 also remain elusive. The nation expended nearly $150 billion on sewage treatment facilities between 1972 and 1990, and some of the grosser water pollution that killed most of the commercial stocks of fish in the Great Lakes and turned rivers and coastal waters into open sewers has been reduced substantially.

But a large proportion of the nation's surface waters—perhaps as much as a half—remain useless for fishing and dangerous for swimming because of the pollutants that continue to be poured into them.[20] Once rich estuaries such as Chesapeake Bay are in serious decline because of pollution; their harvest of fish and shellfish has dwindled sharply. Oil spills, medical wastes, plastic refuse, and other human detritus force us to close beaches; our wastes kill fish, porpoises, seabirds, and other marine life. Sludge, industrial wastes, and other contaminants continue to be dumped into the ocean. Although the deep salt water is resilient, toxics and heavy metals are entering the marine food chain. Plastics and garbage continue to litter the surface and endanger sea mammals and birds.

Underground water supplies, on which about half the country depends for its drinking water, are seriously threatened and their contamination may present a future health problem of serious dimensions. Farm chemicals, contaminants from toxic waste dumps, septic systems, leaking underground gasoline storage tanks, and other hazardous materials are leaching into these aquifers and in a growing number of areas rendering their water unsafe for consumption.

The experience of Frank Kaler, who lived in a small, red brick bungalow that stood alone at the edge of a field in South Brunswick, New Jersey, is one that is repeated all too frequently around the country. "My wife brought me a cup of coffee and it tasted so terrible that I nearly threw it at her," he told me in 1979. "It was bitter and had a sheen on the surface and smelled so bad that I gagged." Kaler soon realized it was not his wife's fault: his well was poisoned. But it was months before New Jersey health officials confirmed that a long list of industrial wastes from a nearby landfill had contaminated the aquifer and turned his water into a reeking chemical cocktail.[21]

Toxic Substances: The nation has not mastered its chemical dependence. It is not, however, for want of trying. The Toxic Substances Control Act of 1976, widely referred to by the evocative name of TOSCA, was supposed to keep really dangerous substances off the market. The Resources Conservation and Recovery Act was intended to control toxic substances from the time they were produced until they were safely disposed of—"from the cradle to the grave." The Comprehensive Environmental Response, Compensation, and Liability Act of 1980—the Superfund—was enacted by Congress to clean up abandoned wastes in the urban and rural landscapes.

These laws have not fully worked, at least not yet. Efforts to protect Americans and their surroundings from chemicals are foundering in a haphazardly administered welter of confusing rules and procedures. Government administrators are hampered by inadequate data, frequent resistance by industry, and conflicting political, economic, and ideological considerations.

The General Accounting Office estimated that there may be as many as 425,000 potentially hazardous waste sites in the country.[22] Although most of the potential chemical emergencies had been addressed by 1990, fewer than a hundred of the nation's dangerous abandoned toxic waste sites had been completely cleaned up. While the EPA accelerated the process of dealing with these sites after William K. Reilly took over the agency in 1989, the remedies often continued to be inadequate.

The nation is even further from finding answers to the awesome dilemma posed by the radioactive wastes created in the production of nuclear weapons and nuclear power. No one wants to be a neighbor to life-threatening waste materials that will remain radioactive for hundreds of thousands of years.

More than three decades after publication of *Silent Spring* and twenty years after Congress passed sweeping legislation mandating the regulation of pesticides, the nation's food supply continues to be sprayed, soaked, and powdered each year with a billion pounds of toxic chemicals designed to kill insects, weeds, and other organisms. It is ironic that the percentage of the nation's crop loss to insect damage is no lower today, according to data from the Agriculture Department, than it was in the early 1940s, when a tenth of the volume of pesticides was used on crops.[23] Now as then, about a third of the nation's crop is lost to pests. The growing immunity of insects and weeds to the insecticides and herbicides we use and the destruction of natural predators by the same substances used on the pests has put the nation's agriculture on a chemical treadmill. Millions of pounds more of these chemicals are used in homes and gardens, hospitals and factories.

A report by the World Resources Institute found that more than

300,000 farmers a year in this country are affected by pesticide poisoning. The World Health Organization estimated that at least 5,000 people in the world die each year as a result of exposure to agricultural chemicals. Many of the pesticides already barred in this country are exported by U.S. manufacturers.[24] Some of these chemicals make their way back here as residues on imported foods or as air pollution from Mexico and the Caribbean. Chemical residues continue to show up in our fruit and vegetables, our bread and meat.

Some eminent scientists have joined the chemical industry in complaining that environmentalists exaggerate the dangers of pesticide residues on food. In several instances the EPA, after weighing additional evidence, has reversed a decision to ban an agricultural chemical it had ordered off the market after environmentalists' complaints. But there can be little doubt that chemicals that kill insects and weeds can also harm people, particularly if they are not used properly. In recent years, not only consumers and environmentalists but also farmers and even industry are beginning to ask whether crops could not be protected with a substantially reduced volume of expensive and potentially dangerous substances.

Solid Waste: By the mid-1980s, 160 million tons of garbage was being generated each year, more than half a ton for every man, woman, and child in the country. Municipal waste dumps were increasingly overwhelmed.[25] The inevitable consequences of a high-consumption, throwaway economy finally began to catch up with us. Per capita production of solid waste in this country is twice that in Japan. New York City's Fresh Kills landfill became a mountain of garbage, the highest point on the eastern seaboard. With land costs soaring near urban areas, it became difficult, if not impossible, to find space for new dumps. Tipping fees for dumping garbage in landfills rose from a few dollars a ton to well over $100. The garbage barge *Mobro*, filled with 3,100 tons of refuse from Long Island, roamed the seas for months seeking a place to get rid of its cargo and, in the process, becoming a symbol of the nation's garbage dilemma. Our throwaway society is being buried in its own debris.

Recycling is part of the solution—but only part. As Denis Hayes noted, our garbage dumps are richer than our mines. Among industrial countries, the United States has the poorest recycling record. Per capita, we recycle less than half the Japanese total. In recent years a growing number of communities are adopting recycling programs and finding that they reduce the urgency of the problem and buy time for seeking a permanent solution. But the continuing lack of markets for recycled materials, technological obstacles, and the sheer volume of the waste make recycling only a partial solution.

The only effective answer, it is now clear, is not to produce the stuff, or to make as little as we can. To the greatest extent possible we must reduce waste by using different processes or materials. Consumer products should be made durable. Packaging, a major component of the domestic waste stream, can be reduced substantially. When William K. Reilly took over the EPA in 1989, he made "pollution prevention" one of his chief goals.

Biotechnology: This is one of the most difficult new issues. The potential benefits of genetic engineering and other applications of the new genetics could, of course, be enormous. More productive strains of food and fiber, biological pest controls, new gene pools for species on the verge of extinction, more effective pharmaceuticals, new ways of disposing of waste, and new industrial processes are only some of the possibilities opened by human command of the building blocks of life. But the potential dangers of the new technology are also huge. Most frightening is the possibility of harm to human life through the release of an accidentally manufactured pathogen. The problem is how to prevent genetic engineering from endangering humans and their environment without standing in the way of progress.

Energy: Many of the most intractable of the nation's environmental problems involve the production and consumption of energy—now chiefly derived from oil, coal, natural gas, and nuclear reactors. The combustion of coal is of course a major cause of air pollution, including acid rain and the carbon dioxide that contributes so heavily to the greenhouse effect. While the federal government is heavily subsidizing the coal mining and utility industries' efforts to develop "clean coal technology," much of the coal burned today is still "dirty" in that it sends sulfur, nitrogen, carbon dioxide, and solid particles into the air. Although such technology eventually may enable coal to be burned without emitting high levels of the sulfur that causes acid rain, there is, as of this writing, still no commercially viable technology available that prevents carbon from rising into the atmosphere.

The age of petroleum is surely drawing to an end. Few experts quarrel seriously with estimates that, for all practical purposes, recoverable oil reserves in the United States will be depleted within a few decades to the point where it will no longer be economical to extract.[26] While there are still huge reserves in the Middle East, it is questionable whether they would be able to meet the growing world demand much beyond the middle of the next century. Moreover, the United States has learned painfully the consequences of placing its economy and national security at the mercy of oil suppliers in unstable, potentially hostile foreign countries. In 1991, the United States and its allies committed over a million of their men and women and billions of dollars to a war in the Persian Gulf brought on, in part at least, by the need to ensure access to the oil of the Middle East. By the end of the 1980s the United States was spending a total of over $420 billion a year on oil, coal, natural gas, and other sources of energy[27] and importing roughly half of its oil supply. The trend is expected to curve upward.

Instead of preparing for the day when we run out of oil, however, the United States is pursuing policies that are bringing that day rapidly closer and will necessitate a chaotic transition. Those policies are also guaranteed to harm the environment. As domestic reserves run down, federal policy has encouraged oil companies in their frantic, hugely expensive efforts to find and exploit new reserves. It has given incredibly short shrift to conservation and the development of new and renewable sources of power.

The search for oil has carried industry prospectors into remote and ecologically fragile areas—the Outer Continental Shelf and the North Slope of Alaska—and onto pristine public forest and rangeland. We have seen some of the results of this ruthless effort to wrest the last economically recoverable reserves of domestic oil from our land and oceans, this "last dance of the dinosaurs," as Jay Hair called it. The sullied beaches, the fouled water, the dead and dying birds and mammals coated with viscous crude oil, and the at least temporarily lost fisheries of Santa Barbara Channel and Alaska's Prince William Sound were tragic and inevitable consequences of the desperate scramble to squeeze the last of our oil from the earth.

In response to persisting problems, as well as to the emergence of even more demanding global challenges—such as the greenhouse effect, the destruction of the ozone shield, deforestation, and the loss of biodiversity—the environmental community is gradually shifting its agenda. As the 1990s began, however, it was not clear whether the political climate in the United States would accommodate the urgent demands of this new agenda.

Writing in 1989, Thomas Berry, the widely admired eco-theologian, found that "in the last three years of the 1980's a vast change of consciousness seems to be sweeping over the entire human community, a change in all our professions and institutions, a change away from our plundering industrial order to a functional ecological order. We begin to realize that we are members not simply of a human community but of a larger community, the multi-species community, that encompasses the entire world of the living and indeed the entire complex of all those beings that constitute our homeland planet, Earth."[28]

With all its problems and shortcomings, environmentalism appears, in the last years of the century, to have the support of an increasingly well-informed public. The movement is at last well armed with experience, professional cadre, legislative tools, and national and international networks to move ahead on a broad front to protect land, preserve life, and confront ecological threats on a global as well as national scale.

But success against the powerful forces that continue to oppose it is by no means assured. The problems it faces are increasingly complex. The national organizations have yet to blend their agenda with the broader social agenda of economic and racial equity. They are still unable to tap effectively the potential strength of the grass-roots activists. Other pressing issues demand room on the stage of national and international policy. And even the land and the wildlife it supports, the focus of traditional conservation for a century now, continue to come under assault.

REBUILDING

THE

HOUSE

Trend is not destiny.
—René Dubos

As a new millennium approaches, time to save and rebuild the environment is running down. Some alarmed environmentalists and scientists fear we have no more than a decade or so of grace. Others give us a half century. Still others believe there will be no collapse of our habitat but a long, slow descent into a biological twilight over the next century or two.

But as René Dubos once observed, "trend is not destiny." The genius that has enabled humankind to master nature and intervene in the process of evolution through technology and social organization can extricate us from the ecological quicksand.

The essential message of environmentalism is not catastrophe but hope. The environmentalists have established a broad but clear agenda for us. They have told us what the solutions are. We are almost awash in answers. We can extricate ourselves from our ecological peril by stabilizing population, conserving resources, preventing pollution, and preserving and restoring nature.

We know what we have to do. All we lack is the wisdom and the will to do it. All that stands in our way is human nature and its works over the last 10,000 years or so.

Environmental historian Donald Worster has pointed out that the nation's economic and social institutions have accommodated the impulse to protect the environment, "up to a point." American culture, he said, has always found favor with the ideals of cleanliness and beauty when such ideals did not get in the way of making money.

"But it is altogether premature to assume that such accommodation implies deep cultural change," Worster wrote. "To say the least," he added, "it is highly problematical whether, on balance, there has been a radical change to environmental protection in this society or even whether what has been achieved will survive into the next century."[1]

Progress cannot be made with regulatory Band-Aids, blind faith in the invisible hand of the market, or other facile remedies. There must be changes in our institutions, in our economic systems, in technology, and in social relationships in ways that reflect our hard-won understanding of the changing balance between human beings and nature. It is, in short, time for society to catch up to the accelerated pace of evolution in the physical world created by human numbers and human power.

To state such goals would appear to set our imperfect society a hopeless task. One has only to look at our economy in disarray, our deadlocked government, the growing power of special interests, our inattentive media, a struggling educational system, poverty and class strife, the political passivity of large segments of the American people, their lack of care about the future, and the age-old ambivalence between love of the land and greed, to realize the immense obstacles that stand in the way of the broad social changes that are called for by the urgency of the environmental problems. Added to these is the difficulty in bringing the nations of the world together to address the threats to the global environment. Not to mention the emotional and intellectual hurdles that we humans, just a few thousand years from huddling around fires in our caves seeking refuge from the terrors of wild nature, must leap in order to readjust our relationship to the natural world.

Differentiating between "hope" and "expectation," the philosopher Ivan Illich said, "I for one see signs of hope in the lifestyles of subsistence peasants or in the network of activists who save trees here, or plant them there. But I admit that I am unable to envisage how, short of a devastating catastrophe, these hope-inspiring acts can be translated into 'policy.' "[2]

That, of course, is what the environmental movement is seeking to do. The environmental impulse, building on the ideas and leadership of farsighted men and women in the nineteenth and twentieth centuries, and expressed through an expanding and increasingly popular movement, could be the agency of sweeping political and social transformation. We have seen how environmentalism has already led to substantial change in our laws, our institutions, and our personal behavior. It has produced a large cadre of informed, trained activists. As the movement continues to grow in strength, it could have the potential to become the instrument of a political evolution that will enable us to establish, as Nathan Gardels put it, "equilibrium between man and nature, and between future and present."[3]

Environmentalism provides a way of acting, of overcoming the passivity of individuals in a mass civilization. It is a different way of thinking about such basic issues as what constitutes progress and how people ought to live. By showing us that we can tame our machines and make them useful without being harmful, environmentalism points toward a civilization advancing with the help of careful science and sensible technology. Environmentalism just may be the threshold of a true post-industrial society.

As a nation, we have yet to cross that threshold. Support for environmental goals and values remains broad but shallow. The political fallout from short-term crises such as economic downturns or the Persian Gulf war demonstrate how easily the attention of the American people can be diverted from environmental problems, how quickly our concerns revert to short-term self-interest. It is clear that the old industrial order is still largely in command. The environmental movement, despite enormous expenditures of talent and effort, and some real progress in limiting pollution and the destruction of resources, has not achieved the fundamental reforms vital to assure our ecological security over the long run.

In the early 1990s it is apparent that the environmental movement in the United States, while still growing and vital, is running up against the limits of its ability to achieve social change using its traditional tools. To achieve the basic reforms necessary to reach its goals, the environmental movement itself will have to evolve. There must be a fourth wave of environmentalism.

For much of this century, the movement has been functioning as an ecological emergency squad, responding to crises and seeking to plug a leaking statute here or fill a regulatory gap there. In the future, instead of simply lecturing, or lobbying, or demonstrating, or haggling, or litigating to protect public health and natural resources, the environmentalism activists almost certainly must move forward to acquire the *power* necessary to achieve fundamental change. To do so they will have to tap the latent support that is repeatedly demonstrated by the opinion polls to build an effective political base—a base strong enough to counter the financial power wielded by those interests that oppose environmental reform. Political leaders must be presented with a clear choice between addressing our environmental ills and being replaced.

Little has changed since Gifford Pinchot commented the better part of a century ago that "there is no reason why the American people cannot take into their hands again the full political power which is theirs by right and which they exercised before the special interests began to nullify the will of the majority."[4]

Gus Speth, the president of the World Resources Institute, predicted that the environmental movement is moving toward a political breakthrough. "I believe that the United States is going to have what we really haven't had yet. We talk about the greening of technology, and the greening of this and the greening of that. We really haven't had a greening of politics in the United States."[5]

Speth is probably right. The electorate, tired of the Tweedledum and Tweedledee ineptitude of the entrenched political parties, probably would welcome a change of direction. Such a desire was demonstrated by the startling public support for the presidential candidacy of billionaire Ross Perot in 1992. But the environmental movement will not achieve the kind of deep political power it needs easily or overnight, if at all. In the absence of proportional representation, a Green Party, particularly one pasted together from a green political movement as splintered as the one in the United States, would find it almost impossible to place its candidates in office except very occasionally in isolated local elections. Even less likely is a successful revolutionary effort by radical environmentalists.

If environmentalism is to gain genuine power, it will have to do it the old-fashioned way—by building coalitions brawny enough to compel the political system, including the two major parties, to adopt its agenda. The environmentalists must be able to command the same kind of respectful attention as business and industry in city halls, statehouses, Congress, and the White House.

To begin with, ways must be found to close the gap between the large national environmental organizations and the grass-roots groups whose members comprise an army of millions ready to be mobilized in the war for political power. As Lois Gibbs pointed out, the community-based groups often succeed where the national organizations fail. They do so, she insisted, by rejecting the "soft path" of negotiation and compromise with governments and corporations and instead taking the harder path of direct political confrontation.[6] Negotiation and compromise can be more useful tools for the environmentalists when they can come to the table with strength equal to that of their opponents.

The national organizations have the knowledge, professionalism, and experience in the niceties and not-so-niceties of national, regional, and statewide politics. They can reinforce the grass-roots activists with an array of skills that can be used where direct political confrontation would be unproductive overkill. They bring their own substantial and relatively affluent membership into the political arena.

A step in this direction was made in 1990 when the "Gang of Ten," an informal but exclusive club of major national environmental groups, disbanded and its members sought to enlarge their outreach to a wider segment of the movement. But it was a small step on what will have to be a long journey.

When the national and grass-roots environmentalists forge themselves into a unified force—if they ever do—they would constitute a formidable new presence on the national political stage. Parties and elected officials would be required to pay more respectful attention to their issues. But even a unified environmental movement would be far from possessing the commanding political power requisite for attaining fundamental social reform. A much broader coalition is required.

To make the political breakthrough necessary to achieve their goals, the environmentalists *must* make common cause with other sectors of our society that have a stake in changing the political and economic status quo. Potential allies include the poor, minorities, women, industrial workers, and other vulnerable groups whose vital interests demand significant social change. The movement surely should explore joining forces with businesses that require a clean environment and efficiently used resources to prosper, and with conservatives fed up with the corporate socialism that is the hallmark of today's PAC-financed realpolitik.

It will not be easy. It will not happen overnight. But a new majority coalition, with the environmental movement as one of its major building blocks, is no pipe dream—it is a real possibility.

First, however, the environmental organizations must put their own houses in order. The great failure of much of the national movement in recent years, in my opinion, has been its unwillingness or inability to take up the causes of social justice in the United States. This failure is all the more dismaying because one of the deepest roots of contemporary environmentalism lies, as we have seen, in the activist civil rights/peace/women's tradition of the 1960s.

Opponents of the environmental movement often brand it as "elitist." For example, William Tucker's book *Progress and Privilege*,

published in 1982, called environmentalism "the politics of aristoc-
racy." Tucker described the environmental movement as "essentially
a suburban agrarianism" espoused by those who have achieved a high
level of comfort and security and want to preserve their privileged
position by blocking further economic and technological progress.[7]
Such arguments, deliberately or out of ignorance, overlook the fact
that almost all Americans, particularly the poor and underprivileged,
are the victims of environmental degradation. It is a point of view
that fails to recognize that pollution is a serious public health concern
and that misuse of resources is a threat to our national security. It is
a perspective that is out of touch with reality.

Unfortunately, it is true that the leadership of national environmental groups *is* largely white, male, and well educated, with incomes
above the national average. This description, however, would fit activists in virtually every social movement. As one study concluded,
"people who are politically active, whether in environmental or any
other issues, tend to be uniformly drawn from the upper middle
class."[8] While relatively well-to-do, few of today's national environmental activists could be considered rich. The tradition of wealthy,
highborn amateurs of the early conservation years is long since gone.
Sociologists Denton Morrison and Riley Dunlap point out, moreover,
that "the *opponents* of environmentalism come much closer to being
an elite than do core environmentalists. Most of the most vocal, co-
ordinated opposition comes from top levels of corporate management.
Such objections to environmental reform are hardly above suspicion
as representing upper-class interests, even if frequently couched in a
rationale of concern for general, including underclass, welfare."[9]

The imbalances in the social composition of the leadership and
staffs of the national environmental organizations cannot, however,
be simply dismissed. One of the reasons that there are not more
representatives of minority groups is that the leaders of the groups
have not, until very recently, taken the trouble to reach out to those
communities. I am not sure of the reasons for this, but I doubt that
they reflect conscious racism. I suspect that many of the environmentalists are so confident that they are doing the Lord's work that

it did not occur to them that they have other obligations to society.

Most of the environmental organizations have recently started to take steps to change "the whiteness of the green movement," but one senses they are doing so basically out of a sense of obligation or in response to criticism. In reality, the environmentalists need the knowledge, talent, street smarts, practical experience, political energy, and militancy of angry outsiders from minority communities more than the minorities need the environmentalists.

Early in 1990 leaders of civil rights and minority community organizations wrote to the major national environmental groups asking them not only to change their hiring practices but to play an active role in addressing the environmental evils afflicting the poor and oppressed. "You must know as well as we do," the letter said, "that white organizations isolated from our Third World communities can never build a movement."

Environmentalists are often charged with opposing economic growth that creates jobs and economic projects, including housing, that help the poor. They are also accused of selfishly blocking economic development of public lands that could benefit all of society.

Some members of groups on the radical fringe are no-growth advocates, but modern environmentalism does not seek to halt economic growth; on the contrary, one of its overriding goals is to be sure that economic growth can be sustained over the long run. It therefore presses for an economy that makes prudent use of natural resources. The corporate critics who charge elitism are often those whose practices pollute and waste resources and thus compromise the nation's long-term economic prospects, who themselves eliminate thousands of jobs by moving their plants to foreign countries where the cost of labor is low, or who abandon block after block of inner-city housing.

Many of the environmentalists, however, are too often insensitive to the economic consequences of their programs, particularly as they affect workers, minorities, and the poor. During the 1990 congressional debate over amendments to the Clean Air Act, for example, the environmental lobbyists in Washington only belatedly and weakly supported economic assistance for miners in the high-sulfur coal industry whose jobs would be eliminated by the new rules for reducing acid rain. Much the same could be said about the environmentalists' campaign to save the endangered spotted owl and the ancient forests of the Northwest that are the bird's only habitat. While pursuing their worthy goal, they provided only late and inadequate proposals for protecting the jobs of workers in the timber industry and preserving the logging communities that depended on the old-growth forest for their livelihood.

Environmental regulation as now practiced does have a negative, if relatively small effect on the gross national product and on the creation of jobs over the short term. But as Morrison and Dunlap assert, "there is no inherent reason why environmental protection and social justice must constitute conflicting social goals. The challenge is to develop social policies which promote *both*."[10] It is a challenge the environmental movement must accept.

Today's environmentalists are not indifferent to injustices such as poverty and racism. Many have a deep personal concern. But involved in the pressing, sometimes overwhelming task of dealing with environmental crises, they push aside the issues of social and economic equity as someone else's immediate business. At least some of the organizations hold back from broader social activism because they fear it would jeopardize their funding from corporations or government sources or alienate their more conservative constituencies.

Environmentalism will not be able to claim full legitimacy for its aims, however, until it addresses the even graver social ills of poverty, hunger, prejudice, and economic inequity. Bertolt Brecht said it in *The Threepenny Opera*: "First feed the face and then talk right from wrong." It is not enough for the environmental groups to demand that the old-growth forests of the Northwest be preserved to save the spotted owl or call for an end to the burning of high-sulfur coal to reduce acid rain. It is also incumbent upon them to come up with carefully worked-out, politically acceptable, economically viable, and timely programs for preserving the communities that depend on logging and to make sure that displaced coal miners are protected against economic disaster. Environmentalists need not put jobs, housing, discrimination, drugs, or homelessness at the top of their list of priorities. But they need to recognize that these problems are an important part of their agendas.

It is unlikely that the comprehensive reforms needed to protect the environment can ever be achieved without redressing those wider social problems. Environmental degradation and social injustice, as we have already seen, arise from essentially the same flaws in our social structure.

Political power cannot be built on a base of dispirited, impoverished people struggling to stay alive in crime-ridden urban ghettos, in barrios or rural slums. As the Reverend Jesse Jackson, the indefatigable herald of the Rainbow Coalition, said: "You cannot separate environment from empowerment. Toxic waste dumps are put in communities where people are the poorest, the least organized, the least registered to vote. If you are poor you are a target for toxic waste. If you are unregistered to vote you are a target."[11]

Preserving open spaces and public lands is vital, but conservationists must try to assure that those amenities are broadly available to all Americans. Of course, the claim by those who wish to profit from the public lands and develop every inch of green space that only rich elitists oppose them is hypocritical and false. The national parks and forests and other public lands are used for enjoyment today chiefly by middle- and working-class vacationers, while the well-to-do can go to the parks or to Acapulco, St. Moritz, or their summer homes on Martha's Vineyard. But these lands must also be open to the children of Watts and Harlem, for whom a tree or a blade of grass is today an all too exotic species.

Widening their agenda in this way will be difficult for the national environmental organizations. Many of them draw much of their membership and financial support from the more well-to-do people or from corporations, where support for social activism tends to be thin or negative.

But environmentalism could be a potent democratizing force. If the house that shelters us all is crumbling, we can unite to try to save and rebuild it. The ground must be made fertile for the planting of entirely new political seeds, making it possible to raise a formidable popular coalition able to win elections at the local, state, and national levels and to push environmental issues to the forefront of the national agenda.

Then what? Assuming that the environmental movement attains the will, the means, and the strength to exercise decisive power over American politics and government, how does it use that power? How does it try to build an ecologically rational as well as socially just society?

Certainly by making wiser budget choices, enacting more effective laws, ensuring honest and rigorous enforcement of those laws, and appointing dedicated public servants to oversee them. But laws and rules, as the last twenty years have demonstrated, are insufficient by themselves. Waste, inefficiency, avarice, shortsightedness, indifference, cannot be legislated out of existence.

The starting point, I firmly believe, must be a reevaluation of some of our economic assumptions. I am no economist and I am not presumptuous enough to propose any sweeping new economic theories. But anyone who has followed environmental problems over the years can hardly fail to trace many of their causes to flaws in our day-to-day economic practices. A key step in our effort to save the environment, in my view, is dealing with those shortcomings.

Free-market capitalism has proven to be a resilient and effective system for producing and distributing goods and services. In practice, however, markets are frequently managed and manipulated and their "freedom" is illusory. Only a cursory look at the United States economy—with its huge budget and trade deficits, its unemployment, its badly skewed distribution of wealth, its savings and loan debacles, its irrational subsidies and other malfunctions—demonstrates that it is far from a perfect system. A rising tide, contrary to popular wisdom, not only often fails to lift all ships, it can also cause extensive damage to coastal ecosystems. One can believe in and support the free market without regarding it as an object of worship to be defended by a holy war at any word of criticism or suggestion of reform.

One failure of the system is that it does not reasonably account for ecological values. Environmental degradation and resource depletion are issues that are largely unaddressed by our economic yardsticks. Today's market indicators do not assign a negative value to pollution or the expenditure of natural resources. They do not place a fair or realistic value on unspoiled natural systems or human health. If we are to preserve the environment from destruction, we must get the costs of production and consumption right, and then adjust prices to reflect the true costs.

One way to get at this dilemma is "full-cost pricing," an approach that, as the 1990s began, was getting increased scrutiny from economists and even many businessmen. The idea would be to add the costs of pollution and the depletion of resources to the selling price of any product. An example offered by energy expert Amory Lovins would be to impose a surcharge on autos that guzzle gasoline and to offer rebates on fuel-efficient cars.

An ecologically sound society must also reexamine the prevailing economic notion of progress. One need not oppose economic growth to ask: Growth for what? Growth for whom? The gross national product is a highly doubtful measure of national and human welfare. Does a healthy economy really require the continual expansion of the production of goods and services without regard to the necessity and utility of those products and their impact on health and the natural environment? Does it make sense for us to spend well over $100 billion a year to repair the ravages of pollution and then count that sum as growth, as progress, because it adds to the GNP?

An ecologically sound economy should adopt policies that encourage, not growth for its own sake, but growth that provides for the real needs of its citizens with an absolute minimum of waste and pollution.

Progress is not achieved solely by stimulating consumer wants and accumulating profits. Are not many of our economic goods really economic bads? Is our mass economy really making us happier as individuals, more stable and secure as a society? Are not the degradation of our environment, social inequity, and social ills such as drugs and crime related to the failures of our economic and social systems?

We need different definitions of economic growth to measure progress. Instead of using the GNP—the gross production of goods and services—as our most sacred indicator, we must substitute new measures of national well-being that account for the depletion of resources, the destruction of nature, the welfare of human beings, and real national progress over the long run.

The idea is not to abandon our economic system but to strip it of those parts that threaten not only the long-term health of the environment but the long-term health of the economy as well. Sustainable development may now be regarded as a cliché, but it is really an expression of responsibility for and faith in the future.

Our mullahs of free-market orthodoxy who condemn long-term economic and environmental planning as sacrilege are shortsighted and are voices of generational selfishness. "Their eyes are fixed upon the present gain and they are blind to the future." By looking indifferently at the pollution of the commons and the exhaustion of resources, those indifferent to the true costs of environmental protection could be the gravediggers of American capitalism if they had their way. Those who demand economic policies that can be sustained in future generations are the true champions of the free market.

With proper planning and prudence, there need be no limits to economic growth. We are not truly constrained by what Kenneth Boulding called a "spaceman" economy, one that can expand so far and no farther in a hermetically sealed system. As Barry Commoner and others have pointed out, the earth enjoys a constant supply of new energy from the sun. If we use the earth's resources wisely to put this energy to use, there is no reason that we cannot have a constantly rising standard of living into the foreseeable future.

The new economics will reward husbanding dwindling resources, recycling existing resources, and restoring land, water, and other natural systems that have already become degraded and unproductive. Progress will be redefined to mean reducing poverty and providing a steadily rising quality of life for a stable or diminishing population. The wealth that is created out of natural resources must be shared more equitably. Provision will be made for preserving open space, biological diversity, and the beauty of nature, all of which will be recognized as representing long-term economic as well as aesthetic value. The natural systems that sustain life will have to be protected through careful and constant stewardship.

Revised economic goals will require changes in the way we operate financial markets and in the role of corporations. Our financial practices customarily discount long-term investments. The highest returns are thus made by developing and exploiting resources as quickly as possible. Professor Colin Clark, who teaches applied mathematics at the University of British Columbia, noted that "if dollars in banks are growing faster than a timber company's forests, it is more profitable (indeed, more economical) to chop down the trees, sell them, and invest the proceeds elsewhere."[12]

American corporations are, almost by definition, in thrall to the "tyranny of the immediate," particularly the tyranny of the money and securities markets. Even those corporate executives who want to do the right environmental thing are constrained by the need to produce the best bottom line in the near term to satisfy their shareholders and to make the best use of the money markets. Voluntarism cannot do the job. A giant Du Pont Company can change policy to reward its managers for environmental as well as economic performance, or a Monsanto can pledge to eliminate toxic emissions unilaterally, only because they are in exceptionally strong market positions. But many companies that would like to adopt responsible environmental policies cannot do so because they would then be at a competitive disadvantage with businesses in their industry that choose to plunge ahead in seeking profit and ignore the environmental consequences.

Economic incentives, of course, are one way to influence corporate behavior. If corporate managers were required to include in their annual balance sheets heavy taxes paid on air or water they have polluted, they would no doubt think twice before letting their emissions into the environment. Eliminating subsidies for environmentally

velopments that are bad for the public health, such as
oal mining on public land, superhighway construction,
oduction, and making these activities subject to the
... marketplace would also help.

In recent years there have been an increasing number of proposals to restructure our tax system by partially replacing taxes on
wages and profits—that is to say, taxing work and capital forma-
tion—with taxes on pollution and resource depletion. Such a policy
would have some problems—a pollution tax would be regressive and
require rebates to lower-income families. But it would also raise
revenues by taxing harmful things, such as pollution and resource
depletion, rather than productive things, such as work and investment.

To achieve meaningful, lasting changes in corporate behavior,
however, it probably will be necessary to make substantial changes
in the structure and values of the corporations themselves. This could
be done by revised securities laws that would require companies to
achieve defined levels of environmental performance. Another possibility is the mandatory rewriting of corporate charters to reflect a
set of values similar to the Valdez Principles, a code of behavior that
calls on companies to address the impact of their operations and
products on their employees, their communities, their customers, and
the environment. Corporate behavior may eventually be regulated by
the principle—codified by law—that the health of the common environment takes precedence over the rights of private property. Pun-
ishments for violation of this principle would have to be certain and
severe. When industry tells us that for the good of society we must
accept the level of risk its operations and products generate, it should
be required to justify the claim. It must prove that there is no commercially practicable alternative that can reduce or eliminate risk. It
must show clearly who benefits and who suffers as a result of the
risk.

But within the framework of new legal and ethical norms, corporations would also have to be given the freedom to achieve their
production, financial, and environmental goals as flexibly as possible,
without detailed, day-to-day prescription by government regulators.

Corporations required to adhere to environmental as well as financial standards would, perforce, have to adopt new criteria for developing and deploying their technologies. No longer could a General Motors announce one week that it had developed the prototype of a virtually pollution-free electric car and the next week attack stiffer tailpipe emissions standards proposed in clean air legislation as unattainable. Experience has shown that companies forced by environmental rules to adopt new technologies generally find themselves in a better competitive position after modernizing.

Inappropriate technology—designed solely to maximize efficiency, production, and profits—was a major cause of our descent into ecological jeopardy. Appropriate technology—designed and used with the well-being of humans and the preservation and enhancement of the environment as necessary goals—can be one of the roads out of our predicament. The mainstream of environmentalism embraces technology that does not destroy the garden but quietly and unobtrusively helps cultivate the land and grow safe and healthy crops.

We need not cling to our blind faith in science and technology to realize that, if we are to escape ecological disaster, we will need the tools that only science and technology can provide. But we must think through very carefully all the consequences of using our machines. We must ask ourselves, for example, if we wish to continue to have machines replace human labor when joblessness causes so much human suffering. We must reject technology that destroys life and the means of sustaining life. But as Lewis Mumford stated, "for those of us who are more hopeful both of man's destiny and that of the machine, the machine is no longer the paragon of progress and the final expression of our desires: it is merely a series of instruments which we will use in so far as they are serviceable to life at large, and which we will curtail where they infringe upon it or exist purely to support the adventitious structure of capitalism."[13]

The power of computers to store and communicate knowledge gives us a strong push down the road to an environmentally sustainable technology. The space program can help monitor the earth and after that is done can carry humans to the planets. Other technologies—new energy sources such as photovoltaics, a panoply of energy-saving appliances, vehicles, and other devices, genetic engineering, durable new materials and new methods of reusing old materials, superconductors, perhaps safe nuclear fusion, and many other feats of wizardry—will be pulled out of the hat to serve both the economy and the environment.

Freeing ourselves of the machinery of the industrial age and replacing it with a technology that serves both organic nature and human society is today's mission into the wilderness. It will be a demanding task. Our choices must be careful ones.

"For each specific technology," the economist Hazel Henderson admonished, "we might ask whether it is labor-intensive, rather than capital- and energy-intensive, and how much capital is required to create each workplace. Does it dislocate settled communities and cultural patterns, and if so, at what social cost? Is it based on renewable or exhaustible resource utilization? Does it increase or decrease societal flexibility? Is it centralizing or decentralizing? Does it increase human liberty and widen the distribution of power, knowledge and wealth in societies or concentrate them? . . . What risks does it pose to workers, consumers, society at large and future generations?" If a technology produces irreversible and intergenerational risks it should be "assumed socially unacceptable until proven otherwise. The very shifting of burdens of proof to the producers of technological hardware in itself constitutes an important paradigm shift toward greater human maturity and responsibility for future generations."[14]

Social justice, political power, economic reform, corporate accountability, and technological evolution—these are the building blocks of an ecologically sound society in the United States. But the edifice cannot be raised without a deeper devotion of the American people to environmental goals and values. As former EPA administrator Lee M. Thomas said, our response to the environmental threats that confront us "must involve a personal commitment from each of us to live environmentally ethical lives—not because it is a requirement of law but because it is an essential component of our inherent responsibility to ourselves, our neighbors, our children and our planet. In fact, environmental laws will not be effective unless they are supported by a widely accepted environmental ethic."[15]

The time may be nearly at hand. A restless, discontented, increasingly fragmented American people is, I think, groping for new values, a new center to our lives. That center has shifted several times over the course of our nation's history. The first Europeans came here to plant a garden in the freedom of a fresh new world. That dream was replaced by belief in Manifest Destiny and the optimism and opportunity of the frontier. Then came the industrial revolution, which elevated mass production, consumption, the corporation, and the worship of the machine into a paramount position in our value system.

Consumerism now seems to be growing increasingly stale and dissatisfying as a value around which to build our lives. At the same time we are becoming more and more aware of the peril created by our own works and of how far we have distanced ourselves from nature. Environmentalism has shown us that the world need not be this way. And it is pointing us in a new direction, toward a new set of values that would lead us to live more gently on and harmoniously with this planet.

In *Man and Nature*, George Perkins Marsh asked, "Could this old world, which man has overthrown, be rebuilt, could human cunning rescue its wasted hillsides and its deserted plains from solitude or mere nomad occupation, from bareness, from nakedness, and from insalubrity, and restore the ancient fertility and healthfulness . . . ?" His answer was that such rebuilding "must await great political and moral revolutions in the governments and peoples . . ."[16]

Now, more than a century and a quarter later, those political and moral revolutions may be taking place. The critics of environmentalism, the Julian Simons and Herman Kahns who contend that we need not fear ecological disaster because human intelligence, resourcefulness, and ingenuity will find the solutions, may have been right—but right in a way they did not intend. Humans *are* responding to the devastation that human works have created. They are doing it by creating a new system of values and a new mass movement called environmentalism. In the United States, this movement is advancing—slowly and sporadically—on a broad front. Its ranks are open enough to include radical Earth First! tree huggers and patrician big-game hunters, militant community activists and cool intellectuals cloistered in think tanks, hard-nosed lobbyists and dreamy bird-watchers. It has captured the interest and sympathy of a widening segment of the American public, the pained attention of our business community, and the wary support of our public officials.

Environmentalism has shown enormous resiliency and staying power. It has kept its strength and continued to grow where other recent crusades, including the civil rights, women's, and trade union movements, have been stalled or checked. If it is a revolution, it is a peaceful one that, except for an extreme fringe, eschews radical solutions.

Despite its potential, the environmental movement has yet to exercise its strength decisively. Possibly it may never do so. The forces that oppose it—a minority, to be sure, but one that possesses enormous wealth with which it can exercise control over the nation's political and economic affairs—have given ample evidence that they will not lightly surrender their power.

But I believe that environmentalism will prevail. The alternatives are clearly unacceptable to a rational and democratic society. If we do not replant and rebuild, we bequeath to our children a bleak and dubious future on a crowded, hungry, poisoned, and unlovely planet. And that might not be the worst. As William Ruckelshaus and others have warned, the exigencies of supporting human life in an increasingly degraded, unproductive, and threatening environment could impose pressures on our free institutions heavy enough to break them.

The history of this country is a history of regeneration, of continual social reconstruction. As James Oliver Robertson reminds us, "American destiny was informed, in myth, by one central principle: America is a fresh place, a new beginning, an opportunity."[17] America can still be that place. Today, the frontier, the new beginning, is the challenge of restoring and safeguarding our environment, of re-creating a "fresh place."

Rachel Carson told us there is another road that offers "our last, our only chance to reach a destination that assures the preservation of our earth."[18] Because of environmentalism, we know we must take that road to re-create not only a cleaner, safer, more pleasant environment but also a sustainable economy and a more just and democratic society.

Preface

1. Roderick Nash, *The Rights of Nature* (Madison: University of Wisconsin Press, 1989), p. 55.
2. Aldo Leopold, *A Sand County Almanac* (New York: Oxford University Press, 1948), p. 203.

1. The Garden and the Wilderness

1. J. K. Galbraith, *The Affluent Society* (Boston: Houghton Mifflin Company, 1958).
2. Murray Bookchin, *Our Synthetic Environment* (New York: Colophon, 1974), p. 217.
3. Leopold, op. cit., pp. 216–17.
4. Frederick Jackson Turner, *The Significance of Frontier in American History*, reprinted in Daniel J. Boorstein, ed., *An American Primer* (Chicago: University of Chicago Press, 1966), p. 547.
5. Charles A. Beard and Mary R. Beard, *The Rise of American Civilization* (New York: The Macmillan Company, 1941), Vol. 2, p. 760.
6. *Journals and Other Documents on the Life and Voyages of Christopher Columbus*, trans. and ed. by Samuel Eliot Morison (New York: Heritage Press, 1963), p. 87.
7. Ibid., p. 88.

8. Leo Marx, *The Machine in the Garden* (New York: Oxford University Press, 1964), p. 3.

9. James Oliver Robertson, *American Myth, American Reality* (New York: Hill and Wang, 1980), pp. 41, 42.

10. Francis Parkman, *Pioneers of France in the New World* (Boston: Little, Brown and Company, 1905), p. 39.

11. David B. Quinn and Alison M. Quinn, eds., *The First Colonists* (Raleigh: North Carolina Department of Cultural Resources, 1982), p. 2.

12. William Cronon, *Changes in the Land* (New York: Hill and Wang, 1983), p. 25.

13. Stewart Udall, *The Quiet Crisis* (Salt Lake City: Peregrine Smith Books, 1988), p. 54.

14. Quoted in Robert McHenry and Charles Van Doren, eds., *A Documentary History of Conservation in America* (New York: Praeger Publishers, 1972), p. 172.

15. Marx, op. cit., p. 41.

16. Perry Miller, *Errand into the Wilderness* (Cambridge: Harvard University Press, 1956), p. 15.

17. Quoted in Ray Allen Billington, *Land of Savagery Land of Promise* (New York: W. W. Norton & Company, 1981), p. 10.

18. Cronon, op. cit., p. 5.

19. Robertson, op. cit., p. 72.

20. McHenry and Van Doren, op. cit., p. 117.

21. Richard A. Bartlett, *The New Country* (New York: Oxford University Press, 1974), p. 22.

22. Ibid., p. 23.

23. Cronon, op. cit., p. 74.

24. Ibid., p. 83.

25. Bruce Catton and William B. Catton, *The Bold and Magnificent Dream* (Garden City, N.Y.: Doubleday & Company, 1978), p. 191.

26. Ibid., p. 138.

27. Samuel Eliot Morison and Henry Steele Commager, *The Growth*

of the American Republic (New York: Oxford University Press, 1956), Vol. 2, p. 56.

28. David Cushman Coyle, *Conservation* (New Brunswick, N.J.: Rutgers University Press, 1957), p. 8.

29. James Fenimore Cooper, *The Pioneers* (New York: New American Library, 1964), p. 434.

30. Henry Nash Smith, *Virgin Land* (Cambridge: Harvard University Press, 1950), p. 62.

31. Nash, op. cit., p. 63.

32. Marx, op. cit., p. 125.

33. Quoted in *American Heritage Book of Indians* (New York: American Heritage Publishing Co., 1961), p. 203.

2. SUBDUING NATURE

1. Quoted in David Freeman Hawke, *These Tremendous Mountains* (New York: W. W. Norton & Company, 1980), p. 66.

2. Quoted in Udall, p. 22.

3. Marion Clawson, *The Federal Lands Revisited* (Washington, D.C.: Resources for the Future, 1983), p. 15.

4. Ibid., pp. 16–17.

5. U.S. Department of the Interior, Bureau of Land Management, *Public Land Statistics*, p. 2.

6. Bernard Shanks, *This Land Is Your Land* (San Francisco: Sierra Club Books, 1982), p. 36.

7. Ibid., p. 39.

8. Ibid., p. 41.

9. Smith, op. cit., p. 190.

10. Catton and Catton, op. cit., p. 155.

11. Beard and Beard, op. cit., Vol. 2, p. 574.

12. Ibid., p. 575.

13. Smith, op. cit., p. 196.

14. Marx, op. cit., p. 187.

15. Cronon, op. cit., p. 126.

16. James MacGregor Burns, *The Vineyard of Liberty* (New York: Alfred A. Knopf, 1981), p. 526.

17. Bernard Bailyn et al., *The Great Republic* (Boston: Little, Brown and Company, 1977), p. 445.

18. McHenry and Van Doren, op. cit., p. 276.

19. Morison and Commager, op. cit., Vol. 2, p. 132.

20. Ibid., Vol. 2, p. 90.

21. Shanks, op. cit., p. 42.

22. Duane Smith, *Mining in America* (Lawrence: University of Kansas Press, 1987), p. 3.

23. Ibid., p. 12.

24. Bartlett, op. cit., p. 263.

25. Duane Smith, op. cit., p. 45.

26. Marx, op. cit., p. 194.

27. Bailyn, op. cit., p. 457.

28. Morison and Commager, op. cit., Vol. 2, p. 125.

29. Quoted in Ron M. Linton, *Terracide* (Boston: Little, Brown and Company, 1970), p. 199.

30. Charles William Griffin, Jr., *Taming the Last Frontier* (New York: Pitman Publishing Corporation, 1974), p. 5.

31. Excerpted in Walter Havighurst, ed., *Land of the Long Horizons* (New York: Coward-McCann, 1960), p. 372.

3. THE AWAKENING

1. Van Wyck Brooks, *The World of Washington Irving* (Philadelphia: Blakiston Company, 1944), pp. 182–83.

2. Quoted in Roderick Nash, *Wilderness and the American Mind* (New Haven: Yale University Press, 1967), p. 97.

3. John Mitchell, "A Man Called Bird," *Audubon*, Vol. 89, No. 2 (March 1987), p. 87.

4. Nash, *Wilderness and the American Mind*, p. 44.

5. Keith Thomas, *Man and the Natural World* (New York: Pantheon Books, 1983).

6. Nash, *The Rights of Nature*, p. 36.

7. Bartlett, op. cit., p. 239.

8. Quoted in McHenry and Van Doren, op. cit., p. 277.

9. Francis Parkman, *The Old Régime in Canada* (Boston: Little, Brown and Company, 1904), pp. 377–78.

10. Brooks, op. cit., pp. 424 ff.

11. Marx, op. cit., p. 216.

12. Jean Jacques Rousseau, *Discourse on Inequality*, Vol. 24 of the Harvard Classics (New York: P. F. Collier & Son, 1909), p. 124.

13. Jean Jacques Rousseau, *The Fall from Nature*, quoted in McHenry and Van Doren, op. cit., pp. 21–22.

14. Miller, op. cit., p. 211.

15. Quoted in Brooks, op. cit., p. 462.

16. Quoted in McHenry and Van Doren, op. cit., p. 176.

17. Ralph Waldo Emerson, *The American Scholar*, in Vol. 5 of the Harvard Classics (New York: P. F. Collier & Son, 1909), p. 7.

18. Ibid., *English Traits*, pp. 346, 412, 416.

19. Ibid., *Nature*, p. 247.

20. John Passmore, *Man's Responsibility for Nature* (New York: Charles Scribner's Sons, 1974), p. 176.

21. Henry David Thoreau, *Walden* (London: J. M. Dent & Sons, 1930). From the introduction by Walter Raymond, p. viii.

22. Ibid., p. 22.

23. Quoted in Nash, *The Rights of Nature*, p. 36.

24. Henry David Thoreau, *The Maine Woods* (New York: Thomas Y. Crowell, 1909), p. 92.

25. Quoted in McHenry and Van Doren, op. cit., p. 178.

26. Ibid.

27. Thoreau, *Walden*, p. 146.

28. Quoted in Nash, *The Rights of Nature*, p. 37.

29. Quoted in ibid.

30. Thoreau, *Walden*, p. 78.

31. George Perkins Marsh, *Man and Nature*, ed. by David Lowenthal (Cambridge: Harvard University Press, 1965). For the biographical data on Marsh, I am indebted to Professor Lowenthal's masterful introduction.

32. Ibid., p. 43.
33. Ibid., p. 36.
34. Ibid., p. 34.
35. Ibid., p. xxiv.
36. Ibid., p. 40.
37. Ibid., p. 52.
38. Ibid.
39. Ibid., p. xxii.
40. *The Papers of Frederick Law Olmsted*, Charles Capen McLaughlin, editor in chief. Vol. 1: *The Formative Years* (Baltimore: Johns Hopkins University Press, 1977). From Dr. McLaughlin's introductory essay, "Frederick Law Olmsted: His Life and Work."
41. Ibid., p. 46.
42. Clawson, op. cit., p. 28.
43. Diane Zaslowsky, *These American Lands* (New York: Henry Holt & Co., 1986), p. 15.
44. Udall, op. cit., p. 97.
45. Quoted in McHenry and Van Doren, op. cit., pp. 290–91.
46. Henry Nash Smith, op. cit., pp. 196–99.
47. Quoted in James MacGregor Burns, *The Workshop of Democracy* (New York: Alfred A. Knopf, 1985), p. 163.
48. Clawson, op. cit., p. 28–29.
49. Coyle, op. cit., p. 31.
50. Quoted in Udall, op. cit., p. 105.
51. Ibid.
52. Quoted in McHenry and Van Doren, op. cit., p. 304.
53. Edmund Morris, *The Rise of Theodore Roosevelt* (New York: Coward, McCann & Geogheghan, 1979), p. 385.
54. Stephen Fox, *John Muir and His Legacy* (Boston: Little, Brown and Company, 1981), p. 124.
55. Udall, op. cit., p. 130.
56. McHenry and Van Doren, op. cit., p. 303.
57. Fox, op. cit., p. 28. I am indebted to Dr. Fox's excellent biography for much of the data about Muir's life.
58. Ibid., p. 43.

59. Ibid., p. 52.
60. Ibid., p. 116.
61. Ibid., p. 99.
62. Quoted in Nash, *Wilderness and the American Mind*, p. 138.
63. Michael P. Cohen, *The History of the Sierra Club* (San Francisco: Sierra Club Books, 1988), p. 9.
64. Fox, op. cit., p. 144.
65. Quoted in Robert C. Paehlke, *Environmentalism and the Future of Progressive Politics* (New Haven: Yale University Press, 1989), p. 192.

4. KEEPERS OF THE HOUSE

1. Henry Adams, *The Education of Henry Adams* (New York: Book League of America, 1928), p. 465.
2. Ibid., p. 496.
3. Ibid., p. 388.
4. Ibid., p. 497.
5. Ibid., p. 498.
6. Milton Russell, "Environmental Protection for the 1990's and Beyond," *Environment*, Vol. 29, No. 7 (September 1987).
7. C. B. Squire, *Heroes of Conservation* (New York: Fleet Press Corporation, 1974), p. 40.
8. James MacGregor Burns, *Roosevelt: The Lion and the Fox* (New York: Harcourt, Brace, 1956), p. 155.
9. Max Nicholson, *The Environmental Revolution* (London: Hodder & Stoughton, 1970), p. 181.
10. Udall, op. cit., p. 141.
11. Horace M. Albright, as told to Robert Cahn, *The Birth of the National Park Service* (Salt Lake City: Howe Brothers, 1985), p. 324.
12. Douglas H. Strong, *Dreamers and Defenders, American Conservationists* (Lincoln: University of Nebraska Press, 1971), pp. 151–75.

13. Samuel P. Hays, *Beauty, Health, and Permanence* (Cambridge: Cambridge University Press, 1987), p. 22.
14. Fox, op. cit., p. 147.
15. Albright and Cahn, op. cit., p. 36.
16. Ibid., p. 310.
17. Fox, op. cit., p. 197.
18. *Wilderness*, Vol. 48, No. 169 (Summer 1985), p. 36.
19. Nash, *Wilderness and the American Mind*, p. 203.
20. John G. Mitchell, "In Wilderness Was the Preservation of a Smile," *Wilderness*, Vol. 48, No. 169 (Summer 1985), p. 17.
21. Ibid., p. 9.
22. Nash, *The Rights of Nature*, p. 64.
23. Leopold, op. cit., p. 130.
24. Ibid., p. 215.
25. Wallace Stegner, "Living on Our Principal," *Wilderness*, Vol. 48, No. 168 (Spring 1985), p. 17.
26. Ibid.
27. Donald Fleming, "Roots of the New Conservation Movement," *Perspectives in American History*, Vol. 6 (1972), p. 18.
28. Stegner, op. cit., p. 15.
29. Shanks, op. cit., p. 200.
30. Fox, op. cit., p. 309.
31. Stewart Udall, interview with author.
32. Fleming, op. cit., p. 80.
33. Lewis Mumford, *Technics and Civilization* (New York: Harcourt, Brace & World, 1962), p. 366.
34. René Dubos, *So Human an Animal* (New York: Charles Scribner's Sons, 1968), p. 16.
35. Ibid., p. 201.
36. Ibid., p. 26.
37. Gerard Piel and Osborn Segerberg, Jr., eds., *The World of René Dubos* (New York: Henry Holt & Co., 1990), p. xiv.
38. Fairfield Osborn, *Our Plundered Planet* (New York: Random House, 1948), p. 199.
39. Fleming, op. cit., p. 58.

40. Paul Ehrlich, *The Population Bomb* (Rivercity, Mass.: Rivercity Press, 1975).

41. Paul R. Ehrlich and Richard L. Harriman, *How to Be a Survivor* (New York: Ballantine Books, 1971).

42. Donella H. Meadows, Dennis L. Meadows, Jorgen Randers, and William W. Behrens III, *The Limits to Growth* (New York: Universe Books, 1972), pp. 23–24.

43. Bookchin, op. cit., p. lvii.

44. Ibid., p. xix.

45. Barry Commoner, interview with author.

46. Barry Commoner, *The Closing Circle* (New York: Alfred A. Knopf, 1971), p. 56.

47. Barry Commoner, interview with author.

48. Ibid., p. 299.

49. David Brower, interview with author.

50. Cohen, op. cit., pp. 424–25.

51. Quoted in Squire, op. cit., p. 87.

52. Russell Train, interview with author.

53. Fox, op. cit., p. 240.

54. William O. Douglas, *A Wilderness Bill of Rights*, in McHenry and Van Doren, op. cit., p. 190.

55. Frederic P. Sutherland and Vauter Parker, "Environmentalists at Law," quoted in Peter Borelli, ed., *Crossroads* (Washington, D.C.: Island Press, 1988), p. 188.

56. Tom Turner, "The Legal Eagles," in Borelli, op. cit., p. 52.

57. Ibid.

58. Squire, op. cit., p. 62.

59. Hays, *Beauty, Health, and Permanence*, p. 4.

60. Ralph Nader, interview with author.

61. Ibid.

62. Fox, op. cit., p. 305.

63. Rachel Carson, *Silent Spring* (25th anniversary ed.; Boston: Houghton Mifflin Company, 1987).

64. Ibid.

65. Ibid., p. xi. From the foreword by Paul Brooks.

66. Ibid., pp. 1–3.
67. Ibid., p. 15.
68. Ibid., p. 6.

5. SAVING OURSELVES

1. Quoted in *Congressional Quarterly*, October 30, 1970, p. 2728.
2. John C. Whitaker, "Earth Day Recollections: What It Was Like When the Movement Took Off," *EPA Journal*, Vol. 14, No. 8 (July–August 1988).
3. Denis Hayes, keynote speech to "You Can Make a Difference" Conference, Stanford University, January 22, 1989.
4. Gladwin Hill, "Activity Ranges from Oratory to Legislation," *The New York Times*, April 23, 1970.
5. Joseph Lelyveld, "Mood Is Joyful Here," *The New York Times*, April 23, 1970.
6. Ibid.
7. Borelli, op. cit., p. 78.
8. Gaylord Nelson, interview with author.
9. Ibid.
10. Denis Hayes, interview with author.
11. Richard Ayres, interview with author.
12. James Gustave Speth, interview with author.
13. Ibid.
14. Hays, *Beauty, Health, and Permanence*, p. 542.
15. Denton E. Morrison, "The Environmental Movement in the United States: A Developmental and Conceptual Examination," prepared for Riley E. Dunlap and William Michelson, eds., *Handbook of Environmental Sociology*.
16. Michael McCloskey, interview with author.
17. Hayes, op. cit.
18. Peter Bahouth, interview with author.
19. Jim Robbins, "FBI Charges Four with Attack on Power Line," *High Country News*, Vol. 21, No. 12 (June 19, 1989), p. 1.

20. Arne Naess, "Deep Ecology and Ultimate Premises," *The Ecologist*, Vol. 18, Nos. 4/5 (1988), p. 130.
21. Lynn White, Jr., "The Historical Roots of Our Ecological Crisis," *Science*, Vol. 155 (March 10, 1967), pp. 1203–7.
22. Passmore, op. cit., p. 34.
23. René Dubos, "Franciscan Conservation versus Benedictine Stewardship," in David Spring and Eileen Spring, eds., *Ecology and Religion in History* (New York: Harper & Row, 1974), p. 120.
24. Fleming, op. cit., p. 75.
25. Carl Casebolt, telephone interview.
26. Wendell Berry, "God and Country," in *Christian Ecology*, proceedings from the first North American Conference on Christianity and Ecology, April 1988, p. 16.
27. Jennifer Parmelee, "Pope Says Environmental Misuse Threatens World Stability," *The Washington Post*, December 6, 1989.
28. Ibid.
29. Nash, *The Rights of Nature*, p. 120.

6. The Environmental Revolution

1. William D. Ruckelshaus, "Environmental Regulation: The Early Days at EPA," *EPA Journal*, Vol. 14, No. 2 (March 1988).
2. William Ruckelshaus, interview with author.
3. Martin H. Belsky, "Environmental Policy Law in the 1980's: Shifting Back the Burden of Proof," *Ecology Law Quarterly*, Vol. 12 (1984), p. 101.
4. John Adams, interview with author.
5. J. William Futrell, interview with author.
6. Ibid.
7. Thomas Jorling, interview with author.
8. Devra Davis, interview with author.
9. Quoted in Thomas, op. cit., p. 18.
10. William Clark, written comments to author.
11. *Time*, June 12, 1989.

12. Gaylord Nelson, interview with author.

13. John Adams, interview with author.

14. U.S. Department of Commerce, Bureau of Economic Analysis, *Survey of Current Business*, June 1989, p. 19.

15. *Survey of Current Business*, February 1986, p. 40.

16. Paul Portney, interview with author.

17. *Ambio*, Vol. 18, No. 5 (1989), p. 274.

18. Dale W. Jorgenson and Peter J. Wilcoxen, *Environmental Regulation and U.S. Economic Growth*, Harvard Institute of Economic Research, Harvard University, October 1989.

19. Paul Portney, interview with author.

20. Edward J. Mishan, *Technology and Growth*, p. 16.

21. Ibid., p. 164.

22. Brian Tokar, "Social Ecology, Deep Ecology and the Future of Green Political Thought," *The Ecologist*, Vol. 18, Nos. 4/5 (1988).

23. C. A. Gerstacker, chairman of Dow Chemical Company, in address to Detroit Economic Club. Printed in *Congressional Quarterly*, March 8, 1972.

24. William Clark, interview with author.

25. Russell Train, interview with author.

26. James Range, interview with author.

27. Irving Shapiro, interview with author.

28. Ibid.

29. E. S. Woolard, "Remarks before the American Chamber of Commerce in the United Kingdom," May 4, 1989.

7. SAVING LAND

1. U.S. Department of Agriculture, Economic Research Service, *Our Land and Water Resources: Current and Prospective Supplies and Uses*, Misc. Publication 1290 (Washington, D.C.: U.S. Government Printing Office, 1974).

2. U.S. Environmental Protection Agency, *Environmental Backgrounder—Wetlands*, November 1988.

3. "Program Aims to Rescue Everglades from 100 Years of the Hand of Man," *The New York Times*, January 20, 1986, p. A20.

4. U.S. Department of Agriculture, *Soil, Water, and Related Resources in the United States: Status, Condition and Trends*, March 1981.

5. *State of the Environment* (Washington, D.C.: Conservation Foundation, 1984), p. 161.

6. U.S. Department of Agriculture, *National Agricultural Lands Study*, Final Report, 1981, p. 8.

7. Stephen D. Blackmer, "Whose Woods Are These? . . . The Future of New England's Forests," *The Environmental Forum*, November–December 1988, p. 21.

8. Thoreau, *The Maine Woods*, p. 104.

9. Quoted by John Carey, "The Changing Face of America," *National Wildlife*, April–May 1986, p. 20.

10. *Annual Report of the Council on Environmental Quality 1987–88*, p. 363.

11. Shanks, op. cit., p. 3.

12. John B. Oakes, " 'Bye, National Parks," *The New York Times*, June 7, 1985.

13. Shanks, op. cit., p. 141.

14. "Wildlife Refuges," *The New York Times*, May 29, 1984, p. A1.

15. "The Battle for the National Forests," *The New York Times*, "News of the Week in Review," August 13, 1989, p. 1.

16. Hays, *Beauty, Health, and Permanence*, p. 127.

17. "A Rising American Impulse to Leave the Land Alone," *The New York Times*, "News of the Week in Review," June 11, 1989, p. 6.

18. Robertson, op. cit., p. 113.

19. "A Forgotten Legacy: BLM Lands in the West," *The Wilderness Society*.

20. "Some Measure the Nation's Progress by What Is Not Built," *The New York Times*, "News of the Week in Review," 1986.

8. SAVING LIFE

1. Roger L. DiSilvestro, *The Endangered Kingdom* (New York: John Wiley & Sons, 1989), p. 15.

2. McHenry and Van Doren, op. cit., p. 93.

3. Bartlett, op. cit., p. 34.

4. McHenry and Van Doren, op. cit., p. 272.

5. Thomas, op. cit., p. 242.

6. Nash, *The Rights of Nature*, p. 122.

7. Christopher D. Stone, *Should Trees Have Standing?* (Los Altos: William Kaufmann, 1974), p. 51.

8. Herman Melville, *Moby Dick* (Garden City, N.Y.: Garden City Publishing Company, 1937), p. 662.

9. Edward O. Wilson, *Biophilia* (Cambridge: Harvard University Press, 1984), p. 139.

10. Passmore, op. cit., p. 187.

11. Ibid., p. 194.

12. Nash, *The Rights of Nature*, p. 161.

13. Michael J. Bean, "The 1973 Endangered Species Act: Looking Back Over the First 15 Years," *Endangered Species Update*, Vol. 5, No. 10 (August 1988), p. 4.

14. "The Law Saves a Few Species from Oblivion," *The New York Times*, "News of the Week in Review," November 27, 1988, p. 8.

15. Sarah Fitzgerald, *International Wildlife Trade: Whose Business Is It?* (Washington, D.C.: World Wildlife Fund, 1989), p. 3.

16. Roger L. DiSilvestro, *Fight for Survival* (New York: John Wiley & Sons, 1990), p. 235.

17. William O. Pruitt, Jr., *Wild Harmony* (New York: Nick Lyons Books, 1967), pp. 78–79.

18. Michael Bowker, "Caught in a Plastic Trap," *National Wildlife*, May–June 1986, p. 22.

19. "As Ozone Is Depleted, Much of Life Could Go with It," *The New York Times*, "News of the Week in Review," April 17, 1988.

20. Thomas A. Lewis, "Will Species Die Out As the Earth Heats

Up?" *International Wildlife*, Vol. 17, No. 6 (November–December 1987), p. 18.

21. Paul Ehrlich, "The Loss of Diversity, Causes and Consequences," in E. O. Wilson, ed., *Biodiversity* (Washington, D.C.: National Academy Press, 1988), p. 23.

22. Edward O. Wilson, interview with author.

23. Jay Hair, interview with author.

24. Thomas Lovejoy, interview with author.

9. AVERTING GLOBAL DISASTER

1. Barbara Ward and René Dubos, *Only One Earth* (New York: W. W. Norton & Company, 1972), p. 2.

2. Ibid., p. 12.

3. *Our Common Future*, Report of the World Commission on Environment and Development (New York: Oxford University Press, 1987).

4. J. A. Lutzenberger, keynote address to the International Meeting of Parliamentarians, Washington, D.C., April 30, 1990.

5. "Environment: Traditional Definitions of National Security Are Shaken by Global Environmental Threats," *The New York Times*, May 29, 1989, p. 24.

6. *Our Common Future*, p. 27.

7. "U.N. Parley Will Examine How Environment Has Done in the Last 10 Years," *The New York Times*, May 3, 1982, p. A10.

8. Alan B. Durning, "Mobilizing at the Grassroots," *State of the World 1989* (New York: W. W. Norton & Company, 1989), p. 154.

9. "Suddenly, the World Itself Is a World Issue," *The New York Times*, "News of the Week in Review," December 25, 1988, p. 4.

10. Linda Starke, *Signs of Hope* (New York: Oxford University Press, 1990), p. 155.

11. Lester R. Brown, *Building a Sustainable Society* (New York: W. W. Norton & Company, 1981), p. 8.

12. *Our Common Future*, p. 5.
13. Mustafa K. Tolba, interview with author.
14. Ibid.
15. Gro Harlem Brundtland, interview with author.
16. Ward and Dubos, op. cit., p. 218.

10. THE COUNTERREVOLUTION

1. Julian Simon, *The Ultimate Resource* (Princeton: Princeton University Press, 1981).
2. Julian L. Simon and Herman Kahn, *The Resourceful Earth* (New York: Basil Blackwell, 1984), p. 1.
3. *Mandate for Leadership III: Policy Strategies for the 1990's* (Washington, D.C.: Heritage Foundation, 1988).
4. Michael E. Kraft, "A New Environmental Political Agenda," in Norman J. Vig and Michael E. Kraft, *Environmental Policy in the 1980's* (Washington, D.C.: CQ Press, 1984), p. 29.
5. Steve Weisman, "Reagan, Assailing Critics, Defends His Environmental Policies as Sound," *The New York Times*, June 12, 1983.
6. "Watt Battled a Rising Tide," *The New York Times*, October 10, 1983, p. 1.
7. "Interior Secretary Declares U.S. Needs an Inventory of Resources," *The New York Times*, April 29, 1981.
8. Jonathan Lash et al., *A Season of Spoils* (New York: Pantheon Books, 1984), p. 16.
9. Ibid., p. 5.
10. J. Clarence Davies, "Environmental Institutions and the Reagan Administration," in Vig and Kraft, op. cit., p. 145.
11. "New Environmental Chief Vows to Ease Regulatory Overburden," *The New York Times*, June 21, 1981.
12. "Environmental Agency: Deep and Persistent Woes," *The New York Times*, March 6, 1983, p. 1.
13. Lash, op. cit., p. 113.
14. Quoted in Udall, op. cit., p. 257.

15. "Reagan's Rogues," *Sierra*, Vol. 73, No. 6 (November–December 1988), p. 21.

16. "36% Cut in Budget Reportedly Urged for Ecology Unit," *The New York Times*, November 19, 1981, p. 1.

17. "Environmental Council Cutbacks: What Price Efficiency?" *The New York Times*, April 18, 1981.

18. "Reagan Order on Cost-Benefit Analysis Stirs Economic and Political Debate," *The New York Times*, November 7, 1981.

19. Ibid.

20. "Tacoma Gets Choice: Cancer Risk or Lost Jobs," *The New York Times*, July 13, 1983, p. 1.

21. William Ruckelshaus, "Risk, Science and Democracy," *Issues in Science and Technology*, Vol. 1, No. 3 (1985), p. 29.

22. Samuel Epstein, "Losing the War Against Cancer," *The Ecologist*, Vol. 17, No. 2 (March–June 1987).

23. Edith Efron, *The Apocalyptics* (New York: Simon and Schuster, 1984).

24. "Administration Drafting New Policy on Regulating Cancer-Causing Agents," *The New York Times*, December 4, 1982, p. 32.

25. Lash, op. cit., p. 131.

26. Ibid., pp. 152–55.

27. Hays, *Beauty, Health, and Permanence*, p. 307.

28. *The Report of the President's Commission on Americans Outdoors* (Washington, D.C.: Island Press, 1987), p. 14.

29. "Reagan Years Are Seen as Stalemate by Environmentalists and Their Foes," *The New York Times*, January 1, 1989, p. 1.

30. Morrison, op. cit., p. 26.

11. The New People's Army

1. Borelli, op. cit., p. 10.

2. William Ruckelshaus, interview with author.

3. *The Gallup Poll News Service*, Vol. 54, No. 3 (May 17, 1989).

4. Lois Gibbs, interview with author.

5. Sam Love, "Times Are A-Changing," *Environmental Action*, Vol. 16, No. 7 (May–June 1985), p. 4.

6. "Plans to Build 2 Waste Plants Upset Many in Poor Section of N. Carolina," *The New York Times*, April 1, 1986, p. A18.

7. Ibid.

8. *Reagan, Toxics and Minorities*, A Policy Report by the Urban Environment Conference, September 1984, p. i.

9. *Toxic Wastes and Race in the United States: A National Report on the Racial and Socio-Economic Characteristics of Communities with Hazardous Waste Sites* (Commission for Racial Justice, United Church of Christ, 1987).

10. Richard Grossman, interview with author.

11. Saul Alinsky, *Rules for Radicals* (New York: Random House, 1971).

12. Ralph Nader, interview with author.

13. Borelli, op. cit., p. 288.

14. Paehlke, op. cit., p. 273.

15. Ibid., p. 5.

16. Anna Bramwell, *Ecology in the 20th Century: A History* (New Haven: Yale University Press, 1989), pp. 3–4.

17. Ibid., p. 248.

18. Ibid., p. 13.

19. Samuel P. Hays, "From Conservation to Environment: Politics in the U.S. Since World War II," in Kendall E. Bailes, ed., *Environmental History* (Lanham, Md.: University Press of America, 1985), p. 225.

20. Nash, *The Rights of Nature*, p. 56.

21. Lester W. Milbrath, *Environmentalists: Vanguard for a New Society* (Albany: State University of New York Press, 1984), p. 15.

22. Riley Dunlap, interview with author.

23. Ibid.

24. Ralph Nader, interview with author.

25. Lois Gibbs, interview with author.

12. THE THIRD WAVE

1. Thomas H. Kean, "Remarks at National Press Club Luncheon," November 15, 1988.
2. "Congress Clears Alaska Lands Legislation," *CQ Almanac*, 1980, p. 575.
3. Richard Darman, "Keeping America First: American Romanticism and the Global Economy," Second Annual Albert H. Gordon Lecture, Harvard University, May 1, 1990.
4. Riley E. Dunlap, "Trends in Public Opinion Toward Environmental Issues: 1965–1990," paper presented at the annual meeting of the American Association for the Advancement of Science, New Orleans, February 15–20, 1990.
5. "Movement Turning to Politics," *The New York Times*, January 26, 1986.
6. Jay Hair, interview with author.
7. Interviews with author.
8. James Gustave Speth, "Environmental Security for the 1990's . . . in Six Not-So-Easy Steps," *Issues and Ideas*, World Resources Institute, January 1990.
9. Commoner, *The Closing Circle*, p. 216.
10. David Foreman, "It's Time to Return to Our Wilderness Roots," *Environmental Action*, Vol. 15, No. 5 (December–January 1984), pp. 24–25.
11. Commoner, *The Closing Circle*, p. 186.
12. Richard Grossman, interview with author.
13. Jay Hair, interview with author.
14. "Environmental Groups Told They Are Racists in Hiring," *The New York Times*, February 1, 1990, p. A20.
15. Ibid.
16. Barry Commoner, *Making Peace with the Planet* (New York: Pantheon Books, 1990), p. 38.
17. Denis Hayes, Keynote speech to "You Can Make a Difference" Conference, Stanford University, January 22, 1989.
18. Lee M. Thomas, "Administrator's Overview," *Environmental*

Progress and Challenge: EPA's Update (U.S. Environmental Protection Agency, August 1988), p. 3.

19. William Ruckelshaus, speech before the Vermont Natural Resources Council, September 10, 1983.

20. Barry Commoner, interview with author.

21. "Toxic Chemicals Loom as Big Threat to the Nation's Supply of Safe Water," *The New York Times*, August 13, 1981, p. B6.

22. "Extent of Nation's Potential Hazardous Waste Problem Still Unknown," Report of U.S. General Accounting Office, December 17, 1987.

23. "Pesticides Finally Top the Problem List of E.P.A.," *The New York Times*, March 6, 1986.

24. Ibid.

25. "Facing America's Trash: What Next for Municipal Solid Waste?" Office of Technology Assessment, June 1989.

26. "Peering into the Energy Future and Sighting Gas Shortages," *The New York Times*, February 22, 1987.

27. "Energy Index," *Greenpeace*, Vol. 13, No. 2 (March–April 1988), p. 17.

28. In foreword to Jay B. McDaniel, *Earth, Sky, Gods & Mortals* (Mystic, Conn.: Twenty-third Publications, 1990), p. viii.

13. REBUILDING THE HOUSE

1. Donald Worster, "Conservation and Environmental Movements in the United States," in Bailes, op. cit., pp. 258–59.

2. Ivan Illich, interview in *New Perspectives Quarterly*, Vol. 6, No. 1 (Spring 1989), p. 23.

3. Nathan Gardels, "A New Ecological Ethos," *New Perspectives Quarterly*, Vol. 6, No. 1 (Spring 1989), p. 3.

4. Quoted by Michael Frome in *Defenders*, Vol. 63, No. 4 (July–August 1988), p. 6.

5. Interview with author.

6. Quoted in Borelli, op. cit., p. 244.

7. William Tucker, *Progress and Privilege: America in the Age of*

Environmentalism (Garden City, N.Y.: Anchor Press/Doubleday & Company, 1982).

8. Paul Mohai, *A Case for Environmental Non-Elitism: An Analysis of Social Movement Participation Through Integration of Social Psychological and Resource Mobilization Perspectives* (Department of Forest Resources, Utah State University).

9. Denton E. Morrison and Riley E. Dunlap, "Environmentalism and Elitism: A Conceptual and Empirical Analysis," *Environmental Management*, Vol. 10, No. 5 (1986), pp. 581–89.

10. Ibid.

11. Jesse L. Jackson, "The Right to Breathe Free," speech prepared for Earth Day tour, March 30–April 3, 1990.

12. Quoted by Sandra Postel, "Toward a New 'Eco'-Nomics," *WorldWatch*, Vol. 3, No. 5 (September–October 1990), p. 23.

13. Mumford, op. cit., p. 365.

14. Hazel Henderson, *The Politics of the Solar Age: Alternatives to Economics* (Indianapolis: Knowledge Systems, 1988), p. 353.

15. Lee M. Thomas, "Speaking Frankly," *EPA Journal*, Vol. 14, No. 4 (July–August 1988), p. 9.

16. Marsh, op. cit., p. 44.

17. Robertson, op. cit., p. 29.

18. Carson, op. cit., p. 277.

Adams, Henry. *The Education of Henry Adams*. New York: Book
    League of America, 1928.
Albright, Horace M., as told to Robert Cahn. *The Birth of the National
    Park Service*. Salt Lake City: Howe Brothers, 1985.
Alinsky, Saul. *Rules for Radicals*. New York: Random House, 1971.
American Heritage Book of Indians. New York: American Heritage
    Publishing Co., 1961.
Bailyn, Bernard, et al. *The Great Republic*. Boston: Little, Brown and
    Company, 1977.
Bartlett, Richard A. *The New Country*. New York: Oxford University
    Press, 1974.
Beard, Charles A., and Mary R. Beard. *The Rise of American Civili-
    zation*. New York: The Macmillan Company, 1941.
Billington, Ray Allen. *Land of Savagery Land of Promise*. New York:
    W. W. Norton & Company, 1981.
Bookchin, Murray. *Our Synthetic Environment*. New York: Colophon,
    1974.
Borelli, Peter, ed. *Crossroads*. Washington, D.C.: Island Press, 1988.
Bramwell, Anna. *Ecology in the 20th Century*. New Haven: Yale
    University Press, 1989.
Brooks, Van Wyck. *The World of Washington Irving*. Philadelphia:
    Blakiston Company, 1944.

Brown, Lester R. *Building a Sustainable Society*. New York: W. W. Norton & Company, 1981.

———, ed. *State of the World 1989*. New York: W. W. Norton & Company, 1989.

Burns, James MacGregor. *The Vineyard of Liberty*. New York: Alfred A. Knopf, 1981.

———. *The Workshop of Democracy*. New York: Alfred A. Knopf, 1985.

———. *Roosevelt: The Lion and the Fox*. New York: Harcourt, Brace, 1956.

Cahn, Robert. *Footprints on the Planet*. New York: Universe Books, 1978.

———, ed. *An Environmental Agenda for the Future*. Washington, D.C.: Agenda Press, 1985.

Carson, Rachel. *Silent Spring*. 25th anniversary ed.; Boston: Houghton Mifflin Company, 1987.

Catton, Bruce, and William B. Catton. *The Bold and Magnificent Dream*. Garden City, N.Y.: Doubleday & Company, 1978.

Clawson, Marion. *The Federal Lands Revisited*. Washington, D.C.: Resources for the Future, 1983.

Cohen, Michael P. *The History of the Sierra Club*. San Francisco: Sierra Club Books, 1988.

Commoner, Barry. *The Closing Circle*. New York: Alfred A. Knopf, 1971.

———. *Making Peace with the Planet*. New York: Pantheon Books, 1990.

Comp, T. Allan, ed. *Blueprint for the Environment*. Salt Lake City: Howe Brothers, 1989.

Cooper, James Fenimore. *The Pioneers*. New York: New American Library, 1964.

Coyle, David Cushman. *Conservation*. New Brunswick, N.J.: Rutgers University Press, 1956.

Cronon, William. *Changes in the Land*. New York: Hill and Wang, 1983.

DiSilvestro, Roger L. *The Endangered Kingdom*. New York: John Wiley & Sons, 1989.

———. *Fight for Survival*. New York: John Wiley & Sons, 1990.

Dubos, René. *So Human an Animal*. New York: Charles Scribner's Sons, 1968.

Efron, Edith. *The Apocalyptics*. New York: Simon and Schuster, 1984.

Ehrlich, Paul. *The Population Bomb*. Rivercity, Mass.: Rivercity Press, 1975.

——— and Richard L. Harriman. *How to Be a Survivor*. New York: Ballantine Books, 1971.

Emerson, Ralph Waldo. *The American Scholar* and *English Traits*, essays in the Harvard Classics. New York: P. F. Collier & Son, 1909.

Ferguson, Denzel, and Nancy Ferguson. *Sacred Cows at the Public Trough*. Bend, Ore.: Maverick Publications, 1983.

Fitzgerald, Sarah. *International Wildlife Trade: Whose Business Is It?* Washington, D.C.: World Wildlife Fund, 1989.

Fleming, Donald. "Roots of the New Conservation Movement," *Perspectives in American History*, Vol. 6 (1972).

Fox, Stephen. *John Muir and His Legacy*. Boston: Little, Brown and Company, 1981.

Galbraith, J. K. *The Affluent Society*. Boston: Houghton Mifflin Company, 1958.

Griffin, Charles William, Jr. *Taming the Last Frontier*. New York: Pitman Publishing Corporation, 1974.

Havighurst, Walter, ed. *Land of the Long Horizons*. New York: Coward-McCann, 1960.

Hawke, David Freeman. *These Tremendous Mountains*. New York: W. W. Norton & Company, 1980.

Hays, Samuel P. *Beauty, Health, and Permanence*. Cambridge: Cambridge University Press, 1985.

———. "From Conservation to Environment: Politics in the U.S. Since World War II," in Kendall E. Bailes, ed., *Environmental History*. Lanham, Md.: University Press of America, 1985.

Henderson, Hazel. *The Politics of the Solar Age: Alternatives to Economics*. Indianapolis: Knowledge Systems, 1988.

Leopold, Aldo. *A Sand County Almanac*. New York: Oxford University Press, 1948.

Marsh, George Perkins. *Man and Nature*, ed. by David Lowenthal. Cambridge: Harvard University Press, 1965.

Marx, Leo. *The Machine in the Garden*. New York: Oxford University Press, 1964.

McDaniel, Jay B. *Earth, Sky, Gods & Mortals*. Mystic, Conn.: Twenty-third Publications, 1990.

McHenry, Robert, and Charles Van Doren, eds. *A Documentary History of Conservation in America*. New York: Praeger Publishers, 1972.

McKibben, Bill. *The End of Nature*. New York: Random House, 1989.

McLaughlin, Charles Capen, ed. *The Papers of Frederick Law Olmsted*, Vol. 1. Baltimore: Johns Hopkins University Press, 1977.

Meadows, Donella H., Dennis L. Meadows, Jorgen Randers, and William W. Behrens III. *The Limits to Growth*. New York: Universe Books, 1972.

Melville, Herman. *Moby Dick*. Garden City, N.Y.: Garden City Publishing Company, 1937.

Milbrath, Lester W. *Environmentalists: Vanguard for a New Society*. Albany: State University of New York Press, 1984.

Miller, Perry. *Errand into the Wilderness*. Cambridge: Harvard University Press, 1956.

Morison, Samuel Eliot, ed. *Journals and Other Documents on the Life and Voyages of Christopher Columbus*. New York: Heritage Press, 1963.

——— and Henry Steele Commager. *The Growth of the American Republic*. New York: Oxford University Press, 1956.

Morris, Edmund. *The Rise of Theodore Roosevelt*. New York: Coward, McCann & Geogheghan, 1979.

Morrison, Denton E., and Riley E. Dunlap. "Environmentalism and

Elitism: A Conceptual and Empirical Analysis," *Environmental Management*, Vol. 10, No. 5 (1986).

Mumford, Lewis. *Technics and Civilization*. New York: Harcourt, Brace & World, 1962.

Nash, Roderick. *The Rights of Nature*. Madison: University of Wisconsin Press, 1989.

———. *Wilderness and the American Mind*. New Haven: Yale University Press, 1967.

Nicholson, Max. *The Environmental Revolution*. London: Hodder & Stoughton, 1970.

Paehlke, Robert C. *Environmentalism and the Future of Progressive Politics*. New Haven: Yale University Press, 1989.

Parkman, Francis. *Pioneers of France in the New World*. Boston: Little, Brown and Company, 1905.

———. *The Old Régime in Canada*. Boston: Little, Brown and Company, 1904.

Passmore, John. *Man's Responsibility for Nature*. New York: Charles Scribner's Sons, 1974.

Peskin, Henry M., Paul R. Portney, and Allen V. Kneese, eds. *Environmental Regulation and the U.S. Economy*. Baltimore: Published for Resources for the Future by Johns Hopkins University Press, 1981.

Piel, Gerard, and Osborn Segerberg, Jr., eds. *The World of René Dubos*. New York: Henry Holt & Co., 1990.

Pruitt, William O., Jr. *Wild Harmony*. New York: Nick Lyons Books, 1967.

Quinn, David B., and Alison M. Quinn, eds. *The First Colonists*. Raleigh: North Carolina Department of Cultural Resources, 1982.

Regenstein, Lewis. *America the Poisoned*. Washington, D.C.: Acropolis Books, 1982.

Repetto, Robert. *The Global Possible*. New Haven: Yale University Press, 1985.

Robertson, James Oliver. *American Myth, American Reality*. New York: Hill and Wang, 1980.

Rousseau, Jean Jacques. *Discourse on Inequality*. Vol. 24 of the Harvard Classics. New York: P. F. Collier & Son, 1909.

Schumacher, E. F. *Small Is Beautiful*. New York: Perennial Library/ Harper & Row, 1973, 1975.

Shanks, Bernard. *This Land Is Your Land*. San Francisco: Sierra Club Books, 1982.

Simon, Julian. *The Ultimate Resource*. Princeton: Princeton University Press, 1981.

———— and Herman Kahn. *The Resourceful Earth*. New York: Basil Blackwell, 1984.

Smith, Henry Nash. *Virgin Land*. Cambridge: Harvard University Press, 1950.

Squire, C. B. *Heroes of Conservation*. New York: Fleet Press Corporation, 1974.

Stone, Christopher. *Should Trees Have Standing?* Los Altos: William Kaufmann, 1974.

Strong, Douglas H. *Dreamers and Defenders, American Conservationists*. Lincoln: University of Nebraska Press, 1971.

Thomas, Keith. *Man and the Natural World*. New York: Pantheon Books, 1983.

Thoreau, Henry David. *Walden*. London: J. M. Dent & Sons, 1930.

————. *The Maine Woods*. New York: Thomas Y. Crowell, 1909.

Tucker, William. *Progress and Privilege: America in the Age of Environmentalism*. Garden City, N.Y.: Anchor Press/Doubleday & Company, 1982.

Turner, Frederick Jackson. *The Frontier in American History*. Reprinted in Daniel J. Boorstein, ed., *An American Primer*. Chicago: University of Chicago Press, 1966.

Udall, Stewart. *The Quiet Crisis*. Salt Lake City: Peregrine Smith Books, 1988.

Vig, Norman J., and Michael E. Kraft. *Environmental Policy in the 1990's*. Washington, D.C.: CQ Press, 1990.

————. *Environmental Policy in the 1980's*. Washington, D.C.: CQ Press, 1984.

Ward, Barbara, and René Dubos. *Only One Earth*. New York: W. W. Norton & Company, 1972.

White, Lynn, Jr. "The Historical Roots of Our Ecological Crisis," *Science*, Vol. 125 (March 10, 1967).

Wilson, Edward O. *Biophilia*. Cambridge: Harvard University Press, 1984.

————, ed. *Biodiversity*. Washington, D.C.: National Academy Press, 1988.

World Commission on Environment and Development. *Our Common Future*. New York: Oxford University Press, 1987.

Worster, Donald. "Conservation and Environmental Movements in the United States," in Kendall E. Bailes, ed., *Environmental History*. Lanham Md.: University Press of America, 1985.

Zaslowsky, Diane. *These American Lands*. New York: Henry Holt & Co., 1986.